VOICES of
SOUTHEAST ASIA

Also Available from M.E. Sharpe, Inc.

Voices of South Asia
Essential Readings from Antiquity to the Present

Edited by Patrick Peebles

VOICES of SOUTHEAST ASIA

Essential Readings from Antiquity to the Present

George E. Dutton, Editor

Routledge
Taylor & Francis Group

LONDON AND NEW YORK

First published 2014 by M.E. Sharpe

Published 2015 by Routledge
2 Park Square, Milton Park, Abingdon, Oxon OX14 4RN
711 Third Avenue, New York, NY 10017, USA

Routledge is an imprint of the Taylor & Francis Group, an informa business

Library of Congress Cataloging-in-Publication Data

Voices of Southeast Asia (Dutton)
 Voices of Southeast Asia : essential readings from antiquity to the present / edited by
George E. Dutton.
   pages cm.
 In English, chiefly translated from Southeast Asian languages.
 Includes bibliographical references.
 ISBN 978-0-7656-3666-9 (hardcover:)—ISBN 978-0-7656-2076-7 (pbk.:   )
   1. Southeast Asia—Civilization. 2. Southeast Asia—History—Sources. 3. Southeast Asian
literature—Translations into English. I. Dutton, George Edson, editor of compilation.
II. Title.

DS625.V65 2014
959—dc23   2013035419

ISBN 13: 9780765620767 (pbk)
ISBN 13: 9780765636669 (hbk)

Contents

Introduction

A survey of Southeast Asian literature such as this begs the question of whether such a body of writing exists. Are there sufficient geographical, cultural, and even temporal links that give such a body of literature genuine coherence? This question grows out of the long-standing debates about whether Southeast Asia is a meaningful label rather than an academic or geopolitical convenience. In literature, as in other areas of culture, Southeast Asia features several significant divisions that would seem to doom attempts to impose coherence upon a place strongly influenced by a series of historically significant cultural inflows. These influences have reflected first the cultures, languages, and literatures that arrived in the region from the Indian Subcontinent, followed not long thereafter by those emanating from the Chinese world to the north. Subsequent influences that dramatically shaped the cultural landscape came first from the Arabic world, sometimes directly and sometimes refracted through a culturally changed subcontinent, and later from Europe, first in the form of merchants and missionaries, and later as full-blown colonialism. This series of successive and overlapping cultural flows created numerous fissures that run across a region ostensibly linked by geography and historical experience. A brief survey of their impacts may help to clarify.

Chronologically, the earliest influence that penetrated the region was that which flowed from the Indian Subcontinent beginning about 500 BCE. These cultural forces crossed the seas and followed the monsoon winds, making their way into and across what is today the Indonesian archipelago. Visible reminders of this process of "Indianization" are to be seen in monuments such as Borobudur in central Java, but in other regions of the island world as well. These forces also took root on the mainland of Southeast Asia, where Hindu and Buddhist practices and literatures traveled with Brahman priests and the merchants who transported them. Not long after the earliest arrivals of these flows from South Asia, the northeastern perimeter of the region saw the beginnings of Chinese cultural inflows. While the reach of this cultural penetration was limited until the end of the first millennium, the seeds had been planted for a slow expansion and southward migration of this literary influence. The third great flow of literary influence came hand in hand with the arrival of Islam, following the same oceanic trading patterns that had earlier brought Hindu-Buddhist influences. The arrival of Islam began in the thirteenth century in northern Sumatra and the religion and its ancillary culture gradually expanded across the entire island region: reaching as far as what is today the southern Philippines, parts of the eastern Indonesian archipelago, and even the central Vietnamese coast, whose seaward orientation made it a de facto part of the island world of Southeast Asia. Particularly in the Indonesian archipelago, this Islamic literary and cultural tradition substantially displaced the existing Hindu-Buddhist literary base, though elements of the earlier tradition continued to survive.

The result of these multiple cultural flows was a broad tripartite division of the literary landscape, with a Sinicized literary tradition strong in the Vietnamese realm, an Indianized literature dominating in the rest of the mainland world, stretching from Burma through Cambodia, and an Islamized literary tradition defining writing and texts in the island world, encompassing territory from Sumatra across the Malay Peninsula throughout most of the Indonesian archipelago and into Mindanao. Not surprisingly, one finds complex literary hybrids throughout this region, reflecting cultural intersections, and an absence of cultural dogmatism that has long defined Southeast Asia. In short, in literature, as in other realms, Southeast Asia was, to use a long-standing cliché, a crossroads, a place that was cross-fertilized by multiple cultures across a long span of time. Nonetheless, as a starting point for understanding the broad historical literary patterns across the region, this tripartite schema should be borne in mind.

The influences of these multiple literary and linguistic forces manifested themselves in many ways. Some were as simple as expanding the vocabulary of local literatures. New words were introduced that described imported concepts and ideas, and these terms were gradually indigenized, picking up local inflections. Other influences were broader, including the introduction of entirely new literary genres and traditions, ranging from Buddhist pedagogical texts to Confucian morality poems to Islamic genealogical narratives and eventually to the European novel. These new genres typically arrived in the form of literary examples from their places of origin, and subsequently inspired local writers to produce their own materials in emulation of these forms. Thus, as with most other external cultural influences, Southeast Asians domesticated these new literary forms, making them distinctly their own. It was not merely genres, but also storylines that were brought into the region and then transformed and localized. Examples abound, but two will suffice to illustrate this pattern.

The first example is the Indian epic the *Ramayana*, a tale of princes, princesses, demons, and anthropomorphized monkeys. This tale was taken up in numerous parts of Southeast Asia, though especially among the mainland peoples, where its characters and storyline were retained, but its locale was indigenized, and numerous references to local personalities were also included. At times, one even sees drastic changes in the main characters, including a Lao version in which the demon Ravana becomes not the villain as in the original story, but the hero, in the form of a refined Lao prince.[1] The second, and much later, example can be found in the early nineteenth-century Vietnamese epic masterpiece the *Tale of Kieu*. This extended poem, by Nguyen Du, was an adaptation and retelling of a minor Chinese tale that Du had read while serving as an emissary to the Chinese court in the early 1800s. The resulting verse thus rested on a substructure of Chinese literature, even as the tale itself was distinctly Vietnamese, both in terms of its sensibilities and even more significantly in its written form, which combined an indigenous script with a distinctively Vietnamese poetic meter. It achieved widespread popularity in the nineteenth century, its circulation primarily oral, for the vernacular poetic form made its transmission relatively straightforward. This was very much in keeping with long-standing Vietnamese oral traditions. These examples are but two of the innumerable instances of Southeast Asian literary borrowing and transformation. Such patterns of literary transmigration and transformation are hardly unique to the Southeast Asian context, of course, for the adaptation and localization of literature is an ancient tradition. And yet, these types of literary borrowings are a particularly significant aspect of the Southeast Asian cultural landscape.

Southeast Asian Literary Forms and Features

The range of literary forms found across Southeast Asia is immense, especially given that scholars in the region have a broad view of what constitutes "literature." Thus, a wide range of religious texts fits into this category, as do such things as legal texts, inscriptions, and even historical chronicles. This highly catholic approach to defining literature means that a work such as this can provide only the smallest glimpse of a very rich tradition. Indeed, for the purposes of this volume I exclude almost entirely a profoundly important part of the tradition, namely shorter poetry. Poetry in particular is a critically important component of this literary realm, for several reasons. The first is that in many of these cultural traditions, poetry was regarded as the highest form of literary output, whatever the subject. The ability to write in verse reflected a certain refinement and skill that lay well beyond the production of mere prose. Every kind of text imaginable was written in verse—religious, literary, political, historical, and so on. However, poetry is a considerably more complex entrée into the world of Southeast Asian societies and culture, requiring a scholarly apparatus that lies beyond the scope of the present volume. The bibliography does include numerous volumes of poetry in translation that interested readers may consult.

There is another important element of verse, however, that is significant for this volume: namely that verse is closely linked to orality, to voices. Writings in verse are thus more literal echoes of the "voices" of Southeast Asia's past than prose works. While verse might have been the preferred literary form for the literate elite, it was simultaneously of great value to the nonliterate common person, for literature in verse was substantially easier to transmit to larger segments of the society. The vocal nature of verse, in which sound and rhythm were critically important, lent itself quite naturally to easy memorization and subsequent recitation to others. In this fashion, works of literature could be readily transmitted to many people and across distances even in the absence of paper, and especially in the absence of the ability to read. This volume's focus on "voices" is particularly reflected in the earlier works, especially those prior to the twentieth century, many of which were composed in long verse. While it was the rare individual who could memorize an entire epic poem or drama, many could commit portions or episodes of such works to memory.

Southeast Asian National Literatures

Southeast Asia today, in the second decade of the twenty-first century, comprises eleven independent nations. As such, the region encompasses eleven national literatures. Such literary traditions are both organic and artificial. They are organic in the ways in which they are linked to the past through shared languages, cultural touchstones, and common social practices and understandings. They are artificial because the nationalist project in each country has carefully sought to define and delimit particular "national" literatures and to create, self-consciously or by default, canons of such literatures. Such canons deliberately include certain works, while just as self-consciously excluding others. These canons shift over time as a result of political changes, new scholarly trends, and the needs of particular groups in these societies, but the fact of national canons remains very much alive. Numerous factors go into establishing these literary canons, including the language in which texts are written. Thus, for instance, Vietnamese academics once debated whether materials written in Chinese characters could be included in a Vietnamese literary canon. The decision ultimately to recognize such works as part of the canon reflected as much practical as literary considerations, for to eliminate such works would wipe out most of the pre–twentieth-century Vietnamese literary heritage.

More complicated questions hinge on whether works must be by Southeast Asians writing in their own countries, or whether they can be writing in other locations. If so, must they be writing about their homelands? Perhaps even more importantly, must they be writing in their national language or in one of their homeland's many subnational languages? While José Rizal wrote most of his famous 1880s novel, *Noli Me Tangere* in Europe, and in Spanish, it is not merely part of the canon of Philippines national literature but virtually its cornerstone. Does a novel written in Dutch by a Javanese exile in the Netherlands belong to a "national literature"? Does a work by a Filipina writing in English in California belong to this literature? For that matter, does a work by a non–Southeast Asian writing in and about a part of Southeast Asia belong? Where does George Orwell's *Burmese Days* fit? There are no correct answers to such questions, but rather multiple answers that depend on myriad factors. The point is that defining "national," much less "regional," literatures is a complex process, one that is politically and emotionally charged, and that hinges on a great many different variables.

The many languages and cultural influences, as well as the reality of the modern diaspora, have all complicated the situation.

This volume thus faces the challenge of somehow representing a "Southeast Asian literature" across a broad span of history. Clearly, such an endeavor is hopeless. Yet, in what follows, I seek to present a sampling of significant texts that give a hint of the richness of a literary tradition that often finds itself in the shadow of its neighbors in South and East Asia. In making selections I have tried to offer both geographical and temporal balance, not favoring any particular countries and also seeking to provide selections that balance the modern with the pre- and early modern materials. From the perspective of the modern nations of Southeast Asia, one cannot hope for true balance in terms of literary representations, so this collection does contain more literature from certain countries than others, and much of it is from the past century. This is a function of numerous factors, chief of which is disparate sizes and populations of the countries of the region. Thus, one is much more likely to find a deep literary heritage in a place the size of modern Burma, with a population in excess of 60 million people, than a tiny place such as Singapore, with fewer than 4 million. Similarly, smaller and/or relatively lightly populated modern nations such as Brunei, East Timor, Laos, and even Cambodia offer considerably more limited options as one selects literature. At the same time, issues of preservation and balances between oral and written traditions also affect such considerations. Thus, despite its size and modern population, the literature of the Philippines does not go back in time as far as that of Vietnam, Burma, or Thailand, there being relatively little surviving domestic written literature from before the nineteenth century. This is largely a function of an emphasis on orality as the means for composing and transmitting "literature."[2]

Another factor to be borne in mind is that in an anthology of this type, I can only hope to present the tiniest fraction of the extant literary traditions of the region. As such, the reader is cautioned in exploring these selections not to regard them as somehow representative of particular national or linguistic literatures. While any given piece may contain within it certain elements common to a particular region or time period, it cannot be said to stand for the larger sweep of literatures from that part of Southeast Asia. At best, these selections might be regarded as a kind of sampler—one whose diverse range can but hint at the richness of the vast Southeast Asian literary traditions.

Themes

The readings selected for this volume are necessarily diverse, and feature several important themes found across Southeast Asia. While not unique to the region, these themes are instrumental to understanding the region's societies, their literary forms, and their belief systems. Among the core themes is the response and adaptation to the arrival of external cultural influences. Just as they have done with religion, architecture, and political forms, Southeast Asian peoples absorbed literary forms and stories from elsewhere and then set about transforming them. From ancient epic poems of the Indian Subcontinent to nineteenth-century French novels, in each case these literary forms inspired local writers to emulate and then to transform these genres into something distinctly Southeast Asian. The transformation was partly in modification of the form, though this was perhaps less dramatic than the transformation of the storylines, the characters, and the settings. Strange people and places were replaced with ones familiar to local audiences, while writers also incorporated local concerns and beliefs about the interaction between people and their environment.

While the indigenization of imported literary forms is a broad trend, particular themes here include the exercise of power and its consequences, relations between men and women, relations between rulers and their subjects, and the role of the supernatural. The earlier texts are often concerned with questions of power and governance. They describe how rulers come to take their positions, the challenges and rivals they face, and the deeds they have accomplished. These texts often include elements of the supernatural or the fantastic: spirits, ghosts, magical weapons, demons. Many of these stories contain elements of the supernatural or the spiritual. They reflect a belief in local spirits, in the Buddha, in Indic deities, but they also question the institutional manifestations of these spiritual powers. The heroes of these tales often have superhuman abilities, most commonly strength. These texts are extremely revealing of the ways in which power was understood to exist, how it was wielded, and by whom. These were also morality texts that illustrated both proper and improper behavior. They illuminated political relations, such as the interactions between rulers and their followers. Also they described the relations between children and their parents, and between friends. The political organization of these societies is also revealed in the dynamic between rural areas and the centralized elite.

The last decades of the nineteenth century and then a flourish in the early twentieth saw the advent of two transformative literary genres—the novel and the short story. These literary forms, inevitably in prose rather than verse, marked a new direction in literary expression. Not only had the form changed, but the content as well. Novels and short stories became vehicles for commenting on the radical changes of the modern, often introduced under conditions of colonialism. They offered critiques of the colonizers to be sure, but also measures of self-criticism as well as attacks against collaborators, urban parvenus, and even once-sacred groups like monks. Numerous stories or excerpts in this volume dwell on family dynamics: the relationships between husband and wife, between children and their parents. We see the tensions in family life caused by economic hardship, by the obligations of social status, and by the challenges of daily life in its many forms. We see human nature on display, again within families, but also within the larger society. We see people who do things they regret and things they are proud of. We see authors who poke fun at the powers that be, and others who poke fun at their own societies. In all of this we learn about them and about ourselves—about what it means to be human—for in so many of these stories we see not strange people from distant lands, but fellow human beings whose experiences of life are often uncannily like our own.

Notes

1. Patricia Herbert and Anthony Milner, eds., *Southeast Asia, Languages and Literatures: A Select Guide* (Honolulu: University of Hawaii Press, 1989), p. 72.
   2. Ibid., pp. 159–160.

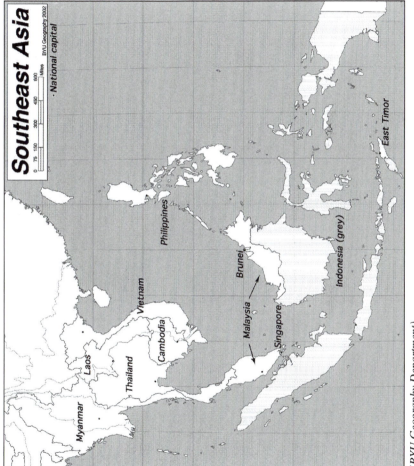

(*BYU Geography Department*)

VOICES of
SOUTHEAST ASIA

Kawi Inscription from Java

~ *894, Indonesia* ~

Anonymous

This inscription is one of the more than 3,000 such texts that survive on the Indonesian islands from the period between the fifth and the end of the ninth centuries. Such inscriptions were issued by rulers, and often carved upon stone pillars (stele) or, less commonly, engraved upon metal plates. Texts carved into stone are an extremely important element of the Southeast Asian written record, and such writings have been found throughout much of the region from northern Vietnam to Cambodia and across many of the islands of what is today the Indonesian archipelago. While there is a vast Southeast Asian literary tradition that was written on paper, palm leaves, and other such surfaces, the inherent vulnerability of these materials meant that texts that were not regularly recopied would typically disappear. Texts carved in stone, however, survived, and, importantly, did so in unaltered form. These words preserved in stone offer us a direct glimpse into a specific moment in the literary record.

This particular inscription, which dates from the final years of the ninth century, was unearthed near the modern city of Surabaya on the northeastern coast of the island of Java. It was written in the Kawi script, a locally modified version of the Sanskrit writing system introduced to the islands in the wave of Indianization that began in the first centuries before the Common Era. This influx of cultural elements included not only Sanskrit, but also Indian texts written in that script. Other prominent cultural elements included eclectic Indian religious traditions, featuring

3

elements of Hinduism and Buddhism, and amalgamations of the two. All of these Indic cultural elements took root in the island world of Southeast Asia, creating the backdrop against which this text was produced.

The inscription dates from the time of the early Mataram kingdom, which united central and eastern Java in the wake of the decline of the earlier Sailendra realm (seventh century to ninth century). Mataram grew as a power from the eighth century and reached its height in the ninth and tenth, before collapsing by the beginning of the eleventh. This text is a paean to the attributes and accomplishments of a particular prince, Raja Kunakua. More generally, however, it is a tale of war and peace, of threat and triumph, of rulers and subjects. As the writer of the text notes, its purpose is to edify those who read it, that they might learn from and be inspired by the account of the Raja and his family. In this respect the inscription has much in common with other such stone engraved texts in Southeast Asia, which often served both political and didactic functions. The inscription recounts events in which the ruler was involved, the challenges that his realm faced from both mortal and demonic forces, and how he was able to prevail against them. It speaks of his virtues and abilities, and of his praiseworthy sons, whose accomplishments both aided their father and reflected positively upon him. The text also describes Raja Kunakua's meeting with and subsequent marriage to a daughter of his conquered foe. Marriage between rival clans was a classic mechanism by which Southeast Asian political figures would consolidate their military successes in a lasting way. The text is noteworthy for its florid language, which is partly a function of the early nineteenth-century translation, but at the same time reflects a particular form of expression deemed suitable for tales of a noble ruler.

Questions

1. What rhetorical techniques does this text use to draw people's attention and to underscore its message about the leader who has ordered its inscription?
2. What does the selection tell us about the qualities of a good leader? How do rulers demonstrate their virtues toward their subjects?
3. How were the conquered people dealt with in the aftermath of the fighting, and what does this tell us about the dynamic between victor and vanquished?

4. What can we infer from this inscription about differing gender roles and expectations?

***

Kawi Inscription from Java

"An Inscription from the Kawi or Ancient Javanese Language, Taken from a Stone Found in the District of Surabaya on Java." Trans. John Crawfurd and Sir Stamford Raffles. In A.H. Hubbard, *Verhandelingen van het Bataviaasch genootschap der kunsten en wetenschappen.* (Batavia: Government Printing Press, 1816), vol. 8, pp. 8–16.

Prosperity! Attend to what is related, and which gives excellence in this world. Wisdom is banished by death; and worth of every kind is terminated by it. Make not light of these matters, but learn what is fitting, and enlighten your mind, for this life is of no account, it is attended with uncertainty, and death is its end.

For this reason, the intelligent have composed this narrative, renowned in assemblies, scented like scattered flowers. If you understand what is here related, you attain excellence. The efforts of tyranny are as the tears of the virgin in the embraces of old age. The assailant burns with desire, the assailed shows no return. Affairs accomplished in this spirit are full of difficulty. It is unbecoming of men to shed tears, which are enemies to valor; in every situation let them behave with meekness, which resembles the stream of water that falls from the mountains and refreshes every object around. Attend to these things, and you will thereby acquire an accession of wisdom; do not alter your copy, and thus the excellence of your narrative will be displayed. Observe well this instruction in your conduct.

It is related of Raja Kunaka that he was a Prince renowned for his penetration, of gentle conversation, a lover of religion and a confirmed Sugata.* His love for his people was great. The whole country was loud in his praise. He was skilled in directing the labor of his people and a strict observer of his word; the country prospered under him. The king directed this stone to be written upon, that men might behold what was

---

*A reference to the Buddha.

inscribed, which is replete with wisdom, that they might improve thereby. When the king fabricated this monument he took the advice of his chiefs and nobles on the excellent things inscribed upon it. All this has been divulged that the ignorant may be informed. Learn thou to judge of things from their appearance, for you have been instructed. Adorn the places of excellence, the temples of the gods, by which you will diminish the number of your enemies, who will bow to and serve you.

The king has acquired strength from the valor of his sons Sri Makuja Wasa and Wardana, beautiful in person and mild in disposition. Should you search the world round you would not find the equals of the two Princes, their valor is equally conspicuous; and their knowledge of the Sastras so complete that to understand them demanded no study. Their whole conduct and demeanor cooled and refreshed all around them. All women felt the intoxication of love for them, and wished themselves united to them, saying in their hearts, how skilled to give delight, they wished us in their arms, and their fame is renowned throughout the earth.

For this reason do thou learn the wisdom which is thus renowned. All the kings who became acquainted with the two princes were desirous of joining them. Fear not death. The king's sons had no dread of princes their equals, for the affections of the whole country went with them. The people who felt the unceasing bounty of the princes, and the effects of their wisdom and abilities, were glad and happy.

Relate the appearance of the kings preparing to go into the presence of the princes. It was at the time of day when the sun rides over the tops of the mountains. Excellent was their demeanor, fitting was their discourse, and they were presented with betel. They feasted and drank down to the lowest of the people, whose hearts were exceedingly rejoiced, and they ate to satisfaction.

The country was populous and prosperous. Let the relation proceed.

There was a king's son whose name was Dadrawisa Madya, who rebelled against their authority, a war commenced. The prince fled. He was pursued and again gave battle. He was ruthless and made no account of his enemy. The king saw the beauty of the young prince, but marked how different his conduct was from a man of high birth. Be it related. When the king ordered his forces to be assembled to proceed quickly to the city to expel the wicked, he proceeded forthwith and arrived at the gate of the kings of demons, and made offerings to the gods.

The armies fought and the forces of the demon king were destroyed by the charge of their enemies. Some had their necks twisted off; those who escaped ran away, terrified at the flight of missile weapons falling like rain. The few who had courage to make a stand were dispatched at once. The flight of the weapons was countless. The defeated forces hid themselves in the ditches and hollows, pursued unremittingly by the weapons of their enemies. The king Sri Jalalaga Dewa was killed. There was no one to contend with the army of men, no one firm to his station. Those who were seized yielded at once and begged for mercy, surrendering to the conqueror their wives and children. Thus the battle ended which had continued for half the duration of man.

Let the story of the destruction of the conquered country be related. He replaced the nobles in their stations as before. His wisdom sought the good of the country. He elected governors and arranged for rebuilding the city. The country was divided into three parts under three heads.

The body of the king's son was decked out and prayers offered up for it according to the practice observed by the dead. His wives, all of exquisite beauty, wished to follow him in death. They bowed and kissed his feet. They seemed determined to follow his fortune, to make it their own, and not to survive him.

"Alas!" exclaimed they, "do not forget the expressions of our sincerity. We are fatherless; we will serve thee; we are pleased that you take us along with thee. You are our Guru. For you were skilled in the arts of love, and knew how to give joy to the heart." Such were the words of the afflicted. "We will wed no more; we will acknowledge the authority of no other lord. We will not make a second marriage, for you alone knew the arts of love. We dread the thoughts of being subjected to another's authority. We are inexperienced, and ignorant of the most approved conduct." The times were changed. Let a spectacle complete in every respect be related, describing a narrative of excellence.

The story proceeds to say, when the kings went forth to exercise themselves, their train slowly following, they arrived at the village of Jawaya, having deep ravines to the left side, within which were seen rare objects. They halted, delighted to observe pandan flowers floating in order upon the water, as if they had been obeying an order to that effect. The appearance of the sky and of the clouds seemed preparing to usher in the height; the day closed and it became dark. They assembled in the forest and lighted great torches to prepare against the wild beasts, and after some time the bounty of the king was distributed, excellent food, and all kept awake. It was passing cold; all trembled and their arrangement was broken. In the morning they again put themselves in order, and prepared to march forward. The king was presented on the way with gifts. The people sounded the praise of the king's sons, wishing they might have no rivals, that they might have no occasion to retreat from the battle, but that their enemies might be terrified at their presence, that their aspect might be bright and not turn pale in the battle, and that their rank might be exalted.

It is related that there was a female of passing excellence, her beauty was far-famed, she was without blemish; all men felt the pangs of love for her, and she became the constant object of their discourse. Her whole demeanor was becoming; her excellence fitted her to be the consort of a king, the gift of the gods to him. That king was just in his conduct towards his subjects; as long as he reigned no wickedness was committed in the country. His people were happy and rich, the effects of his bounty. His liberality towards the poor and dependent was without interruption. His learning was moreover complete; assuredly of the Devas. Whatever he imagined was right. He was therefore loved and feared throughout the country.

This prince possessed discernment of talent above all the princes his equals in power. He was ready to pardon those who erred. His religious austerities in search of the prosperity of his country were so great that he did not allow himself to sleep. Criminals disappeared without effort. His knowledge equaled that of a Pandita (a teacher). An enemy came renowned for his skill in war. He invaded the country. The numbers of his army were unknown. His adverse forces commenced a nocturnal combat with equal valor, none flinching. The darkness of the night increased. The king's army charged the enemy in a body, dealing out and receiving cuts and stabs, shrieking and shouting. The king's army could not withstand the darts that were showered upon them, they began to flinch but could not find the gate; the army was vanquished, many were killed; those maimed dreaded the anger of the king like a sage. The discomfiture of his force is not related. The army was thrown into confusion with a noise like the fall of a mountain, or like the sea inundating a city. Thus happened the defeat of the king's army, and in this manner was the power transferred to other hands. The women were met mourning the death of the fallen king.

She who dwelt on the loss of her lord was found motionless from grief, in beauty like the goddesses Ratti or Supraba. Her breasts were

Borobudur was constructed by the Sailendra dynasty in the eighth and ninth centuries in central Java. It was an important pilgrimage site for the devout who would ascend the monument in circular fashion around the succeeding levels. The monument is richly carved with scenes from the Buddha's life, instructing visitors as they make the journey toward the top and enlightenment. *(Author's collection)*

superior in loveliness to ivory. Her complexion excelled burnished gold glittering. Such was the spouse of the fallen prince. Forthwith arrived the victorious king in anxious search for the princess.

He found her under the shade of a tanju tree by a mound raised in shape of a mountain, where pious austerities are performed. Her maids mourned their fallen lord, their countenances pale with grief. Thus also the surrounding flowers and plants, as if they too wished to perish and partake the fortunes of the prince. The king wondered at the sight. He praised the place of worship. In front it was studded with pearls and precious stones. The skill displayed gave pleasure to the heart which excited to devotion. The victor approached the princess and her attendants. The conquerors seized the attendants. A scene of plunder ensued. The Nayakas laid their hands on such as were fitting to become their wives. The beautiful with rising bosoms were seized by the chiefs. The king laid his hands on the princess and welcomed her to his bed.

Shwegugyi Pagoda Inscription

~ *1141, Burma* ~

King Alaungsithu

The Shwegugyi pagoda inscription is representative of a particular Southeast Asian literary tradition, namely commemorative texts upon the dedication of religious structures. Buddhist temples in particular would have their founding marked in some fashion by a dedicatory text, which was usually inscribed on a stone marker and placed in the temple. Like the earlier inscription from Java, this one is important for having preserved contemporary voices unmediated by centuries of recopying and transmission, as has often been the case with texts preserved on less permanent surfaces. With inscriptions and other stone-engraved texts, we have the original words in their original forms. While they must of course also be read with care, in them students of earlier Southeast Asian literature have "original" texts.

This particular inscription was carved upon a large stone stele in the Shwegugyi (Great Golden Cave) pagoda, which was erected in the sacred city of Pagan in what is today central Burma. Situated on the banks of the Irawaddy River, Pagan was the political epicenter of Burmese kingdoms from the latter half of the ninth century until its decline and abandonment under threat from Mongol armies in the late 1200s. From Pagan, Burmese kings could control the Irawaddy basin, its rice crops, and the transportation networks that extended along the river toward the coast. The Shwegugyi pagoda was erected, and the inscription ordered, by King Alaungsithu, whose reign from 1113 to 1167 was one of the longest in the history of mainland Southeast Asia. Alaungsithu ruled during an era of economic prosperity and political stability that marked a high point of the Pagan kingdom. He carried

The plain of Pagan in central Burma is dotted with thousands of Buddhist temples, erected by pious rulers of the dynasty based there. The construction of these temples was an act of religious devotion and a mark of kingly power. Construction would be commemorated by inscriptions placed inside them, and temples would then become sites of worship and devotion to the Buddha and local spirits. *(Author's collection)*

out extensive temple and other public building projects, of which the Shwegugyi pagoda was among the most prominent. He was also a dedicated Buddhist ruler who took very seriously his responsibilities as the moral center of his realm. He traveled widely during his reign promoting Buddhist projects and undertaking acts of merit. He is linked to the Shwegugyi pagoda not only because he built it and raised this inscription, but also because it was here that he was eventually murdered by a son impatient to gain control of the throne. Alaungsithu was later entered into the Burmese pantheon of spirits, or *nats*, for his many contributions to Buddhism, and his spirit continues to be revered by contemporary Burmese.

The Shwegugyi pagoda inscription represents simultaneously a dedication of the new pagoda and a kind of policy statement by the ruler who erected the structure. The text suggests the ways in which Burmese rulers sought to associate themselves with Buddhism and with the figure of the Buddha in particular. Buddhism arrived in mainland Southeast Asia in the first millennium and was practiced in various forms across its numerous kingdoms. Of these various forms, it was the Theravadin tradition (or Way of the Elders), that eventually became established as the predominant mainland form. While it had been taken up by some rulers as early as the sixth or seventh centuries, it was not until the eleventh century that the Way of the Elders became more widespread. It was at that time that the Burmese ruler King Anawratha (r. 1044–1077) took up the Theravadin tradition from the southern Burmese Mon kingdom, and it gradually spread across the mainland. Today the Theravadin tradition dominates Buddhist practice throughout mainland Southeast Asia, with the exception of the central and northern portions of Vietnam, where variants of Mahayana Buddhism prevail.

The language of this inscription reflects the king's desire to be understood in terms of a striving for the perfection, compassion, and wisdom of the historical Buddha. Such interconnection between the Buddha and rulers dates to the reign of Ashoka (r. 304–232 BCE), who ruled over the Mauryan Empire in South Asia. This linkage between rulers and Buddhism became a central feature of mainland Southeast Asian kingdoms as well. Indeed, it is a phenomenon that has manifested itself historically from the earliest arrival of Buddhism in Southeast Asia, and continues to the present time, albeit in altered form. This inscription, like many such literary texts, has numerous objectives. While it is a policy statement, it is also a didactic text, one that begins by sketching out the process by which the Buddha progressed toward his final enlightenment through several lifetimes, finally transcending desire in his incarnation as the Gautama Buddha. This temple inscription is equally a kind of admonition to the subjects of the Pagan kingdoms' rulers, laying out what is expected of them while warning about what would befall those who transgress these teachings. Finally, it also represents an enumeration of the aspirations toward which all Buddhists should strive.

Questions

1. What does this text reveal about the aspirations of this ruler of Pagan in his role as leader of his country?
2. What challenges do those who aspire to Buddha-hood have to overcome?
3. What impact might such a text have on those who read it, and what purpose would its message possibly serve?

***

Shwegugyi Pagoda Inscription

Archaeological Survey of India. Taw Sein Ko and
Emanuel Forchhammer, comp. *Inscriptions of
Pagan, Pinya and Ava.* (Rangoon: Superintendent of
Government Printing, 1899), pp. 73–76.

Honor and reverence to the Buddha, whose wisdom is as vast as the earth
and is pure, and who has led in the paths of the excellent law all human
beings, *devas*, and *brahmas* and other beings, who could not of their own
accord find their way across the slough and the grove of desire. I adore
this Buddha, whose law and monkhood are incomparable.

The present world is honored with five Buddhas. Four, who were more
eminent than men, have already appeared, and of these I shall proceed
to enumerate briefly the excellent attributes of Gautama Buddha, who
was replete with all wisdom and who was a scion of the Sakya family
of kings: Let the righteous hearken to me.

The Buddha, who is of great renown and who is the object of worship
of the three superior beings, acquired the 30 kinds of virtue not only in
one, but in several existences, by performing the three kinds of meritorious deeds, namely, that for the world in general, that for his relations,
and that for the attainment of Buddhahood. He was the fountain of mercy
and was full of diligence. One of his virtues was the performance of the
five kinds of charity in the interests of the world. As King Vessantara,
his constant delight was the furtherance of the welfare of others, and as
he chose the chief of the ten kinds of virtue, he became, on his demise,
an inhabitant of the highest abode of *nats* excelling them all in glory.
While there, a host of *nats* from different parts of the universe approached
him with the request that he might assume Buddhaship, and it being in
accordance with his own wish, the embryo Buddha looked ahead with
the five kinds of visions, and on his next birth became a member of the
Sakya family. The glorious and wise embryo remained as a man in the
abode of men for 29 years and then renounced the world to become a
Rahan and thus to acquire omniscience. He performed several acts of
penance, and his origin was as good as that of the previous Buddhas. He
resided at the foot of a banyan tree near the Neranjara river, and lived on
the milk offered him as alms. Subsequently he approached the beautiful
and excellent throne under the Bodhi tree and having seated himself
thereon exercised the four kinds of diligence. While the Bodhisat, who

was more excellent than the three kinds of superior beings, was thus occupied, he beheld the *nat* Mara, with a host of mercenaries, approach him with the courage of the king of lions. But he was totally unmoved; he destroyed the gate of desire, and thus overawed the evil *nat* and his host. The victorious, imperturbable, wise and diligent Bodhisat then passed the three watches of the night exercising his omniscience. During the last watch or that immediately preceding the dawn he reviewed all of his previous births. Being more excellent than the five kinds of *Muni* and having acquired omniscience, he merited the title of Buddha. The emitter of the rays of wisdom, having acquired knowledge of every law, joyfully recited the stanzas beginning with the *Anekajat Samsaram* and passed seven days on the throne. He thus emerged from all sorrow, accomplished his task of becoming Buddha, and ceased from all passion, and was content, glad, and joyful, with his mind set upon the welfare of men and *nats*.

The wise, righteous, and justly famous King Alaungsithu, who is able to disperse his own enemies and those of his people and Religion as the glorious and rising sun disperses darkness, fear, and cold, has been ruling Pagan in accordance with the ten kingly precepts. Knowing that in the three worlds it is exceedingly difficult to become a Buddha or a man and have the opportunity of hearing the law of the righteous preached, the wise King Alaungsithu had this beautiful and lofty cave-pagoda build and adorned with several small pagodas and statues of *nats* in honor of the excellent and virtuous Buddha Gautama. Being desirous of saving the three kinds of superior beings from the miseries of *samsara*,* the king further had a wonderfully beautiful and pleasing image made, which exactly resembled the living Buddha, the adorable, the wise, and the possessor of the five kinds of clear-visioned eyes. After the completion of this pagoda and image, His Majesty caused a complete copy of the Tripitaka (the Buddhist canon) to be prepared, and during the dedication ceremonies offered suits of robes to several monks, and cheerfully ministered to their other material wants with his own hands. An intense desire to become a Buddha then seized the king and His Majesty accordingly expressed the following prayer:

"Gautama attained Buddhaship by acquiring the ten kinds of virtue and was thus enabled to liberate all sentient beings from the bonds of desire. May I, in future, be in a position to do likewise.

---

*Samsara is the Buddhist concept of perpetual cycles of death and rebirth.

"The all-wise Buddha comprehended the mysteries of the law and propounded them without effort. He was the disburser of gifts to the multitudes of suppliant *brahmas* and *devas* who flocked to him from the ten thousand universes, while he was with Annalakondhanna Thera in the highly pleasant Isipatanamigadavum grove, the resort of the flying *rishis* and the feathered world, after he had himself travelled a distance of 30 yojanas with incomparable diligence, and was thus the means by which many attained Nirvana. May I be able to do likewise.

"The excellent Buddha, whose origin was as good as his predecessors, was well versed in the Yamakas and could therefore prophesy as only Buddhas can. From his body emitted variously brilliant rays of brown, gold, red, white, and scarlet, and six other kinds of resplendent rays penetrated with great rapidity to all quarters in different ways, lighting up the darkness everywhere. He succeeded in persuading by various means several heretics who despised Nirvana and were on their way to the four forms of destruction blinded with their own vain beliefs and misled by the thought that they were Buddhas themselves, but who were in reality far from the path leading to the abode of the *nats* and to Nirvana. Moved by a heart full of great and tender mercy towards all sentient beings, the Buddha brought many who were in abject misery from several other universes to this, and exerting his power placed them in a line on Mount Meru, walked along on their heads, and thus healed them all. May I be able to work miracles of this nature.

"Having performed the above miracle, the Buddha proceeded to the slab of rock known as Pandhakampata in Tavatimsa, the abode of the 33 Sakkas, and having seated himself thereon in divine glory administered the draught of blessing to several *nats* and *brahmas* and preached the Abhidhamma law to an assembly of *nats* headed by the one who was previously his royal mother. May I have the opportunity to perform a similar deed.

"The Buddha who resided on the summit of Mount Meru, attended by a brilliant retinue, performed several miracles for the enlightenment of the world. May I, in future, be able to do likewise.

"After having preached to the assembly of *nats* in Tavatimsa, the Buddha descended to this continent and preached several sermons to men, *brahmas*, ogres, *nats*, brahmins, *nagas*, elephants, and heretics who thought themselves Buddhas. May I become such a Buddha.

"The Buddha whose origin is as excellent as that of his predecessors, performed the whole of the five kinds of duties incumbent on all Buddhas. May I be able to do so."

Viet Dinh U Linh Tap

~ *1329, Vietnam* ~

LY TE XUYEN

The Vietnamese literary tradition is a hybrid, combining elements of indigenous tales and oral traditions with introduced Chinese genres and elements. Not only genres and subjects, but also writing systems overlapped. Until the introduction of the romanized alphabet by European missionaries in the middle of the seventeenth century, Vietnamese wrote using either Chinese characters or a locally modified version of such characters known as *chu nom* (southern characters). This modified script was used to write vernacular texts, those reflecting the local spoken language, and was frequently used for composing poetry. The earliest surviving Vietnamese literary works are Buddhist-inflected poems from the eighth and ninth centuries, which were joined in the twelfth by court histories and then slowly various collections of tales.

Among the earliest Vietnamese literary works in prose is the *Viet Dinh U Linh Tap* (Compilation of the Departed Spirits of the Vietnamese Realm), compiled in the early fourteenth century by Ly Te Xuyen, a Vietnamese official. The collection features twenty-seven short tales, each of which examines a particular historical, mythical, or legendary figure who played some critical role in the early historical development of the Vietnamese peoples and was subsequently transformed into a spirit. The focus on these particular spirits was determined by historical circumstances. It was these, among a wide range of local spirits, whom the Tran Dynasty (1225–1400) rulers regarded as having been instrumental in helping the Vietnamese defeat three separate Mongol invasions between 1257 and 1294. The author categorizes these spirits under three broad headings: sovereigns (both legend-ary and historical, though not broken down in this fashion in the text), worthy ministers who served these sovereigns, and nature spirits. This compilation has subsequently become the primary written source of many of the Vietnamese myths regarded in modern time as having originated in the primordial oral tradition. While it is entirely possible that the core of some of these tales may lie in much earlier oral ac-counts, this text marks the moment at which their particular elements took on a historical fixity.

Each of these tales collected by Ly Te Xuyen provides a measure of "biographical" information about its titular spirit and then describes details of a manifestation of that spirit's power. The tales thus reinforce the popular perception of the efficacy of each spirit by describing its power. Many of these spirits had temples erected for them to which Vietnamese would travel to pay homage and make sacrifices. The belief in spirits and their protective powers was, and still is, a central part of Vietnamese belief systems, and has survived alongside the addition of later "world religions" such as Buddhism, Confucianism, Daoism, and even Christianity. As such, this text might be regarded as a survey of a pantheon of the Vietnamese spirit realm at the time of its creation.

The three biographies included below represent different types of spirits. The first is that of the historical figure Phung Hung, an indig-enous leader of the Vietnamese who challenged the Tang dynasty domination of the region that the Chinese referred to as Annam (the Pacified South). The second tale is that of the famous eleventh-century general Ly Thuong Kiet, noted for his military feats in vanquishing both the kingdom of Champa to the south and the forces of the Chinese Song dynasty to the north. (Champa was a kingdom occupying the coastal territory of what is today central and south-central Vietnam. It was gradually taken over by the Vietnamese between the eleventh and the eighteenth centuries.) The third is the tale of two spirits, those of the seas and of the mountains, and recounts their epic struggle in a contest for the hand of the king's daughter. The tension between the mountains and the seas is a classic theme in Vietnamese culture, making this tale particularly noteworthy for its juxtaposition of these two elements. The conclusion of the tale also provides an explanation for the sometimes violent storms of the fall and winter seasons—the water spirit's revenge upon the land that defeated it.

Questions

1. In what ways does the supernatural world intrude upon the world of mortals, and how does this serve to shape the course of events?
2. How do people interact with the natural world?
3. What are these stories trying to tell the reader about characteristics of early Vietnamese society and its fundamental concerns?
4. How does religion guide the actions of people, and in what ways does it manifest itself in these stories?
5. Where does power come from in these stories? How does one acquire it, and how does one display it, or prove that one has it?

***

Viet Dinh U Linh Tap

> Ly Te Xuyen. *Departed Spirits of the Viet Realm*. Trans. Brian E. Ostrowski and Brian A. Zottoli. (Ithaca, NY: Cornell University Southeast Asia Program, 1999), pp. 11–14; 34–36; 75–77. Reprinted with the kind permission of the publisher.

Phung Hung
(The Great Father-and-Mother King)

According to the *Records of Giao Province* of King Trieu, the King was of the Phung line and was named Hung. For generations, his ancestors had passed down the tribal chieftainship of the Bien Kheo barbarians of Duong Lam province. They were called "quan lang." A well-propertied family, they were powerful in their sphere. Hung was of extreme strength and courage, able to fight tigers and push buffalo. His younger brother, called Hai, was also of great strength, able to carry thirteen thousand pounds of stones or a small ten thousand-peck boat for over ten miles. The Di and Lao all feared their names.

In the Duong Dai Lich era [766–780], because our army of An Nam was in turmoil, the brothers went together to patrol the neighboring regions. These all fell to them, and wherever they went, there were none who did not scatter. Hung was satisfied and changed his name to Cu Lao; Hai changed his name to Cu Lu. Hung took the title of Metropolitan Lord; Hai took the title of Metropolitan Guardian. Using the strategy of

Do Anh Luan of Duong Lam, they used troops to patrol the provinces of Duong Lam and Truong Phong. The people all followed them. Their power and reputation resounded powerfully.

They released word of their desire to plot against the regional head-quarters. At that time, Protector General Cao Chinh Binh brought troops to attack them, but he could not beat them. Melancholic and exasperated, he fell ill with a stomach ulcer and died. Hung entered the regional headquarters, overseeing affairs seven years before dying. The crowds wanted to install Hai. But the assistant chieftain, Bo Pha Can, who was strong enough to clear away mountains and lift up cauldrons, and whose courage and power were excellent, refused to accede and proceeded to install Hung's son, An, leading a mob against Hai. Hai fled from Bo Pha Can, moving to Chu Nham cave. It is not known what happened to him afterwards. An honored Hung as the Bo Cai Great King. For it is custom in the realm to call the father "bo" and call the mother "cai." For this reason, his name was given like this.

An continued to rule for two years before Emperor Duong Duc Tong [780–805] appointed Trieu Xuong to serve as An Nam Protector General. Xuong entered the scene, sending an envoy with gifts in advance to instruct An. An duly set out the ceremonial guard and a crowd to meet them in surrender. The people of the Phung line were thus dispersed.

Soon after Hung died, his abilities were divinely manifested. He often appeared among the villagers. A thousand chariots and ten thousand horses flew up above the houses and amidst the trees. People in the crowds looked up to see something obscure like clouds forming the five colors of light. The sounds of strings and woodwinds carried far and echoed in the sky. Then there was a sound of shouts and cries, and flags and drums were seen in the distance. A fendered palanquin dazzled the eyes. All of these things in the distance were clear to see. Whenever the region had fearful or joyous matters at hand, in the middle of the night the village notables would first see a supernatural figure announcing the tidings. This figure was made a deity by the crowds.

To the west of the regional headquarters, a shrine was built for worship. Prayers for clear skies and for rain were always divinely answered. Whenever there was suspicion over matters of theft or dispute, ceremonial items were brought before the temple to request an audience and oaths were sworn there. Immediately, ill fortune or blessings were observed. Sellers offered gifts and prayed for large profits, and they were all answered. On every day of thanksgiving to the spirits, people gathered in great numbers and wheel tracks and footprints covered the roads. The appearance of the shrine was magnificent, and the incense has never been extinguished.

When First Lord Ngo founded the county, the northern [Chinese] army came in to pillage. The First Lord was distraught at this, and in the middle of the night he was dreaming when he suddenly saw an old gray-haired man in imposing, formal dress carrying a feather fan and bamboo cane. He declared his name and said, "I have sent ten thousand regiments of spirit soldiers to strategic places, where they are ready to lie in ambush. May Your Lord hasten to advance troops to oppose the enemy. You will have secret assistance, and need not allow yourself to worry." Then, at the victory at Bach Dang [939], there indeed was witnessed the sound of chariots and horses in the sky, and the battle was in fact a great victory.* The First Lord was taken aback, and ordered the construction of a great temple, larger than on the former model. He supplied feather screens, royal banners, bronze gongs, deerskin drums, dancing and singing, and sacrificial oxen in show of gratitude. As things have changed over the successive royal reigns, this has gradually become an old ceremony.

In the first year of Trung Hung [1285], he was appointed Believing and Assisting Great King. In the fourth year [1288], the words "Manifesting Sincerity" were added. In the twentieth year of Hung Long [1312], the words "Revering Righteousness" were added. To this day, his majesty is strongly increasing. The incense is not extinguished.

Ly Thuong Kiet
(Defender-in-Chief, Loyally Assisting, Mightily Militant, Majestically Victorious Duke)

The Duke was of the Ly line and was named Thuong Kiet. He was from the sub-district of Thai Hoa to the right-hand side of the capital at Thang Long.

His father, An Ngu, served as an official and reached the post of Revered Gentleman of the Household. For generations theirs had been a family of hatpins and ivory tablets. The Duke was of many plots and strategies, having the talent of a martial leader. In his youth, he was slender and graceful, refined and elegant. He was lauded spectacularly and appointed Palace Gateman-Usher.

---

*This is a reference to the Vietnamese defeat of a Chinese naval force on the Bach Dang River, near Hanoi, which led to Vietnamese independence from China after nearly 1,000 years of Chinese domination.

This temple to General Ly Thuong Kiet is located in Hanoi. Such temples have been supported by the state and by local communities since the earliest days of Vietnamese history. They commemorate historical figures or spirits of other origins, and are important sites of offerings and devotions. *(Co Xa Linh Tu, Wikimedia Commons, http://en.wikipedia.org/wiki/File:Co_Xa_Linh_Tu.JPG)*

In the reign of Ly Thai Tong [1028–1054], he was promoted to Office Inspector-Manager. Ly Thanh Tong [1054–1072] made him Commandant Grand Guardian. He kept his post with careful reverence, actively following the system of rites and laws and never making the slightest of excesses. He was given the duty to oversee officials and people in the two districts of Thanh Hoa and Nghe An, as well as the five sub-prefectures and three upland villages of the Man and Lao. If there were rebels, he was authorized to quell them. Only Champa was neglectful of its duty to send tribute, so the sovereign himself went to punish them. The Duke obeyed orders to take on additional responsibility as a great general, and was given halberd and flag as he led the vanguard. The Cham lord, Che Cu [1061–1074], was captured alive.

Because of his merit, he was appointed Defender-in-Chief Bulwark of the State. He then accepted the titles of Area Commander with Special Warrant Over the Various Garrisons, Cooperating With Officials of the Secretariat-Chancellery, Supreme Pillar of State, Adopted Brother of the Son of Heaven, Great Bulwark-General of the State, and Dynasty-

Founding Duke. Ly Nhan Tong [1072–1128] ascended the throne and promoted him to Defender-in-Chief Bulwark of the State, employing him as a high official.

Early in the Anh Vu Chieu Thang era [1076–1085], the Duke heard that the Sung (dynasty) wanted to bring down troops to watch our frontier from afar in order to obtain a pretext for military action. The Duke immediately petitioned the emperor, "Sitting and waiting for the enemy to arrive is not as good as striking first to grab the tip of his lance." Thereupon, the emperor ordered the Duke to lead a great army. He destroyed Ung, Kham, and Liem, subduing four forts in those regions, and captured innumerable riches. In the first year of Long Phu [1101], he was given the titles of Palace Attendant Supervising the Department of First-Class Employees and General Administrator of Matters Inside and Outside the Palace.

That winter, he pacified the rebel Ly Giac of Dien province. The Sung retaliated by plundering and winning Luc, Luoc, and other provinces. The Duke gathered his strength and constructed a wall along the Nhu Nguyet River. He retook Vu Binh Nguyen. Upon returning from battle, his praises and rewards were greatly increased.

When he died, he was awarded the posthumous titles of Office Manager of Those Who Enter the Palace, Inspecting and Approving Defender-In-Chief, Manager of Important Security Matters of the Realm, and Duke of the Viet Realm. He was given rice land with ten thousand households, and his younger brother, Ly Thuong Hien, succeeded him in being granted the rank of marquis.

The people were fond of demons and spirits; witches and wizards deluded men. The Defender-in-Chief greatly increased reprimands and fines, sifted out more than half, and sternly did away with vile customs. Consequently, at that time, wherever there were obscene temples, they were always changed into places for offering incense to benevolent deities. The people received great favor from him, and they petitioned to build a temple for his worship. Whenever they prayed, they always received a divine response.

In the first year of Trung Hung [1285], he was appointed Loyally Assisting Duke. In the fourth year [1288], the words "Mightily Militant" were added. In the twenty-first year of Hung Long [1313], the words "Majestically Victorious" were also granted. At this deeply majestic temple, divine responsiveness is increasingly manifest.

The Mountain Spirit and the Water Spirit
(Tan Vien Protecting Sacredness, Saving the Country, Manifesting Divinity and Responding King)

According to Duke Tang's *Records of Giao Chi*, the King was the Mountain Spirit, who enjoyed friendship with the Water Spirit. The Mountain Spirit resided hidden at Gia Ninh cave in Phong province.

King Hung had a daughter named My Nuong, who was of excellent appearance, having the beauty to fell cities. The king of Thuc sent an emissary to request a marriage. King Hung was about to allow this when a great minister and lord of Lac disagreed, saying, "They are only spying on our country!" King Hung feared this would create a rift in relations.

The lord of Lac said, "Your Great Majesty's land is expansive and the people numerous. I beseech you to grant her to he who has strange talents and extraordinary abilities, making him your son-in-law. First arrange your troops to wait in ambush. It is needless to imagine anything better." And so King Hung broke things off with Thuc. Everywhere in the country those having extraordinary abilities were sought for. The King and the Water Spirit both responded to the search. King Hung ordered them examined. The King could penetrate jade and stone. The Water Spirit could enter water and fire. They manifested their divine powers equally well. King Hung was greatly pleased. He told the lord of Lac, "The two gentlemen are both worthy matches. I have only one daughter; which of the two virtuous men shall be chosen?" The lord of Lac said, "Your Majesty should agree with them that whoever comes to marry her first shall be granted her hand." King Hung consented to this. Each was bidden to return and prepare the ceremonial offerings.

The King returned home over the night to bring local products, gold and silver, beautiful girls, rhinoceroses, and elephants. There were also rare birds and beasts, all numbering in the hundreds. By sunrise the next day, he had already made his presentations to King Hung. The king was greatly pleased and thereby granted My Nuong in marriage. The King met her in person and brought her back to live on Mount Loi.

That evening, the Water Spirit also prepared aquatic products, pearls, tortoise shells, valuables, and coral. There were great and fine fish as well, also numbering in the hundreds. The Water Spirit reached the imperial city to set out and present his offerings. Seeing My Nuong had returned to be with the King, the Water Spirit was very angry, leading a mob to pursue them and wanting to reduce Mount Loi to pieces.

The King moved to reside at the peak of Mount Tan Vien. And so later generations were made enemies with the Water Spirit. Each year, he brought autumn rains to strike Tan Vien. The people on the mountain together built a palisade for assistance, and the Water Spirit could not violate it. The King's divine traces are extremely numerous. It is not possible to recount them completely.

In the first year of Trung Hung [1285], he was appointed Protecting Sacredness King. In the fourth year [1288], the words "Saving the Country" were also awarded. And additionally the words "Manifesting Responsiveness" were granted.

Maniyadanabon

～ *Fifteenth Century, Burma* ～

SHIN SANDALINKA

This text was written at some point in the last decades of the eighteenth century, but contains accounts of earlier Burmese rulers, including the one about King Ngazishin (r. 1343–1350) that is reproduced below. The entire volume is centered on episodes involving the court, and particularly the dynamic between rulers and their advisers. The full title of the larger text is "Submissions of Minyaza or Precious Jewel Examples," which makes clear the purpose of the text—namely, to provide examples of particular forms of conduct, policies, and responses to situations with beneficial outcomes. Thus, it was written as a guide to good and successful kingship that could be referred to by Burmese rulers. In this respect, it falls into the Indian tradition of the government handbook, such as Kautilya's noted *Arthashastra* (roughly, "The Science of Politics"), a third-century BCE exemplar of this genre. At the same time, this format echoes that found elsewhere in Southeast Asia, including Vietnam, where nineteenth-century court historians began producing works in the "imperial mirror" genre, which they had borrowed from China. The "imperial mirror" was a similarly didactic format in which the events of the past were commented upon by historians to provide lessons for future rulers.

The *Maniyadanabon* follows a standard formula, which presents a historical king and a problem that he faced, followed by possible solutions, and then historical precedents to explain the correct course of action. These examples were often taken from Buddhist Jataka tales about the previous lives of the Buddha, from various Buddhist scriptures, and even from Burmese folk tales. This particular excerpt contains lessons regarding proper and well-timed speech. It comments on how servants and officials should advise the king, reflecting on when it is appropriate to speak the unvarnished truth, and when it is more suitable to tell a white lie, or at least diverge from harsh realities. These brief episodes are rich examples of the ways in which stories are more than mere tales, but also can serve to impart important lessons. They also illustrate the ways in which the world of the ordinary person (the teller of tales, and transmitter of the Jataka stories) and that of the elite intersect, even if their particular engagements with the stories may be different. Finally, these stories suggest the significant ways in which the worlds of animals and human intersected in both the real and literary realms. The tales feature horses given impressive sounding names; they feature talking lions and birds; they have mythical beasts interacting with humans. In short, this was a world in which animals were never far away, and were presumed to have spiritual qualities that gave them power and significance. It is not surprising, then, that animals would be prominent figures in these stories, and that they would be creatures from which rulers could learn important lessons.

Questions

1. What does this story tell us about the concerns of Burmese rulers? What sorts of issues did they have to contend with?
2. What are the manifestations of royal power, and at the same time, what are the limitations of those powers?
3. What sorts of lessons are being learned in these accounts, and where are the lessons being learned from?
4. What does this form of literature tell us about Burmese society, culture, and political structures?
5. What role does religion play in political life—in other words, how do these two realms intersect?

***

The Maniyadanabon

Shin Sandalinka. *The Maniyadanabon of Shin Sandalinka.* Trans. L.E. Bagshawe. (Ithaca, NY: Cornell University Southeast Asia Program, 1981), pp. 16–23. Reprinted with the kind permission of the publisher.

The First Example: Minyaza's Account of a Pretended Monk in Ngazishin's Time

One day, just as it was nearly time for Ngazishin to call for his dinner, a certain pretended monk came into the front part of the palace to beg for his food and stood there. Ngazishin asked him why he was standing there. When he replied that he was waiting to beg his food, Ngazishin said, "I will send for food," washed his hands and with glad heart handed over to that monk the entire meal that was set out upon his serving tray.

Ngazishin was very happy and said, "He came to beg food well past the usual time—it is almost midday. He must be an *arahat* of exceptional powers and wisdom, who came specially to give me, the king, an opportunity of winning merit."*

He spoke with great joy, and sent one of his servants to follow the monk and to watch him, to see where he went, and to find out all about him. The servant followed and watched, but when the monk handed his begging bowl over to a woman, he saw that he was no good monk, but a fraud. When he saw this the servant thought anxiously, "If I tell the king all about this monk, not only will the kindly feeling that is his present mood be broken up, but I shall lose honor. Since this is so, I must preserve my honor and make the most of the merit which the king has earned by his kind action." With this resolve he returned to the palace.

The king immediately questioned his servant who answered, "Lord of Life, what my glorious lord King said is true, that this must be an *arahat* of exceptional power and wisdom. I followed and watched him, but I could not tell with my sight where he went. The monk simply vanished."

On this report Ngazishin said, "I was sure that I was right," and made the servant his right-hand man. A little later word came to him that the ruler of Pinya had sent him a bay horse and he said, "This is the result of the merit that I earned."

Later on Ngazishin learned that that monk was in fact a fraud. He asked his ministers, "How many kinds of servants are there?"

"There are servants like boats, servants like cattle, servants like parrots, servants like geese, servants like elephants, and servants like horses, they say; six sorts in all," answered the ministers.

---

*An *arahat* is a person of great spiritual accomplishment who is believed to have achieved enlightenment.

"Ministers, among the six sorts, he who reported to me so as to make the most of my meritorious intention is a servant like a parrot," said the king, giving him further praise and rich rewards.

Ngazishin went on to say, "Ministers, as regards my horse, the bay, when I was riding him from Pinya to Kyetthet, we came to Kyettet in Taungdwingyi and as I rode him through a sorghum field in a big turban, it seemed to those who saw that a white egret was flying past; now which of these four horses would be the fastest, my bay, or Nayapatizithu's horse named Kaungginhkwe (Heaven Cleaver), also called Thudawzin, or Alaungzithu's horse named Wutmonmakywe (Doesn't Shake Dust from your Clothes) which drew the famous spirit car, or the Tamil King Eilaya's horse named Beikmanwaya (Temple Weapon)?"

"The bay horse set out from Kyetthet in the morning and by night reached Kyettet in Taungdwingyi, Kaungkinhkwe was ridden out from the Chindwin valley just at sunrise and by the dusk of evening reached Thithseinthitsaya. The horse which drew the spirit car, it is said, came ten times to Pagan bringing champak buds from Mount Popa. Beikmanwaya, it was said, completed a journey of three yozanas," the ministers reported.

"Yes, but which of them was fastest?" asked the king.

"We must reply to Your Majesty's question as follows," said the ministers. "Those in the king's employment, at a time when it is right to speak exactly, must speak exactly, as their master requires. At a time when it is right to minimize, they must minimize. When it is right to exaggerate, they must exaggerate. They have to speak having due regard to time and place and considering the circumstances. If they speak without considering first, without thinking of or respect for the time, they will not attain any intelligent end. In this case, since it would not attain any desirable end, it is hard for us to venture a decision." So saying, they took their leave.

Minyaza's Examples of How, on the Right Occasion, One Should Speak and Keep Silence When Silence Is Right

One should keep this rule in mind and always consider carefully the time and the place; in accordance with this rule one should speak only when the right moment has come. If you speak at the wrong moment, you will receive only mockery and blame from other people. Those who speak out at the right moment will have the praise of wise men and will do well.

It is like this: In the time of King Brahmadatta in Bayanathi there was a certain cross-eyed, gap-toothed Brahman priest. This priest came to know that his wife was deceiving him with another priest who happened to look just like himself. He tried to put a stop to the affair, but could not, and so he plotted to have his enemy killed, not in a way that would involve himself in violence, but by deceiving the King."

"My King," he said, "among all islands, the Zabudeik island takes precedence; among all cities, this royal city takes precedence; among all kings, you, my King, take precedence. It will be well if you will re-hallow and rebuild anew the south gate by which you move out of the city."

The king agreed and gave orders that lucky timbers and anything else that the Brahman wanted should be brought.

"My lord King," he then said, "since tomorrow morning will be a lucky time, I shall set up the gate-posts then. Will you arrange for the offering to the spirits?"

The king asked what was required and he replied, "Since at this moment a spirit of particularly great power is in charge, along with many other offerings a pair of Brahmans of pure race, male and female, with cross-eyes and gap-teeth must be found and killed, and their flesh and blood offered and their bodies buried under the gate posts: then you, my King, will have great prosperity and the city will be properly established."

"Very well," said the King, "I consent."

The Brahman was delighted at the idea that he would be watching the death of his enemy, and went rejoicing home. He could not restrain his words, but called right out to his wife, "Hey you worthless slave, after today who will you take your pleasure with? Tomorrow I'm having your lover sacrificed and killed."

"He's done nothing, why should he be killed?" she asked.

When her husband explained how he had arranged for him to be killed, the Brahman's wife sent a messenger to run quickly in secret to her lover. When he had heard the whole story this couple of Brahmans, who, it must be remembered, looked just like the wronged husband, ran away together.

In the morning, not knowing that his enemy had in fact escaped, the Brahman priest went early to the king's palace; there he told them that in a place called such-and-such there was a Brahman of such-and-such an appearance and that he should be brought. The king sent his servants, but they reported that the man had fled. They were told to find another one like him, but though they went round the whole city searching they could find none and reported that except for the Brahman priest there was nobody else.

The king felt that it would not be right to put his Brahman priest to death, but his ministers submitted that because of the priest the gates had been taken down and that if they could not be replaced that day the city would not be safe; if a Brahman were not buried that day, it would be another year, and if there were no gate for a whole year, would their enemies not use the opportunity? "Would it not be best to make another Brahman the priest and bury this one under the gate-post?"

"Whom should I appoint to be priest?" asked the king.

"Young Tetkariya, this Brahman's pupil, would be a good choice," suggested the Ministers.

Tetkariya was summoned and given the position of priest, with many offerings and much esteem. When this had been done, in order to arrange for the hallowing of the place where the gate was to be set up, the young man Tetkariya, who was to become the Buddha in the future, went to the place of the gate and inspected it. Then he had a pit dug and had it surrounded with wicker screens. Afterwards, on the king's authority, he bound the old Brahman priest and brought him to the building. When he was put inside the screens, the Brahman priest looked at the pit and could not maintain his countenance.

"I was a fool," he said to the Buddha-to-be, "I did not hold my tongue and told how my enemy would be destroyed, and so I have encompassed my own death."

"It is not only, teacher, because you failed to hold your tongue that you are brought to a desperate state. Other people too must come to it," he answered. "Teacher do not be afraid; I have a plan to give you your life—but watch what you say in future!"

"The crucial moment has not yet come!" he then announced. He let the day pass, and at dead of night a dead goat was brought and he made the offering to the spirits from that goat's flesh and sent his teacher far away.

In this story, the Brahman, by not guarding his tongue when he should have waited for the right time to speak, brought himself near to his own death, but was saved and set right by the young man Tetkariya, the Buddha-to-be.

This Is Another Example

As for loss by failing to guard one's tongue, Keithayaza, the Lion King, said to a young lion who was born from his own affair with a lady jackal, "Do not call out! If you make a noise and the creatures of the forest hear, they will say you have a jackal's voice and cease to respect you. Keep silence and I will give you a thousand forests."

In spite of this offer, he did not keep silence but called aloud. The forest creatures all heard and ceased to give respect and he did not get his thousand forests. The Lion King saying that to stay silent is worth a thousand forests is an example.

In this story the young lion failed to get his thousand forests by failing to guard his tongue and stay quiet.

As an example of the benefit which comes from remaining silent and speaking only when a point is reached when speech is called for, in the land of Bayanathi a certain hunter went to the Himawunta forest and as he set traps in all sorts of ways he caught a pair of Keinnayas (half-bird/half-human) and presented them to the king. The king had never seen such creatures as this pair of Keinnayas before and was delighted with them; he asked, "What are these creatures good for?"

He was told, "When they sing, they can sing with the most beautiful voices, and when they dance, nobody can dance like they can."

The king was pleased and rewarded the hunter. He kept saying over and over to the Keinnayas, "Come on now, sing—go on, dance."

But the Keinnayas thought, "In this business of singing and dancing we can't sing properly in verses and words and letters like people; if he doesn't like our singing and dancing, if he scolds us, it will just be a scolding and even if he kills us it will just be a killing, but if there are too many words, it may give a false impression." So for fear of giving a false impression they remained silent.

But the king at last grew angry and said, "You aren't spirits and you aren't people; it's only as meat for my curry that that slave's son, the hunter, brought you in. I'll have one of you cooked for supper and one for breakfast."

The Keinnayas thought, "The King is angry and will slaughter us for sure. It will be best to speak; now is the time to speak." So the female said, "Great King, a hundred thousand speeches which are not well said are not equal to one which is well said—not worth even a sixteenth. For this reason we were afraid of speaking badly and so kept silent."

When he heard this, the king was very pleased with her and gave orders that the female Keinnaya should be taken to her home in the Himawunta forest and released and that the male should be taken to the royal kitchen for his own breakfast. At this the male Keinnaya said to himself, "If I don't talk, I'll be killed for sure; it's best to speak." So he said aloud, "Great King, all cattle eat the grass and leaves and therefore the rain receives the reverence of all the cattle. People rely upon the savor of the five products of the cattle, and since they maintain their life with them, cattle receive the reverence of all people. In the same way we rely very much upon each other, and if you release both of us we shall return together to the Himawunta forest. Assuredly when we die we shall be separated, but while we live it is not right to separate us. The great king can indeed send this female Keinnaya to the Himawunta forest, but if she is separated from me before it is time for us to die she will pine in most pitiable grief. Please to kill me first and then send her to the Himawunta forest. I did not remain silent out of caprice, but because I could see the fault that lies in verbiage, and so I stayed mum without speaking."

When he heard such words from the two Keinnayas the king was very pleased with them. He housed them in a golden cage and had the hunter convey them carefully back to where he had caught them in the Himawunta forest.

In this matter the two Keinnayas kept a guard upon their tongues and spoke only when the time was right; they were therefore set free from the danger of death.

This Is Another Example

All in all then, the following causes of blame fall upon those who used to talk very much: they fail to remember the order of their talk so as to be consistent; they say things which are not so, but false; they make mistakes and pronounce truth to be false and falsehood true; even when they do speak the truth, others are unwilling to believe them; when they talk excessively, others will not pay attention, and so on. For this reason it is good to speak only when the right time comes. Here is an example of the trouble that can come from overmuch talking.

There was a certain Brahman priest in the land of Bayanathi, and when he went in among the king's courtiers no one else had a chance of saying a word. Ceaselessly he, and he alone, held forth until the king of the country made a deaf mute, who was good at flicking pellets, sit behind a screen with a hole in it in front of the priest as he was talking away. Each time the priest opened his mouth in talking, from behind the screen he flicked a goat's turd into it. In his eagerness to talk the priest did not notice that goats' turds were going into his mouth; they mixed with his saliva and were swallowed until after a whole gallon of goats' dung had gone the king said, "Priest, stop talking now. A gallon of goats' dung has gone in your belly; you'd better go home and sort out your guts."

He went home, took a purge to clear his belly of the goats' dung and evacuated it. But from that time the priest was much ashamed, and though he went to the royal occasions and festivals held around the king, he stayed as quiet as a pot turned upside down.

You must keep these examples in your mind, and not talk on babbling like a never-stopping running brook. If you guard your tongue properly, you will stay quiet and, when you speak, speak well and to the point for the general benefit when the time is right for you to speak.

Truyen Ky Man Luc

~ *Sixteenth Century, Vietnam* ~

NGUYEN DU

This tale is taken from the *Truyen Ky Man Luc* (*Summary Tales of the Strange*) which was written by Nguyen Du in the middle of the sixteenth century. Nguyen Du had been a student of the famed scholar-poet Nguyen Binh Khiem (1491–1585), and had passed the Vietnamese civil service examinations at the highest levels, qualifying him for service as a government official. He composed this collection of tales upon his retirement from government service. The "tales of the strange" genre is one that the Vietnamese adapted from China, where it was very popular. This particular text was written by its Vietnamese author in classical Chinese, but not long thereafter was rendered into the Vietnamese vernacular script, thus increasing its accessibility to local audiences. In all likelihood, many would have heard it read aloud, given extremely limited literacy in sixteenth-century Vietnam, and its translation into the vernacular would have facilitated its popularization.

The story told here illustrates the powerful hold of the world of the spirits and divine figures believed to have control over people's lives and fates. It also shows the Vietnamese sense of the ways in which these worlds interacted with one another. The realm of the divine was not entirely closed off to the world of the mortals, as spirits and deities could enter the world of the living, and, on occasion, the reverse journey might take place. The tale illustrates, too, the concept that divinities might be both benevolent and treacherous, either benefiting or harming the people of the kingdom. Such tales were frequently metaphorical, for the elements of governance seen in the realm of the divine mimicked those encountered in the world inhabited by subjects of the emperor.

Vietnamese were all too familiar with political and administrative structures that could both protect and harm them. The tale reflects this reality,
while expressing the hope for divine justice. The concluding comments
of the king in adjudicating the crime reflect both idealized views of governance and the expectations of women. The ruler notes the official's
failings, notably not using his position to uphold virtuous rule but rather
following the path of debauchery. At the same time, however, the ruler
apportions some blame upon the story's kidnapped wife for her alleged
failure to resist strongly enough the pressures placed upon her by the
genie-official. Thus, although reunited with her husband, she bears this
chastisement, as well as the loss of her son conceived with the genie
during her captivity. The story reinforces the perception of the cruel
realities of governance while underscoring the idealized expectations
of rulers and of their subjects.

Although ostensibly a fable, the story recounted below represents a
not very subtle critique by its author of the ruling Mac dynasty (1527–
1592). The Mac family had seized power from the earlier Le emperors
at the beginning of the sixteenth century and quickly established a
new dynasty. Some scholars, like Nguyen Du and his teacher Nguyen
Binh Khiem, had pledged their allegiance to the new rulers, hoping
that they represented a solution to a state that had descended into
misrule and disarray. Many of these officials, among them Nguyen
Du, soon became disillusioned at the regime's unwillingness to hold
officials accountable for misdeeds, and chose to go into retirement
rather than continue serving the court. In short, while this tale is part of
a long-standing literary genre, it is very much a product of its time.

Questions

1. What is the nature of the relationship between rulers and their
   subjects as illustrated in this story? What does the trial scene
   suggest about the aspirations of both subjects and kings?
2. In what ways do the realms of mortals and divine figures intersect?
   In what ways does the world of the spirits and gods resemble the
   world that ordinary Vietnamese found themselves in?
3. How are gender roles in society illustrated in this tale and what
   do you think of the roles and attributes ascribed to men and
   women?

***

34-43 pgs

Truyen Ky Man Luc

Nguyen Khac Vien and Huu Ngoc, eds. *Vietnamese Literature.* (Hanoi: Red River Press, n.d.), pp. 268–278. Reprinted with the kind permission of the publisher.

The Trial at the Dragon Palace

Of old, in the district of Vinh Lai, Hong Chau province (near coastal northern Vietnam), there lived many aquatic animals. They were the object of worship celebrated in a dozen temples all along the river. As time went by some of them were invested with supernatural powers. Invocations for rain or for fair weather were granted; incense and fires burned without interruption before the altars and inspired in all a respect mixed with fear.

During the reign of Minh Tong of the Tran (dynasty, 1225–1400), Hong Chau was governed by a member of the Trinh family. One day his wife, of the Duong family, on her way to visit her parents, moored her boat near one of these temples. Suddenly two young girls carrying a little gilded box went up to her and said:

"Madam, our Lord has sent us to offer you this small gift as a token of his feelings. In the realm of the Cloud Water your dream of mounting the dragon will soon be fulfilled."

Having uttered these words, they disappeared. The lady opened the box and saw a scarlet union of hearts ribbon with this quatrain:

"Laughing, the beautiful one thrust an emerald pin in her hair.
That vision made me languish with love.
I send you this gift so that tomorrow night in the nuptial
    chambers, by the gleam of the flowered torch
We may bind together this knot of union at the heart of the
    Crystal Palace."

Lady Duong, frightened, immediately left the boat with her servant and returned on foot to her husband. Informed of the adventure, he in turn felt very uneasy.

"The aquatic monster, lustful genie of that temple, wants to carry you off. You must flee from him. From now on do not set foot any more near moorings or along river banks. On stormy or moonless nights we must light lamps and be vigilant."

With such precautions, six months passed and nothing happened. On the night of the 15th day of the 8th month when the Milky Way and the moon shone brightly in a crystal sky, Trinh, overcome with happiness, said to his wife:

"We have nothing to fear in this moonlight bathed by fresh breezes."

Together they partook of a dinner steeped in wine. Inebriated, they then fell into a profound sleep. Suddenly a storm broke out. The heavens were streaked with lightening and resounded with thunderous claps. When Trinh awakened, the doors and windows were still closed, but his wife had disappeared.

Trinh went to the temple near the place where, six months before, his wife had moored her boat. The calm waters of the river spread out under the cold clearness of the moon. On the bank he saw the clothes of his beloved. He was overwhelmed with grief. He stood motionless under the immense sky, his throat contracted, uttering only muffled groans.

Heartbroken, he gave up his position as a mandarin, erected a tomb near Don mountain and shut himself up in a little pavilion. The house was near the bank at a spot in the river where the water churned in a deep whirlpool. Trinh used to climb up above it to contemplate the countryside. He often saw an old man with a light red colored sack leave in the morning and return in the evening. "That's strange!" he thought. "There's neither hamlet nor village in these parts. So where can that old man be going?"

Trinh scoured the region and found only an uninterrupted sandbank, devoid of human shelter, with here and there a few tufts of reeds rustling at the surface of the water. Intrigued, he continued his search and finally found the old man telling fortunes at the Southern Market. Trinh observed him and noticed that, although his face was emaciated, it nevertheless reflected a remarkable lucidity. He thought he must be a man of letters retired from the world, or a Saint who had reached illumination, or an immortal who enjoyed travelling to contemplate nature.

Trinh became friendly with the old man. He invited him to his home every day to entertain him and both of them had good times together. The old man appeared to be moved by Trinh's generosity, but he was never willing to reveal his identity. Questioned, he only laughed, which intrigued Trinh all the more.

One day Trinh got up well before daybreak, hid himself in the reeds and kept watch. In the early morning mist that threw an opaque veil over the countryside, he saw the old man emerge slowly from the water. He ran to him and prostrated himself. The old man, laughing, said:

"I see you're trying to spy on me! Since you have been able to penetrate my secret, I will no longer hide it from you. I am the Lord of the White Dragon. In this year of drought, I have plenty of leisure time to wander about. If the Emperor of Heaven should decree rain, then I would no longer have the time to tell the fortunes of the dwellers of this earthly world."

Trinh said: "Formerly, Lieu Nghi had the pleasure of making an excursion under Dong Dinh Lake; Thien Van had the good luck to take part in a feast at the Dragon Palace.

"Ordinary as I am, could I hope to follow in the steps of the Ancients?"

"Nothing is simpler," replied the Lord.

With the tip of his stick, he traced a figure on the surface of the water. Immediately the river opened, leaving a passage where Trinh entered following his guide. After a half-league march, they arrived at a place full of light and entered into a many-storied palace. The furnishings, the table service, as well as the dishes served at the meal were entirely different from in the earthly world. The Lord received him graciously.

"I never could have imagined," said Trinh, "that a man living in misery like myself might one day set foot in this wondrous country. I was once victim of an extraordinary misfortune; today I make an extraordinary discovery. Dare I hope that the moment has come to avenge myself?"

The Lord asked for explanations. Trinh told him what had become of his wife.

"I venture to call on your supernatural powers to punish the odious monster that the sail may follow its normal course under a fair wind and that I may spring to action like a fox leaning on a tiger. Blessed be our encounter!"

"That Genie," observed the Lord, "even though he is depraved is always at the service of the Dragon King. Each of us rules over a particular domain and none seeks to trespass on the domain of others. None would dare commit the unpardonable crime of provoking conflict."

"Then may I demand justice at the Palace of the Dragon King?"

"The affair is still unclear. If you hasten to set a trial in motion against an all-powerful enemy without sufficient evidence, I fear you will not be able to avenge yourself. It would be better to first send someone for information. But I am afraid I don't have an agent under my orders whom I can rely upon to entrust with this mission. We must think about it."

At that moment, a young girl dressed in blue approached. "I ask to fill this role" she said. With deference, Trinh entrusted her with the mission and handed her an emerald pin as a sign. The young girl went to the temple dedicated to the Genie of the Crested Serpent of Hong Chau. Making inquiries, she learned that, in fact, there was a lady of the Duong family there upon whom the title of "Lady of the Land of Beauty" had been conferred, that she inhabited a crystal palace surrounded by pools of water-lilies, that the Genie bestowed more nuptial favors upon her than upon the other women of the Palace, and that she had given birth to a boy.

The messenger rejoiced, but could not find her way in that palace of many pavilions and several-storied buildings. She resigned herself to waiting before the door. Spring was in full splendor, roses bloomed in profusion like so many little red clouds scattered along the tops of the walls. Affecting carelessness, she picked a few flowers, roughly shaking the branches. The doorman came out, infuriated. She excused herself and, handing him the emerald pin, said:

"I thought these flowers could be picked by anyone, that is why I was gathering them. I confess my mistake. I fear my frail body could not endure being whipped. I beg you to present this gift to the princess so that she may pardon me. I will be eternally grateful to you."

The doorman took the pin to Lady Duong. She scrutinized the jewel for a long time, then simulated anger.

"Who is this badly brought-up urchin who dares ruin my brocade rose garden?"

She gave orders to have the young girl tied up in the apricot orchard. Taking advantage of a moment when no one was around, she slipped in, holding the pin in her hand. "This belongs to Lord Trinh, my former husband," she said, all the while crying. "How did it come into your hands?"

The young girl told her what had happened. "That jewel was handed to me by Lord Trinh. He is right now with the Lord of the White Dragon. Tortured by nostalgia, he even forgets to sleep and eat. He entrusted me with the mission of giving you this evidence of his unfailing determination to discharge the debt of love which binds you both."

Scarcely had she pronounced these words when a servant came to inform Lady Duong that the Genie of the Crested Serpent demanded her presence. She hastened to leave. Early in the morning of the next day she returned, spoke graciously to the messenger and gave her a letter.

"I ask you to tell Lord Trinh that his hapless wife in the distant land of the waters thinks constantly of him. Have him search out all means so that the phoenix may soar once more in the clouds, the steed may return to the border post and I may not grow old in this Palace of the Waters." Here is the content of the letter:

> Alas! The vows we pledged together before the seas and the mountains could not be kept. How unhappy our life is, driven by winds and rains! Across ten thousand leagues of mountains and rivers, I send you these words from my heart. I never cease meditating on my destiny so slight and fragile, on my body so frail and weak. As marriages are sealed by the Heavens, we had hoped to be buried in the same tomb. In the space of one night misfortune bore down upon us and I was cast into the whirlpool. I was not even able to drown myself. That is why I resigned myself to see-ing the moon go down and flowers fade. My clothing is impregnated with ghastly odors, my body and my life are agony. My sorrow is as immense as the ocean and my days as long as years.
>
> Happily, in this state of despair, your message full of solicitude has just arrived. Upon seeing the pin, tears filled my eyes. The arrival of the messenger filled my soul with pain. After this indignity even wild grasses and common flowers make me ashamed, but the boundless Heavens and Earth are witness to my fidelity to our indestructible vows through the many transmigrations. The emerald lies still sullied; deign bring your heart of pure gold to cleanse it.

The young girl in the blue dress returned carrying the news. "Now we can take action," said the Lord of the White Dragon to Trinh.

Together they went towards the Southern Sea and came to a high citadel. The Lord entered first, after having suggested that Trinh wait, at the door. A moment later, Trinh saw a man come out who led him into a palace where a king sat, dressed in red with a belt trimmed with jade and attended by numerous ministers. Trinh prostrated himself and explained his case in heart-rending accents. The King turned to a Minister on his left and told him to send a convocation immediately. Two soldiers hastened to depart. After approximately half a day they returned, escorting a robust man with a red cap on his head over a black face with a rough beard like a spearhead. He prostrated himself in the middle of the court.

"High positions are never conferred at random," said the King in a severe voice, "they are reserved for those who have made themselves useful. Punishment is never imposed lightly, it is reserved for criminals and wrong-doers. Formerly you had merit. That is why I granted you the direction of an entire territory. Charged with the mission of protecting the people, you took advantage of your title to satisfy your lasciviousness. Is that a way to do away with sufferings and remedy the misfortunes of the people?"

The accused attempted to justify himself. "He lives on the earth, I live under the waters. We belong to two separate worlds with no relation one to the other. Nevertheless, trying to do me harm, he dares slander me! If Your Majesty believes his deposition, your Majesty and the Court will be misled by lying accusations and I will be punished without proof. I do not believe that to be a way of sparing the higher from worries, nor of watching over the interests of the lower."

Before the Court, the two parties contradicted each other. As for the accused, he persisted in denying all guilt. The King, perplexed, did not know what to do. The Lord of the Dragon whispered in Trinh's ear:

"Describe your wife, her name, her age, and ask the King to have her brought to the Palace."

Trinh followed this advice. Forthwith the King ordered Lady Duong to be summoned. At sunset, two soldiers led in a beautiful woman, full of grace, in long floating robes.

"Where is your husband?" asked the King.

"My husband is the man dressed in blue. As for the man in red, he is my enemy. Three years ago I was carried off by force by that monster. If your Grace, like the Sun, does not deign to throw light here, my withered soul and my sullied body will bear his shame all my life, unable to look my equals in the face."

The King became angry.

"I cannot imagine such deceit on the part of this brigand! He acted impelled by lechery yet dares deny it with such an affront. For such a crime, he deserves to be put to death."

At these words, a man in a blue robe, the main court clerk, stepped out: "I have heard it said that all reward bestowed from personal prefer-ence constitutes a violation of justice and that all punishment inflicted in anger lacks moderation. The pros and cons must be weighed to find a just solution. The guilty one has always placed his vigor and his talent, as a faithful subject, in the service of peace in that distant land. Though he has committed serious misdeeds, he has nonetheless been able to be of use to the people. Every crime must be punished and in this case, the guilty deserves ten thousand times death. But he relies on Your Majesty's magnanimity to save his life, which would enable him to absolve himself through great deeds. May Your Majesty spare him capital punishment and let him be punished by detention in the black cell."

The King approved and rendered the verdict.

"It is said that men in life are no more than birds of passage following one another. The way of Heaven is infallible: one harvests happiness in doing good, one cannot enjoy peace in doing evil. That is an untransgressible law throughout the centuries. Owing to your past exploits, you were entrusted with the governing of an adjacent province. You should have used your supernatural powers to make the magnanimous virtues of the dragon shine even more. But you followed the vicious nature of the serpent and committed the sin of lechery. Loose living, unpunished, grows worse from day to day, that is why it is necessary to apply a severe and just law. To carry off by force the wife of one's fellow man testifies to unbridled passion. A heavy sentence should be imposed to warn the evil and depraved. As for Lady Duong, even though blameworthy because of the defilement which she should have defended herself against with all her might, she is to be pitied when considering the coercion from which she could not extricate herself. Let her then be returned to her former husband and let her son be left to the guilty father! This sentence is to be executed without error or delay."

After having heard the judgment, the Genie of the Crested Serpent went out, his head bowed. The Ministers of the Court signaled Trinh to retire in his turn. Back home again, the Lord of the White Dragon organized a feast in honor of the reunited couple and gave them gifts of grained rhinoceros horns and scales. The husband and wife prostrated themselves in a sign of thankfulness and returned to earth. They recounted all that had happened to the members of the family who shared in their joy and expressed their astonishment at such an incredible adventure.

Some time later Trinh went to Hong Chau to settle some business. Passing near the temple of the guilty genie, he saw the walls overturned, the steles broken, covered with lichen and moss near a kapok tree whose snowy flakes were blowing in the wind by the light of the setting sun. He questioned the old men there and found out what had happened.

"A year ago," they told me, "one fine morning the rain fell although there wasn't a cloud in the sky and the waters of the river rose and spilled over. A serpent ten meters long with blue scales and a red crest was seen to swim to the surface of the water and make for the North, followed by hundreds of little serpents. Since then, the temple has lost its supernatural powers." Counting on his fingers, Trinh noted that it was the same day on which he had brought action against the genie.

Comment

It was customary that worship be dedicated to the one who checked a great evil or eliminated a scourge. The one who thus benefited from worship should think of the significance of the invocation and act with uprightness each time he heard his name invoked. It was inadmissible to accept offerings and cause the people misfortune. This principle once accepted, the exile imposed on the Genie of the Crested Serpent by the King does not seem sufficient punishment. To fully satisfy justice, he should have acted like Hua Ton, Thu Phi. That is why Dich Nhan Kiet, governor of Ha Nam must be approved for asking the Emperor to destroy one thousand seven hundred temples devoted to evil genies.

Sejarah Melayu

~ *1612, Malaysia* ~

Tun Sri Lanang

Islam began to spread into Southeast Asia in the thirteenth century, first arriving at the northern tip of the island of Sumatra, and then slowly expanding across much of the rest of the island world. The religion was spread primarily from the Indian Subcontinent and chiefly by Sufis, practitioners of a form of mystical Islam readily taken up by Southeast Asian populations already acquainted with worlds of potent spirits and mysticism. Islam took root at various port cities of the Malay Peninsula over the course of the fourteenth and fifteenth centuries, as the leaders of these trading cities used Islam to induce South Asian and Arabic traders to visit their respective ports, but also to enhance their authority, both political and spiritual.

As time passed, these rulers arranged for genealogical accounts to be written of their own origins and those of their respective kingdoms. The *Sejarah Melayu*, written over the course of the sixteenth and seventeenth centuries, is the prime example of the great annalistic tradition of the Malay Islamic kingdoms. It was commissioned by the sultan of Johore, a state located at the tip of the peninsula, at a time when his realm was under assault by the Portuguese. The chronicle was thus an attempt to reflect on the glories of the sultanates to which he was heir. The *Sejarah Melayu* traces the history of the sultanates up to and including the arrival of Portuguese warships from Goa in 1511.

The text combines political and military history with important genealogical accounts as are common to this genre. It is a genre with roots in older Islamic texts, but at the same time, has one foot in the world of Indian epics, including the *Mahabharata*. Some of the names found in the *Sejarah Melayu* suggest that its author was familiar with

The Kapitan Keling Mosque was built in Penang, Malaysia, in the early nineteenth century, and is emblematic of the spread of Islam along the Malay peninsula. Its architectural style, combining Arabic domes and minarets with locally inspired tile roofs and rooflines, suggests the ways in which Islam was transformed by its encounter with local cultural and artistic forms. *(Author's collection)*

earlier Javanese adaptations of the *Mahabharata* stories. The tale not only provides an account of the genealogical origins of the sixteenth-century Malay sultans, but also serves to link to them to the Javanese, and particularly the powerful Majahpahit kingdom of the fourteenth through sixteenth centuries. Indeed, the *Sejarah Melayu* suggests that the origins of the Javanese rulers can be traced through the same genealogies that produced the Malay sultans.

This excerpt focuses on the exploits of a powerful prince, Raja Suran, whose armies defeated all opponents as they made their way from India into Southeast Asia, where they clashed with Raja Chulan, the ruler of all of the "lands below the wind," that is, Southeast Asia. Despite offering fierce resistance, Raja Chulan is also defeated, at which point the two rulers' clans are united when a daughter of Raja Chulan is given in marriage to Raja Suran. From this base, and to assert his own military strength, the account speaks fancifully of Raja Suran making ambitious plans to invade China, a seeming logical next step after his ancestors had conquered India, and now Southeast Asia. The *Sejarah Melayu* then offers an explanation for the failure of the Islamized Indian conquerors to extend their reach into northeastern Asia. Thereafter, the tale continues its descriptions of the adventures of Raja Suran, including his visit to a vast kingdom at the bottom of the sea, into whose royal house he marries before returning to his terrestrial realm.

The account is compelling for its evocative descriptions of battle scenes, of the use of elephants and various forms of military hardware. It contains scenes of magic and of the power of the divine. It shows the political dynamics between rulers, in which families were linked through the marriage of princesses to promising political figures. It also provides a sample of the kinds of genealogical records that were often found in the Malay annals. In short, the text demonstrates the ways in which the Malay rulers conceptualized the trajectory of their past. They were, as they saw it, heirs to a series of powerful figures whose armies had shaken the earth, defeated all in their path, and who had, through their enlightened and benevolent rule, consolidated their gains while also ensuring the spread of their Islamic faith.

Questions

1. How does this account reflect the strong genealogical emphases typically found in the Malay chronicles?
2. What does this excerpt reveal about the nature and mechanics of military confrontations in the early modern period?
3. What role does nature play in this account? What kinds of geographical references occur here in terms of locales and topographical features?
4. Where and in what form do references to Islam appear? How does Islamic belief shape the actions of the characters in this tale?

***

Sejarah Melayu

J. Leyden and T.S. Raffles. *Malay Annals.* (London: Longman, Hurst, Rees, Orme, and Brown, 1821), pp. 7–19.

Raja Narsi Barderas married the daughter of Raja Sulan, the raja of Amdan Nayara, who, it is asserted by some, was the grandson of Raja

Nashirwan Adel, the son of Raja Kobad Shah Shahriar, who was raja of the east and west. This Raja Sulan was the mightiest prince of the lands of Hind and Sind, and of all the rajas under the wind (i.e., towards the west, the wind being supposed to rise with the sun). By the princess his daughter, Raja Narsi had three sons:

1. Raja Heiran, who reigned in the country of Hindustan.
2. Raja Suran, whom Raja Sulan took and installed in his own place.
3. Raja Panden, who reigned in Turkestan.

After a short time Raja Sulan died, and his grandson Raja Suran reigned in his place in Amdan Nagara, with still greater authority than his predecessor, and all the rajas of the east and west acknowledged his allegiance, excepting the land of China, which was not subject to him.

Then Raja Suran Padshah formed the design of subjugating China, and for this purpose his men at arms, and the rajas dependent on him, assembled from every quarter with their hosts, the numbers too great to count. With this prodigious host, he advanced against China, and in his course, the forests were converted into open plains; the earth shook, and the hills moved; the lofty grounds became level, and the rocks flew off in shivers, and the large rivers were dried up to the mud. Two months they marched on without delay, and the darkest night was illuminated by the light of their armor like the luster of the full moon; and the noise of the thunder could not be heard for the loud noise of the champions and warriors, mixed with the cries of horses and elephants. Every country which Raja Suran approached, he subdued and reduced under his subjection, until at last he approached the country of Gangga Nagara, the raja of which was named Raja Linggi Shah Johan, and whose city was situated on a hill of very steep approach in front, but of easy access in the rear. Its fort was situated on the banks of the river Binding, in the vicinity of Perak.

When Raja Linggi Shah Johan heard of the approach of Raja Suran, he summoned all his vassals, and ordered the gates of his fortresses to be shut, and stationed his guards for their protection. He also directed his moats to be filled with water. The host of Raja Suran quickly surrounded his fortresses, and attacked them sharply, but were vigorously repulsed. On this, Raja Suran mounted his huge elephant, and approached the gate of the fortress, notwithstanding the showers of spears and arrows with which he was assailed; he struck the gate with his battle mace, and it immediately tumbled down, while the raja entered the fort with all his champions. When Raja Ganggi Shah Johan saw Raja Suran, he seized his bow and struck the elephant of Raja Suran on the forehead, which instantly fell down. Raja Suran quickly sprung up and drew his sword, and struck off the head of Raja Ganggi Shah Johan. After the death of the raja, all his subjects submitted to Raja Suran, who married Putri Gangga, the beautiful sister of Raja Ganggi Shah Johan. From Gangga Nagara, Raja Suran advanced to the country of Glang Kiu, which in former times was a great country, possessing a fort of black stone up the river Johor. In the Siamese language, this word signifies the place of the emerald (Khlang Khiaw) but by persons ignorant of this language, it is usually termed Glang Kiu. The name of the raja of this country, was Raja Chulan, who was superior to all the rajas of the countries lying under the wind.

As soon as he heard of Raja Suran's approach, Raja Chulan summoned all his vassals, and marched out to meet him with a vast army, like the sea rough with waves, and elephants and horses like the islands in the sea, and standards like a forest, and armor plated in scales, and the decorative ribbons on the spears like the *lalang* flower. After having marched about four times as far as the eye can see, they arrived at a river; when he saw Raja Suran's army extending like a forest, on which he said, in the Siamese language, "call them" and this river still bears the name Panggil, which in Malay has this meaning. When the Siamese troops engaged with the troops of Kling, a dreadful noise arose, the elephants rushed against the elephants, and the horses bit the horses, and clouds of arrows flew across each other, and spears pierced spears, and lances encountered lances, and swordsmen encountered swordsmen, and the descent of weapons was like the rapid fall of rain, and the noise of the thunder would have passed unheard in the combat, drowned out by the shouts of the combatants, and the ringing of weapons. The dust ascended to the heavens, and the brightness of the day was darkened like an eclipse. The combatants were all so mingled and blended, that they could not be distinguished from one another, attackers madly encountered other attackers, many stabbed their own friends, and many were stabbed by their own partisans, till multitudes were slain on both sides, along with many elephants and horses. Much was the blood which was shed upon the earth, till at last it dampened the clouds of dust, and the field of combat was light, and the fierce attackers became visible, none of whom on either side would flee.

Then Raja Chulan advanced his elephant, and broke into the ranks of Raja Suran, which exceeded all power of calculation. Wherever he approached the corpses swelled in heaps over the ground, till great numbers of the Kling troops perished and, unable to maintain their ground, they began to give way. He was observed by Raja Suran, who hurried forward to meet him. Raja Suran was mounted on a lofty elephant eleven cubits in height, but the elephant of Raja Chulan was very courageous, and they fiercely rushed together, roaring like the thunder, and the clash of their tusks was like the stroke of the thunderbolt. Neither of the elephants could conquer the other. Raja Chulan stood on his elephant, brandishing his spear which he aimed at Raja Suran; he missed him, but pierced his elephant in the fore flank, from side to side; Raja Suran rapidly discharged an arrow at Raja Chulan, which struck him on the breast, and pierced him to the back, and Raja Chulan fell down dead on his elephant. When the host of Raja Chulan saw their master dead, they quickly took to flight, and were hotly pursued by the Kling forces, who entered with them into the fortress of Glang-kiu. Raja Chulan left a daughter of great beauty named Putri Onang-kiu, whom Raja Suran took to wife, and carrying her with him, advanced to Temasek (today Singapore).

Then, it was reported in the land of China, that Raja Suran was advancing against them with an innumerable army, and had arrived at the country of Temasek. The raja of China was alarmed at hearing this intelligence, and said to his ministers and advisors, "If Kling Raja approaches, our country will be inevitably ruined; what method do you advise to prevent his approach?" Then, a sagacious minister of China said, "Lord of the world, your servant will devise a plan." The raja of China appointed him to do so. Then this minister ordered a vessel to be prepared, filled full of fine needles, but covered with rust; and planted in it trees of the *kesmak* and *bedara* plants; and he selected a party of old and toothless people, and ordered them on board, and directed them to sail to Temasek. The boat set sail, and arrived at Temasek in the course of a short time. The news was brought to Raja Suran, that a boat had arrived from China, and the raja sent persons to enquire of the mariners how far it was to China. These persons accordingly went, and enquired of the Chinese, who replied, "When we set sail from the land of China, we were all young, about twelve years of age, or so, and we planted the seeds of these trees; but now, we have grown old and lost our teeth, and the seeds that we planted have become trees, which bore fruit before our arrival here." Then, they took out some of the rusty needles, and showed them, saying, "When we left the land of China, these bars of iron were thick as your arm; but now they have grown thus small by the corrosion of rust. We know not the number of years we have been on our journey; but, you may judge of them from the circumstances we mention." When the Klings heard this account, they quickly returned, and informed Raja Suran. "If the account of these Chinese be true," said Raja Suran, "the land of China must be at an immense distance; when shall we ever arrive at it? If this is the case, we had better return." All the champions assented to this idea.

Then Raja Suran, considering that he had now become acquainted with the contents of the land, wished to acquire information concerning the nature of the sea. For this purpose, he ordered a chest of glass, with a lock in the inside, and fixed it to a chain of gold. Then, shutting himself up in this chest, he caused himself to be let down into the sea, to see the wonders of God Almighty's creation. At last, the chest reached a land, denominated Zeya, whereupon Raja Suran came forth from the chest, and walked about to see the wonders of the place. He saw a country of great extent, into which he entered, and saw a people named Barsam, so numerous, that God alone could know their numbers. These people were half infidels and half true believers. When they saw Raja Suran, they were greatly astonished and surprised at his dress, and carried him before their raja, who was named Aktab-al-Arz, who enquired of those who brought him, "Where has this man come from?" And they replied, "He is a new-comer."—"Where did he come from?" said the raja. "That," said they, "none of us know."

Then Raja Aktab-al-Arz asked Raja Suran, "Who are you, and where have you come from?"—"I come from the world," said Raja Suran; "and your servant is raja of the whole race of mankind; and my name is Raja Suran." The raja was greatly astonished at this account, and asked if there was any other world than his own. "Yes, there is," said Raja Suran, "and a very great one, full of various forms." The raja was still more astonished, saying, "Almighty God, can this be possible?" He then seated Raja Suran on his own throne. This Raja Aktab-al-Arz had a daughter named Putri Mahtab-al-Bahri. This lady was extremely handsome, and her father gave her in marriage to Raja Suran, to whom she bore three sons. The raja was for some time much delighted with this adventure; but at last he began to reflect what advantage it was for him to stay so long below the earth, and how he should be able to carry his three sons with him. He begged, however, his father-in-law to think of some method of conveying him to the upper world, as it would be of great disadvantage to cut off the line of Secander Zulkar-neini. His father-in-law assented to the propriety of this observation and furnished him with a sea-horse named Sambrani, which could fly through the air as well as swim in the water.

Raja Suran mounted this steed amid the lamentations of his spouse, the Princess; the flying steed quickly cleared the nether atmosphere, and having reached the upper ocean, it rapidly traversed it; and the subjects of Raja Suran quickly perceived him. The minister of Raja Suran came to see on what sort of animal his master was mounted, then quickly caused a mare to be brought to the shore of the sea. On seeing the mare, the steed Sambrani quickly came to the shore, and as quickly did Raja Suran dismount from him, at which the seahorse immediately returned to the sea. Raja Suran then called a man of science and a scribe, and ordered the account of his descent into the sea to be recorded, and a monument to be formed which might serve for the information of posterity, until the day of judgment. The history of this adventure was accordingly composed, and inscribed on a stone in the Hindustani language. This stone being adorned by gold and silver, was left as a monument, and the raja said that this would be found by one of his descendants who should reduce all the rajas of the countries under the wind. Then Raja Suran returned to the land of Kling, and after his arrival he founded a city of great size, with a fort of black stone, with a wall of seven fathoms in both height and thickness, and so skillfully joined that no gaps remained between the stones, but seemed all of molten metal. Its gates were of steel adorned with gold and gems. Within its circumference were contained seven hills, and in the center was a lake like a sea, so large that if an elephant was standing on the one shore he would not be visible on the other; and this lake contained every species of fish, and in the middle was an island of considerable height, on which the mists continually rested. The island was planted with trees, flowers, and all kinds of fruits, and whenever Raja Suran wished to divert himself, he used to frequent it. On the shore of this lake was a large forest, stocked with all sorts of wild beasts, and whenever Raja Suran wished to hunt, he mounted his elephant and proceeded to this forest. The name of this city was Bijnagar, which at the present time is a city in the land of Kling. Such is the account of Raja Suran, but if all his adventures were to be related, they would rival those of Hamdah.

Prince Samuttakote

~ *Seventeenth Century, Thailand* ~

Phra Maharatchakhru

Siam (later Thailand) had been influenced by Theravada Buddhism much like its Burmese neighbor. Its rulers were also powerful patrons of Buddhism and its institutions, and the Thai literary traditions were strongly influenced by Buddhist tales and by the larger patterns of South Asian epics. The epic poem *Prince Samuttakote* was composed beginning in the second half of the seventeenth century, during the reign of King Narai (r. 1656–1688). This was a period often regarded as the "Golden Age of Thai Literature." The tale is a distinctive localization of a particular Buddhist literary tradition, with its origins in the Jataka tales, the numerous stories about the previous lives of the Buddha. These tales are a core element of the popularization of Buddhism across mainland Southeast Asia, where few people would have read, or even seen, the canonical Buddhist scriptures (the *Tipitaka*), but many would have heard, read, or seen illustrations from the Jataka tales. In essence, these tales of the various incarnations of the Buddha before his enlightenment have a powerfully didactic nature, suggesting the types of actions and avoidances that might lead one closer to enlightenment, or at the very least to a better reincarnation.

The tale of Prince Samuttakote belongs to a mainland Southeast Asian variant of the Jataka tradition, for it is not derived from the "canon" of Jataka tales, but rather is part of a collection of "apocryphal" Jataka tales found only in Thailand, Burma, Laos, and Cambodia. Tradition has it that these tales had their origins in the Chiang Mai region of what is today northwestern Thailand, though Hudak notes that the content and form of these tales suggests an Indic origin. In any case, this tale is a dramatic adaptation of one of these Jataka tales into poetic form, and was probably designed for live performance. Although there is no definitive evidence regarding its composer, the poem was said to have been written by Phra Maharatchakhru, who was apparently a teacher and adviser to King Narai, though he may have previously served the king's father. Maharatchakhru died before he could complete the poem, which then may have been continued by King Narai himself before finally being taken up again and completed in the middle of the nineteenth century.

The excerpts below are from the first portion of the epic, composed in the second half of the seventeenth century. It first describes a contest arranged by the King of Romyaburi seeking to identify the most eligible mate for his daughter, and then the marriage that follows once the proper suitor has been identified. In a sequence echoing the Khmer *Reamker*, and thus the Indian *Ramayana* itself, the centerpiece of the contest involves the handling and use of a bow of magical power. As in the *Ramayana*, a single man, in this case Prince Samuttakote, has the ability to pick up and use the bow, and in so doing marks himself as the suitor selected by the fates to have the princess's hand. At this point, however, the story veers away from the *Ramayana*, for the failed suitors do not take their defeat lightly. Instead, they coordinate their efforts and gather an army to challenge the prince, refusing to accept his triumph. Prince Samuttakote rallies his own forces and vanquishes his jealous rivals on the battlefield. The selection concludes with the marriage between the prince and princess.

The tale reveals the deep literary and spiritual influences that have come to Southeast Asia from the Indian Subcontinent. At the same time, however, it reveals the numerous ways in which such influences were localized and adapted to reflect particular indigenous interests and aspirations. Here as elsewhere (e.g., in the Khmer *Reamker*), the Indic tales often serve more as starting points for local literary productions. The characters may be brought over, but even these are often renamed, and the course of their trials and triumphs also bears the marks of the Southeast Asian literary figure who wrote the tale.

Questions

1. What are the signs of authority and power in this tale? What is the task before the suitors for the king's daughter? What is the significance of the central role of weapons in the contest?

2. What are the features of the royal wedding that follows the selection of the groom? What kinds of decorations are used? What are the ritual elements that are included?
3. Nature is frequently referred to in these early epics. What kinds of natural features or elements are found in this selection?

***

Prince Samuttakote

The Tale of Prince Samuttakote: A Buddhist Epic from Thailand. Trans. Thomas John Hudak. (Athens: Ohio University Center for International Studies, 1993), pp. 89–128. Used by permission of Ohio University Press, www.ohioswallow.com.

The Wedding Contest

Then the king of Romyaburi,
The great, royal kingdom
With the power of might
To defeat all enemies,

Arranged the contest
For the royal daughter.
Kings from every continent
Came with their leaders.

The king readied
The iron bow heavy
With such great weight
That fear spread far and wide.

And so he told every king
From every direction with power great,
And with the ability
To battle in every corner,

"Whoever can lift the bow,
Hold it way overhead,
Show his skill with arrows
In ways devised,

To that Lord of Men I'll give
This royal princess
And the wealth and treasure,
Allow them to rule Romyaburi."

Pleased, the kings from all the lands
Readied to contest for victory
On the face of the field.

Groups of kings, powers in war,
Mounted their chariots
And one after another rode out:

First Maturarat
Chariot harnessed with horses,
In his hand a long lance;

Then Kawsoek
His chariot with dragons,
And he with a bow standing forth;

Then Thepanikorn,
A crossbow in hand,
His chariot harnessed with tigers;

Then mighty Mattarat
Riding in a glittering chariot
With the swish of a sword;

Then Thepphitchay
In a chariot with his hands
Swinging a mace of gold;

Then splendid Phitthayut
Rode in a chariot with a tusked lion
With countless capable soldiers;

Then Makottarat
In an adorned chariot
With a ferocious lion;

Then Jittarat in a gold chariot
With two lions
Skilled and powerful;

Then Jitasen, lion-strong,
His chariot swaying
Harnessed with a jamri;

Then Chumpasun set forth
In the zodiac chariot
With giants by the thousands;

Then the giant Nikum
Like Kumphakan, the leader
Of all the giant soldiers.

They mixed extolling their might,
But became discouraged,
Ashamed and abashed.

Each thinking to snatch the lady
In vain attacked many times
Without wavering even once.

None succeeded;
Indifferent they looked on,
Not entering the field.

Samuttakote Shows His Skill

Then Samuttakote appeared
Showing his warrior skills,
His might and his intent.

With the power of a naga (serpent)
Able to battle with special powers
He took to the field.

He seized the iron bow,
Swung the powerful weapon,
And proved his power to all.

Drawing the bow with mighty arrows
The lotus-foot prince drew back,
Showing the bow in the field.

His magic might instilled fear;
As he showed his superior force
In battle on the field.

Like Rama of the Solar Race
He lifted the iron bow
With might and magnificence.

He plucked the string and clear thunder
Echoed across the earth
Shaking every corner.

He grasped a glinting arrow,
Curved and bent
The handsome bow in a flash.

To all directions, he was polite, courteous,
But his power was feared
By enemies across the earth.

He showed his skill
Like Saraphang
Who proved his power long ago.

Quickly he showed his skill with arrows
As the King of the Realm,
Sri Narakup, decreed.

Shooting one arrow he demonstrated:
The shot became a flood
Covering the earth:

Hundreds of graceful arrows,
More than imagined,
Innumerable and countless.

Then he shot an arrow with full strength,
A high powerful shot
That hung in the heavens,

And then spread like falling rain
In the rainy season
And noise reverberated over the land.

To cover the earth and sky,
He shot an arrow
Showing his intent.

He shot one full strength
Into the air as a naga
And then another killing it.

One became a palace room
All across the sky
Shining with arrows.

One became a jeweled orb,
And the soldiers admired
And praised the Lord of the Land.

Then he shot another with full strength
And it became a golden flower
Sparkling over the ceiling.

Flowers hung at the top,
A many-hued jeweled place,
A city of many things.

Every king, soldier, warrior
Praised the prince's power,
His perfect skill and ability.

Then the king ordered hung a hair
From a jamri,
Twisted into knots in a circle,

Far, far out, a full yoot (ten miles)
To those looking it was unclear,
Farther than the eye could see.

He had the prince shoot one arrow
Into the heavens high
To make it evening.

He had the prince quickly shoot an arrow,
Shoot the jamri hair,
Split it in half.

The prince listened, with no hesitation
Shot it flying
To the heavens with skillful tricks,

Created darkness over earth and sky
As though it were midnight,
A day with no moon.

The kings, soldiers, warriors
Milled about in every spot
Confused, startled, frightened.

The prince strung one arrow, a barrier,
Shot it into the sky
Shading all from sight.

It struck one strand of the hair,
Cut it from sight,
Felled it quickly before all.
Deities and ascetics sang praises,
"Victory, victory, fight on fiercely,"
Cries of approval rang out.

They cast heavenly flowers in praise,
And all the enemy
Trembled in hair-raising fear.

News of the majestic power spread,
And the populace and troops,
One after another honored the prince.

Orchestras, trumpets, conches, drums
Sounded gloriously,
Combining in celebration.

King Narakup was jubilant
Every wish completed
To win His daughter.

His heart was satisfied,
All done perfectly
With no desire undone to disappoint.

At once he announced
He'd join his dear child
In union with the splendid youth.

He'd offer her in marriage,
Soon to become queen
For the Lord of the Land.

Unhappy with the outcome of the contest, numerous suitors for the princess' hand raised their armies in battle to challenge Prince Samuttakote, but ultimately unsuccessfully. With the defeat of the suitors, the stage was set for the marriage.

Samuttakote Weds Phintumadi

Romyaburi, nobles of the city,
The Lord of the Realm
Arrayed and readied all
For the splendid ceremony.

Kings gathered from afar
With coteries of ministers
And Brahmins learned
In rites and rituals.

They readied the royal regalia
Marvelous and abundant,
They decorated the city,
That royal earthly site.

Quickly they bedecked
The celestial palace
With nine shimmering gems,
And pure shining sapphires.

Ladies-in-waiting were adorned
More elegantly than city ladies.
Whoever beheld them changed not his mind,
Seeing their shiny radiance.

They compared and divided these handmaidens,
Personal attendants paying respect,
Enough to adorn
The prince and his precious lady.

Glittering gold necklaces,
Jeweled crowns and diadems,
Equal in beauty to the one wearing them,
An excellent figure of beauty,

Elegant crowns, necklace chains
Fell around the neck,
Royal regal raiments,
Adornments and ornaments.

At the time of ceremony,
That auspicious hour,
All duties were set
For the great event.

Their dressing and adorning set
With regalia appropriate for the Lord,
The prince and lady held
A special happiness.

A messenger was sent,
One with great knowledge,
To take the glorious news
With all its details,

To go and pay obeisance
To his Royal Majesty,
His Highness Phintutat,
The King of Kings.

"I'm the messenger
From Romyaburi's king,
Who's all powerful
With great auspicious signs.

I was sent, I, the servant,
To bring the royal news,
For you to come to this land,
Powerful and prosperous.

His Majesty King Narakup,
Ruler and Master of Men,
Gathered all kings together
To give his daughter in marriage.

Numerous nobles beyond count,
Soldiers by the thousands
Were readied in their units
In every part, every place.

He readied the iron bow
Named Sahatsaphan
And gave it to the judge
To be admired midst the field.

He announced to all the kings
Whichever person, whoever,
Could lift the victory bow
And show it to the battlefield,

Any king who could raise it up
And shoot an arrow powerfully
With both skill and art
And show His Majesty, the King of Kings,

Would receive in marriage
The noble virgin, the precious one,
And rule the kingdom, greatest in the universe,
In bliss and happiness.

The noble son of the king,
Prince Samuttakote,
Equal to the great Rama,
The great and fearless warrior,

Raised up the great bow;
And warriors praised him in the field.
He showed his weapon and power
And his fame spread over the earth.

Kings from every corner
Gathered to wrestle away victory.
But he scattered these enemies,
Destroying them in the field.

And then, His Majesty, Lord of Men,
As planned, readied
To perform the ceremony,
Complete in all rites and rituals.

He directs me to welcome you,
Two nobles so loving,
To offer blessings and joy
In the wedding ceremony."

Hearing from the messenger
This royal decree
Was like bathing in ambrosia,
And the queen's heart rejoiced.

Quickly they made ready
The massive elephants and horses
With warriors and soldiers
Like the immortal sun god Athit.

His Majesty and the Queen
Adorned in ornaments
With thousands of ladies-in-waiting
Like stars around the moon

Reached the great land,
The heavenly kingdom,
The city of Romyaburi,
Eternally noble and regal.

They entered the royal city
And His Majesty Narakup set forth
To welcome the Lord of Men,
Phintutat, to join them.

In the royal throne hall,
Proclaimed to thousands,
The two sat together
And talked of the great love.

The queen and the great queen
Both happy and content
Went to their eminent thrones
To speak as old friends.

They gathered together
For the royal son and daughter,
For the one skilled in all ways,
Whose fame spread far.

Spreading over the three worlds,
Orchestra sounds echoed,
All over the vast world
And the magnificent festivities.

All kinds of music played,
Every kind and type
And variety readied
For special entertainments.

With the ceremony completed
The royal princess
And the noble son,
Their fame and honor spread afar.

With the ceremony finished,
The Lord of the Land,
Phintutat, bid farewell.

And His Majesty Sri Narakup
Invited the King of Kings
To return to his city.

He returned with nothing impeding
And the people rejoiced
As they ruled with joy and happiness.

The Protector of the Land and Phintumadi,
The queen content,
Remained happy in body and spirit.

They entered the palace
With glorious ladies
Ready to serve them.

They reveled in joy and affection.
Induced into love play,
They found their hearts' content.

Their fame reached the three worlds;
In every direction, every king
Pronounced their love and perfection.

All the nobles came to offer
A flood of jewels and gems. From every corner,
They came to pay respects.

Happiness and content filled Romyaburi
And midst the people too.
Peace and happiness heaped together
As the populace praised them.

Reamker

~ *Sixteenth–Eighteenth Century, Cambodia* ~

ANONYMOUS

Like the Siamese, their Khmer neighbors also imported and adapted Indic literary tales. The *Reamker* is the Khmer version of the ancient Indian epic the *Ramayana*. This tale arrived in Southeast Asia as part of the literary and linguistic influences that traveled to the region from the Indian Subcontinent as early as in the first centuries before the Common Era. Once in Southeast Asia, the *Ramayana* along with the other great Indian epic, the *Mahabharata*, became a cornerstone of Southeast Asian storytelling and drama. Over time these epics were transformed into vernacularized versions that incorporated local elements, names, places, and cultural practices. Such adaptations were written and rewritten over the centuries, retaining core elements of the epics as they had been transmitted, but constantly changing localized elements of the stories. A good example of this in the Khmer version of the epic is the addition of a scene in which the monkey king Hanuman has an encounter with a beautiful mermaid, Sovann Maccha. This kind of localization was precisely what made this tale relevant and appealing to Khmer audiences, who embraced these obviously local characters.

The *Reamker*, was written at some point in the sixteenth century and revised over the course of the following century. The excerpt below is drawn from the early part of the tale in which we meet the titular figure of the epic, Rama, and his bride-to-be, Sita. It tells of the contest sponsored by Sita's father to identify a husband for her. These early verses combine elements of local kingship practices with classical approaches to marriage arrangements. King Janak's plowing ceremony reflects Khmer practice, in which rulers would carry out this annual ritual designed both to ensure a successful harvest, and symbolically to mark out the ruler's terrain. The contest for Sita's hand has at its center a magical weapon, and the process is one in which the weapon in essence selects the winner. Throughout Southeast Asian history and legend, magical weapons have been markers of kingship, and it was the ability of claimants to power to wield particular weapons that served as evidence of their having been selected by the Gods. Rama's ability to wield magical weapons is again manifested in his encounter with the ogre Ramaparamasur, angered because Rama has taken his own name. The ogre is forced to acknowledge the power of Rama, who can readily take up the demon's bow with a single hand and shoot a flight of arrows from it. The episode illustrates a practical manifestation of the power of Rama, not merely as one who has demonstrated the approbation of the divine, but as one who can use his magical power to defeat those who would threaten humanity.

But then, as in the traditional epic, Rama's luck runs out, and his apparent path to succeed his father is sidetracked by his stepmother. She had previously secured King Mithila's promise to give the throne to her own son rather than to Rama, as had been widely expected. Rama accepts this turn of events cheerfully, and takes his new bride and his brother Lakshman into exile in the forest. Thus begin their adventures, in which Rama and Lakshman spend their days hunting the forest ogres who wreak havoc with the lives of the people of the kingdom, while Sita waits for them in their encampment. When Sita is lured out of the safety of their encampment by a spell cast by a disguised Ravana, she is kidnapped, precipitating a fierce war between Rama and Laskman on one side, and the evil demon Ravana on the other. This war, and the eventual successful rescue of Sita, takes up the last third of the epic, concluding with the three central figures returning to the capital, where Rama is finally permitted to take up his rightful place as ruler of the kingdom.

The *Reamker* has a special place in Khmer literature as being among the earliest surviving literary works from the premodern period. Moreover, the influence of the Indianized epic can be found not only in this written tale, but also in the earlier architecture and iconography of the classical Khmer temples, where figures from the tales have been carved in substantial bass reliefs. It is very likely that the *Reamker* would

Angkor Wat, built in the twelfth century, represents the crowning architectural achievement of the Khmer rulers at the height of their power. The temple is richly decorated with long bas reliefs illustrating numerous classical stories and myths, including elements of the *Ramayana* story, reworked in Cambodia as the *Reamker*. *(Author's collection)*

have been performed in dramatic form as a central part of Khmer royal entertainments.

Questions

1. What are the roles of the divine and the world of the gods in this story? To what extent can mortals control their own fate, and to what extent do divine forces interfere?

2. What does this story tell us about how power is wielded and how it is transferred between people? What are the responsibilities of rulers in this account?

3. What is the role and significance of weaponry, magical or otherwise, in this story? How do magical weapons serve those who wield them, and how do they direct the course of events?

4. How do family relationships figure in this story? Who is bound to whom, and what kinds of obligations do the characters have to their relatives? What challenges do they face as they try to live up to these obligations?

5. How does this telling of the *Ramayana* compare with that found in the Thai tale of Prince Samuttakote written at roughly the same time?

***

Reamker

Reamker (Ramakerti): The Cambodian Version of the Ramayana. Trans. Judith M. Jacob, with Kuoch Haksrea. © Royal Asiatic Society, 1986, reprinted by the Royal Asiatic Society & Routledge, 2006. Reprinted with the kind permission of the Royal Asiatic Society of Great Britain and Ireland.

King Janak of Mithila adopts Sita, found during the royal ploughing ceremony. He holds the contest of the bow, in which Ram is successful.

Then the King of Mithila was carrying out a ceremony in the prescribed way. On an auspicious day in June, he assembled his chief ministers for the turning of the soil in accordance with the ancient tradition so as to bring peace to the people. As he took his golden plough with the royal oxen, his gait was like that of a roaring lion. When he had ploughed as far as the bank of the Yamuna River, there suddenly appeared a divine, golden maiden on a raft, herself in a magnificent lotus-flower, completely perfect, of superlative and remarkable splendor. The king was highly delighted with this, a royal daughter. Then the lord of Mithila assembled his soldiers for an immediate return to the city. He took the young lady, so fine, as his own daughter to his kingdom where he was an excellent ruler of his people. Then he held a ceremony to give her a name and in accordance with the circumstances she was called Sita. Pure and beautiful, she glowed like the full moon. The royal princess, so noble in face and character, was, it was plain to see, unequalled by any of the ten thousand goddesses.

Then the king, master of men, saw his daughter's remarkable, pure loveliness. That learned and august sovereign therefore created by magic a bow and arrow and he made a vow, saying, "If any god of unvanquished power can raise this magic bow with his invincible might, I will give the hand of my beloved Sita, so esteemed, to that god of mighty deeds." Miraculously, in all the ten directions, a tremor went through the earth and through the heaven of the thirty-three, where heat affected the godly throngs.

All the gods, overjoyed, hurried eagerly down together all in disorder from the heaven of the thirty-three. Indra was mounted on Aira, deathless lord of the *nagas*, bright, splendid, elevated.

The God of Fire, exalted, of unconquerable might, rode on a rhinoceros of fire of superlative strength.

The God of the Wind caused havoc in the sky, for, as he came with his horses, there blew a gale such as to bring death. The God of Rain, a huge form, rode on a mighty *naga*, splashed all over with water. And there came Candrakumar, borne on a bird, a patterned gold peacock. Brahm, observer of the religious way of life, strong and mighty ascetic, rode on a royal goose. Nerrati, lord of power, was seated upon an ogre as he set forth. Baisrab, great king and lord, came in his immense, magnificent aerial palace. Isur, whose power, prestige and splendor surpassed all in the three worlds and in the dwelling of the divine lords, was seated upon a great royal ox, having in his divine being infinitely great might and power. All the gods, the *kinnaras* and the ruling princes gazed at the mighty bow, intent upon their attempt to lift it. Isur of unlimited powers, the representatives of the gods, and the kings tried out their physical prowess and were unable to raise the bow. They remained there with His Majesty.

Then the king, master of men, saw Hari, Prince Naray(n) Ram. Perhaps he would be able to raise the magic bow with his strength, for he had force and physical prowess in abundance? Isur, leader of men, saw that all the gods were by now about to return home but Bisvamitr had brought that royal lord and Prince Laksm(n) to the city of Mithila. When they approached him to ask permission to try to raise the bow, the king of Mithila replied, "Prince, do please demonstrate the power of your right arm."

Ram had watched all the kings trying to raise the mighty bow. An eager look came into his fine face. He stepped forward to try what his strength could perform. All the godly hermits and princes watched the mighty deed. Ram, immensely strong and mighty prince of superlative power and prowess, raised the bow of victory! All the gods and men in the world offered their congratulations to that supreme lord whose strength was seen to be tremendous. The prince swung the bow, raising it up and took aim, sending the mighty arrow up high, demonstrating his powers unmistakably. He held out the mighty bow and arrow. Curving like a wheel, they whirled round in his fine hands.

The king of Mithila gives Sita in marriage to Ram. An envoy is sent to his father, King Dasarath, to invite him to the wedding. With his sons, Bhirut and Sutrut, King Dasarath comes to Mithila.

Then, seeing the surpassing strength and power of Ram, the king of Mithila was delighted. He offered his good wishes to him for triumph upon triumph, for the greatest achievements and brought the beloved

Princess Sita, endowed with great qualities, and offered her to Ram, the greatest of all. He and his chief ministers ordered an envoy to arrange the engagement with King Dasarath, instructing the envoy to go and give details to that king in the city of Aiyudhya. This the envoy did. He approached to inform King Dasarath of great esteem, supreme lord among princes, saying, "Bisvamitr, the great hermit of mighty powers, whose achievements are the result of his asceticism, just recently brought the royal princes, Ram and his young brother, to the city of Mithila, where the king had assembled his forces for the raising of the bow of supernatural power. His Majesty made a vow: if any god or prince, of supreme physical force, managed to raise the bow, then in accordance with his vow King Janak would offer the princess called Sita to him.

Then all the gods and princes came forward one by one to try their strength and raise the bow. They could not do it! They remained there in the court of the king's ceremonial hall. But when Your Majesty's son, Ram, master of men, came forward to try the effect of his great power, then, by the might of his arm, he raised the bow and shot an arrow, there in the arena amidst the assembly of learned beings. And there reverberated throughout the earth the sound of a thunderbolt, of a hundred thousand thunderbolts. The mighty sovereign, great King Janak, overjoyed, praising him and wishing him success, is preparing for marriage the dear, noble Sita, to unite her with Ram of great might. I am sent by the king, my master, to inform Your Majesty, protector of the earth, and to invite you to come and enjoy the marriage celebrations."

King Dasarath heard the envoy tell the story of his elder son, how he had demonstrated his surpassing strength, exceeding that of all other princes of all kingdoms in all directions, and his joy was immeasurable. He said, "O my chief ministers and attendants, hear the news told by the envoy about the dear Prince Ram, my elder son. He has strength greater than anyone's in the three worlds! He was able to raise the bow of victory, manifesting his prowess before all men. We heard a sound at that time and thought that it was a hundred thousand thunderbolts striking magnificent Mount Sumeru and that this was why a tremor went through the earth over a distance of 80,000 leagues. But now the envoy tells me about Ram, great among princes, how he raised the mighty bow of supernatural power; how he shot it and it broke with a sound as of a hundred thousand thunderbolts. And now at once the King of Mithila will make preparations for a wedding—auspicious occasion—between Ram and the princess, by name Sita, who will be his first lady. O ministers and generals, please muster a force. Let them mount their horses and yoke their chariots."

Immediately the chief ministers respectfully placed their hands together and praised the prince's merit. They took leave of His Majesty the King and went out to assemble a vast host of soldiers. They made ready the chariots, the big elephants, the horses, all according to the King's command and went to inform King Dasarath. "We have done that which was your bidding. We have diligently organized the troops so that they are neatly arranged in their military divisions." Then the king mounted on a horse-drawn carriage to sit with his three august wives. Bhirut rode on a large elephant, its head held high, accompanying his father. The elephant, decked with bejeweled, golden trappings and a beautiful silk embroidered collar, had brilliant gems placed upon it. Sutrut, regal as a lion, was seated upon an elephant equipped with splendid golden trappings. He held the gold croc proudly, dazzling reflections darting here and there as he moved his outstretched arm and drove off, closely accompanying the king, his father, who was seated in his magnificent gold carriage. The whole infantry force gave a shout and moved forward in procession with the princes to the city of Mithila where, when the king was ready to enter the city, they were ranged rank upon rank. King Janak was delighted that Dasarath, foremost of lords, had arrived. Leaving his glorious gold palace, so fine and perfect, like a domain of the thirty-three, he went to receive that mighty sovereign and great overlord. The two great kings went into the palace, with its bejeweled tiers, and spoke in friendship to each other.

The wedding ceremony of Ram and Sita is held. King Janak then accompanies King Dasarath and Ram as the whole party leaves for Aiyudhya. At the gate of Mithila the ogre Ramaparamasur threatens Ram because he has been given his name. He is reduced to submission.

Then the two masters of men assembled the divinely wise hermits, whose power came from observing the precepts of asceticism, the chief ministers and the Brahmin teachers, who had read right through the three Vedas and the Jyotisar, and had them confer to find an auspicious day, perfect for carrying out the marriage ceremony. When they had found an auspicious day and a time with excellent portents, stable and firm in the signs, the king had music played—strings, trumpets, conches, drums—ordering performances by the various groups, and he led forth his dear Sita, most high, and joined her in matrimony to Ram the god. The two, prince and princess, paid homage to the two great kings. The two fathers, seated on thrones of fine crystal, decoratively bejeweled, felt they knew in their hearts what Prince Ram, master of men, had in mind.

Then the king had the royal drum beaten to assemble the chief ministers and had them muster the military forces and ordered them to select strong elephants, horses and fine carriages, complete with drivers to drive. The ministers hastily bowed low, saluting the king with respect, and, taking their leave, departed to gather at the hall of justice. They took up their stations, all in their places. Here, there and everywhere, they were drawing up the troops of soldiers and saddling the horses, which were provided with fine new saddles. The royal carriage, engraved with a design of flowering creepers, was harnessed with swift horses and waiting in position. They made ready the huge elephants, all harnessed, their embroidered cloths firmly fixed, prettily decorating their foreheads, and gold bands set with jewels decking their tusks. All was quickly finished and put ready and all the drivers and elephants assembled. Every item was prepared. Everywhere the trappings, infinitely numerous, dazzled the eye with their many colors. Next the ministers approached the king and informed him that they had assembled all the troops in readiness, all according to the command of that lord, the great King Janak.

Then the three royal persons, masters of men, called the assembly to choose an auspicious time, excellent in respect of its signs and the accompanying position of the constellations. When this was done and a day was found, a watch, a moment, which, together with the movement of the lunar mansion, was auspicious, the two kings departed from the ancient royal city of Mithila. They ranged their forces with a company of advance troops to guard against an attack. As for Prince Ram's men, he marched them off behind his father, following the forces of the great King Janak, who had his daughter in his care. The whole host, elephants and horses, accompanied those masters of men, the three royal persons, as they set off. Dust was scattered everywhere. The sky was blotted out with darkness in all directions. There was not a ray of light! The sun's shafts were screened, gone. Earth trembled over a distance of eighty thousand leagues.

The kings marched as far as the gate to the open road. The clamor of the infantry, the rumbling of the carriages, the noises made by the elephants and horses, the wafting strains of music and the voices of men rose loudly to the heavens. The sky and the sun were overcast, the rays of light dimmed and darkness filled every corner, a dread and astonishing manifestation of the power of the divine Ram. Then the fierce Ramaparamasur, greatly daring, mighty teacher of the art of the magic arrow, heard, as the news spread, of the victorious power of the supreme lord Ram, elder son of King Dasarath, of his mighty deed thus manifested and how his given name was Ram, the victorious. The ogre gave much thought to that name, regretting it. In a temper, he went boldly and imperiously through the air, armed with all the weapons he could need—he had arrows, a bow and an axe, piercingly sharp, for destruction—with the intention of testing this power which was due to asceticism. A moment later he was upon the forces of the great King Janak and of the father of Ram and Laksm(n). "Hail, Dasarath!" he said, "How is it that you so uncompromisingly gave your son the name Ram which was my name? Your son is a learned man but of no great strength. Such power as he has is to be classed as human and of this world. How dare you set your son up as a god? I would call such behavior extremely provocative. It is an act of aggression, a serious offence. I am going to cut off the life of your son, do him to death this instant."

King Dasarath replied, "O divine hermit, you who are governed by this world's philosophy of truth, with regard to the name of this son of mine, I did not decide it for him from my own ideas. Great sages in their millions with their supernatural powers, all of them being great hermits of learning, assembled and gave him this name. And because this eldest son of mine has mighty power the assembly of all the royal hermits and great men of learning endowed him with this auspicious name, calling him the august, the divine Ram, who has achieved abundant merit. That was how it was."

Then the anger of the ogre Ramaparamasur increased most dreadfully. Furious and full of animosity, he was up and away, rushing through the air towards Ram's force. King Dasarath felt a shock of fear. He was afraid for the life of his son. He wept, beat his breast, his heart feeling tight and full. He moaned, moving restlessly about. Then he sent a brave messenger to ask news of Prince Ram, fearing that he might have been overcome by the physical power of the ogre, that he might be defeated. He might *not* be victorious in battle!

The messenger took his leave and went straight off, close upon the heels of the great ogre. Then Ramaparamasur, ferocious and huge, brandishing his axe and wielding his bow and arrow, flew towards the force of Ram, supporter of the earth, son of the supreme lord Dasarath. Reaching his intended destination, Ramaparamasur went right up to the gate, wielding his axe and bow and arrows and yelled out with loud cries. He stamped his feet on the ground, making the earth tremble. He called out to the master of men, "You ascetic, you! You are ignorant and timid yet thoroughly bad! How is it that you have dared to take my name? For I have great power in my right arm, tremendous physical force.

"Come out and settle your moral debt with me so that it shall not be a cause of trouble and unseemly provocation. If you behave so arrogantly I shall take this axe and strike you, bashing your head in. I shall knock down your glorious pavilion, adorned with jewels, smashing it to pieces instantly but if you bow down in the dust of my feet, placing your hands with palms together, kneeling, then I will forgive you and let you keep on with this life." Ram replied, "O arrogant great godless creature! Where did you come from, flying here through the air? From the skies? From the mountains? From the forests and caves of the vast Hemabant? You come here to my encampment with many demands!" Hearing Ram, Ramaparamasur grew angry. He blazed with indignation. "So!" he said, "how is it that you are not afraid, not agape at my physical strength for deeds of prowess? Am I not the son of a great sage, whose strength is in the precepts, whose manner of life is elevated above ordinary standards, and who is known by the name of King Yamatik? That is the race of my father. You are without understanding, a vulgar ascetic of the forest, a nobody of ill-omened birth. You, with your impudence, do not recognize a grand lord when you see one! Like a blind man, you are confused. You lie when you say that I am a godless creature. This might well be called trouble-making, committing a serious offence."

"O Ramaparamasur," Ram instantly replied, "I may have said that you are a godless creature lacking in gentleness. Well, what you just said could be described as thoroughly offensive! Now it has never been a normal characteristic of hermits to speak rudely, causing annoyance. In all the four continents they speak only with loving friendship towards everyone. They are always most kind, they use words responsibly, they are well-behaved and they follow the Dharma as it is clearly their role to do. But now one would say you are provoking trouble. You are being aggressive, trying to be my rival in heroic deeds. I am in fact the son of the great King Dasarath, supreme among princes—indeed the kings of all kingdoms have submitted to him and pay homage at his feet. As for myself, in the beginning, in the second age of the world, I lived as

Naray(n). All the gods and hermits saw that all kinds of godless creatures were attacking religion and therefore the gods invited me to come and be born as Ram, the strong and mighty, to suppress those evil, godless creatures who were being wickedly oppressive and destructive."

Ramaparamasur then replied without delay to Prince Ram, "Divine Ram! You could be described as very conceited, overconfident and boastful, claiming to be of the race of Bisnu, of Naray(n), master of men, who upheld the burden of the earth. If you are of the race of Hari, the family of mighty Bisnu of great strength and prowess, then come and try to raise my bow which I am holding—if you can! Then I will believe that you are of the esteemed race of Naray(n), lord of the world in the second age."

Then Prince Ram manifested his prowess and the power of his physique. With his left arm only, the supporter of the earth, so mighty, raised the magic bow up aloft and whirled it round. He took great Aggivas, his sharp, powerful arrow and instructed it, together with the bow. He swung the bow up and aimed it towards the body of the ogre. The latter, agape at the deed, felt a sudden shock of dread. Trembling, he raised his hands, palms together, and bowing low in homage, he said, "Please, lord, I beg for my life." "I have already instructed my arrow," Ram said in reply, "and I can shoot it." Ramaparamasur was more and more afraid. His mind went blank and he trembled as, with palms together, he bowed low and said to the lord of compassion, "I beg to be expiated, lord, of all the wrong I did just now. I offer you, supporter of the earth and lord of princes,—for I must reckon with your powerful bow—I offer you all my arrows. Please do not continue to be angry. I would like to invite you, who wield a sharp arrow, to shoot it to gather together my own arrows, which I offer you so that all shall go into your quiver and you, great prince, will manifest your great prowess."

Then the god Ram aimed a sharp and mighty arrow, the great unconquerable Brahmas, shooting it to gather together all Ramaparamasur's arrows on the mountain height of Kailas. They came into his quiver of swift arrows as was the command of Prince Naray(n), master of men. Ramaparamasur raised his hands, palms together, to show his admiration of the perfection of the prince, lord of power. He bowed low, taking leave of the lord, and went through the air to the hermitage which was his own home. Ram, exalted by his mighty deeds and great strength, excelling in efficacious powers, gained a clear and decisive victory over the ogre Ramaparamasur amid the host of soldiers.

The journey to Aiyudhya is completed. A feast is given after which King Janak leaves to return home to Mithila. King Dasarath prepares to hand over the kingdom to his eldest son Ram, but is dissuaded from this by Kaikesi who reminds him of a promise to give the kingdom to Bhirut, her own son.

Then the two princes went to attend upon the two sovereigns. Their father experienced the five joys and delightedly congratulated Prince Ram, praising his achievement, his prowess and his overwhelming victory on this occasion. The three royal persons, protectors of the earth, assembled the vast host of attendants and the four army corps and marched their force, at a time calculated to be the most auspicious, as indicated by the planet Mahamahendr, proceeding all the way to that delightful ancient city, the glorious royal seat of Aiyudhya. The king provided a feast, as was the custom, with the beautiful ladies of the court at hand in attendance. The royal family amused themselves pleasantly, together with the numerous grand counselors and generals. The king provided a banquet for the army, for the men and for every officer of high or low rank. The chaplains, Brahmins and poets offered their respects, their admiration and their congratulations to the prince. Then the king of Mithila took leave of his elder, King Dasarath, and entrusted his daughter, of divine purity, to King Dasarath. This done, he returned to the ancient city of Mithila, to rule his peaceful kingdom with admirable integrity, constantly pondering on meritorious deeds.

Then King Dasarath, foremost of great sovereigns, assembled his court in connection with the transference of the kingdom, the beautiful white umbrella and all the accouterments, the decorative, bejeweled crown and the splendid gold sandals to Ram, his eldest son, for him to rule the land in his place. The king had the city tidied up and the roads, every highway and byway, smoothed and flattened. He bade the military commanders bring their troops by every route to the royal citadels within the king's domain. All the princes of the various countries were to bring their gifts to offer to the master of men. Then the holy hermits, the aged Brahmins, so wise, and the princes and princesses of all countries brought their presents and came to offer them respectfully to the master of men, reciting praises of the virtue and the strength of the mighty Prince Ram. All declared their allegiance to the great prince, Ram, who would now rule the kingdom in place of his father. The king was old now. It was right that he should thus hand over the realm to Ram that he might maintain the royal domain, protect the populace and give them peace. King Dasarath, their chief, seeing all the princes in agreement and so eager in their approval, ordered that an auspicious day should be sought for the crowning of Prince Ram. The king would organize a great feast. He gave instructions for the provision by the various services of all kinds of amusement.

When the auspicious day had already been found for holding the coronation, glorious occasion, then it was that Kaikesi came to speak with the master of men, King Dasarath. "Lord, with regard to your promise, given to me when you were setting off to wage war and demonstrate your prowess, and fight victoriously against King Adityasuriya—you gave me your word that you would give the kingdom to Bhirut to rule, that *he* would reign in place of Your Majesty. But now you are handing it over to Ram. It seems you have no honor. You are not trustworthy." Then Dasarath wept and wailed excessively, unable to control his thoughts until he fell, faint and writhing, as though a fire was being lit in his breast. The sovereign Dasarath collected his thoughts, recalled the incident and gave it consideration. He spoke to Kaikesi. "The reason why I am at this moment preparing for my elder son, Ram, to rule the kingdom and protect the people in my place is that this is in accordance with ancient procedure. It has never in history been the royal custom for the younger to rule before the elder. And moreover, if I gave the kingdom to Bhirut to rule, it is likely there would be trouble, criticism from the people."

Kaikesi, his wife, replied, "Lord, master of men, Your Majesty must be regarded as abandoning, in respect of this matter of honor, the world's code of morality." Dasarath answered her, "Will you please let me ask something of you? I will divide the kingdom of glorious Aiyudhya into two separate parts and give them to my sons, Ram, the elder, and Bhirut to rule, so as to abide by my agreement." Kaikesi, who out of jealousy wickedly persisted in her wrong attitude to the matter, did not like the idea and did not heed it. Anger flared up suddenly in her like the blazing heat of fire. In a furious out burst, she spoke to the master of men. "I am asking you to do as I say, my liege, to give the kingdom to Bhirut. As for your elder son, Ram, and his young brother, Laksm(n), let them go and live in the forest ways, leading the religious life as hermits, keeping the precepts for fourteen years. Let them build up their knowledge of magic practices and then let them return to the city." King Dasarath, supporter of the earth, grieved and beat his breast and writhed in distress at parting from Ram, his eldest son, most beloved, and from that lord, Laksm(n) because of the request of Kaikesi, who opposed his plans and was unrighteous, mean and jealous.

Tale of Kieu

~ *1810s, Vietnam* ~

Nguyen Du

The *Tale of Kieu*, an epic poem, is perhaps the best known Vietnamese literary work. It was written by Nguyen Du (1765–1820), a scholar and court official, whose life spanned the late eighteenth and early nineteenth centuries, a time of dynastic upheaval and transition. The tale takes its name from its central figure, the young woman Kieu, and is a story of love, hardship, and the suffering that Kieu is forced to endure as a result of what she perceives to be her karmic burden from a previous lifetime. The daughter of a modestly well-off family, Kieu lives with her parents, a brother, and a sister. She falls in love with Kim, her next-door neighbor, who is also a friend and fellow student of her brother, with whom he is studying for the court's civil service examinations. Kieu and Kim manage to find a rare opportunity to spend some time alone together, during which they pledge their mutual and undying devotion.

Kieu's life is suddenly upended, however, when her father is ensnared in a plot by corrupt officials and cannot pay off the debt he is alleged to have incurred. Kieu volunteers to accept an arranged marriage to pay off her father's debt, giving up her secret love for Kim. The marriage proves to be a sham, and Kieu finds herself sold into a brothel. This begins a series of debasements for Kieu, who is forced to endure a succession of traumatic relationships, bouncing from brothel to brothel before being taken on as an unacknowledged second wife, and eventually finding herself married to a powerful rebel leader. He arranges an informal court to which he orders that those who have wronged his wife be brought, so that they might face justice. Rather than a conclusion, however, this scene is followed by further suffering before Kieu, having paid her karmic debt, is finally able to return home to her family.

The excerpt here is the opening of the tale, which introduces the core characters, but also foreshadows the major events that are to befall Kieu. There are the hints of a complex fate that lies before her, and the passage ends with the first inklings of love between Kieu and the young scholar Kim. This sets in motion all that is to follow, a tale that ultimately comes full circle, returning Kieu to her family and her love, albeit transformed by her many experiences during the course of her journey.

The tale highlights the complex Vietnamese admixture of belief systems, most notably Confucianism and Buddhism. While Kieu's selfless entry into an arranged marriage to pay her father's debts is a classic example of Confucian-ordained filial piety, her worldview is equally shaped by her belief in Buddhist notions of multiple lives and of the consequences of previous incarnations. The story makes no effort to reconcile these worldviews, which coexist throughout the epic. Although Nguyen Du was a classically trained Confucian scholar who participated in the rituals of that world, like many Vietnamese, he also had strong sense of the role that larger forces played in peoples' lives, for he had lived through a tumultuous time of civil war. The story is peopled with a wide range of figures who dotted the early modern Vietnamese landscape: corrupt officials, earnest students, thoughtful judges, monks, nuns, military figures, lecherous men, and jealous wives. It is, in short, a kind of microcosm of this world, making Kieu a useful introduction both to some of the complexities of the ways in which the Vietnamese viewed their world, and to the social landscape of that world itself.

Nguyen Du's poem was drawn from an older Chinese literary tale of only modest note, a work he transformed through his remarkable facility with the Vietnamese language. Although drawn from the Chinese literary corpus, Nguyen Du made the *Tale of Kieu* distinctly Vietnamese through his use of the Vietnamese poetic six-eight meter, and by writing it in the vernacular, using a modified Chinese script. While Vietnamese scholars had for centuries been writing in classical Chinese, this vernacular-based script was used chiefly for modest private writings, and some measure of shorter poetry. This work represented the culmination of the script's development, a pinnacle of

Vietnamese literary production. After it was written, probably in the first decade of the nineteenth century, the *Tale of Kieu* (sometimes also popularly known for its three main protagonists as the *Kim Van Kieu*) became wildly popular among the Vietnamese populations. Being in verse made the story relatively easy to memorize in a society where access to written materials was extremely limited, and people would routinely learn by heart hundreds of lines of the poem. Even today, it remains perhaps the single best-known and loved work of the Vietnamese literary canon, a story whose innate emotion and drama have easily stood the test of time.

Questions

1. What might this account of judgment and retribution say about this Buddhist society?
2. To what extent does the realm of the supernatural show up in this extract? How does it intersect with the world of the living?
3. What does this excerpt reveal about late eighteenth-century Vietnamese society, its dynamics, and its composition? What kinds of people make up this society?
4. How do past and future meet here in the present? Why does karma matter?

***

Tale of Kieu

Nguyen Du. *Tale of Kieu*. Trans. Huynh Sanh Thong. (New Haven, CT: Yale University Press, 1983), pp. 3–11. Reprinted with the kind permission of the publisher.

A hundred years—in this life span on earth
talent and destiny are apt to feud.
You must go through a play of ebb and flow
and watch such things as make you sick at heart.
Is it so strange that losses balance gains?
Blue Heaven's wont to strike a rose from spite.

By lamplight turn these scented leaves and read
a tale of love recorded in old books.
Under the Chia-ching reign when Ming held sway,
all lived at peace—both capitals stood strong.
There was a burgher in the clan of Vuong,
a man of modest wealth and middle rank.
He had a last-born son, Vuong Quan—his hope
to carry on a line of learned folk.
Two daughters, beauties both, had come before:
Thuy Kieu was oldest, younger was Thuy Van.
Bodies like slim plum branches, snow-pure souls:
each her own self, each perfect in her way.
In quiet grace Van was beyond compare:
her face a moon, her eyebrows two full curves;
her smile a flower, her voice the song of jade;
her hair the sheen of clouds, her skin white snow.
Yet Kieu possessed a keener, deeper charm,
surpassing Van in talents and in looks.
Her eyes were autumn streams, her brows spring hills.
Flowers grudged her glamour, willows her fresh hue.
A glance or two from her, and kingdoms rocked!
Supreme in looks, she had few peers in gifts.
By Heaven blessed with wit, she knew all skills:
she could write verse and paint, could sing and chant.
Of music she had mastered all five tones
and played the lute far better than Ai Chang.
She had composed a song called *Cruel Fate*
to mourn all women in soul-rending strains.
A paragon of grace for womanhood,
she neared that time when maidens pinned their hair.
She calmly lived behind drawn shades and drapes,
as wooers swarmed, unheeded, by the wall.
Swift swallows and spring days were shuttling by—
of ninety radiant ones three score had fled.
Young grass spread all its green to heaven's rim;
some blossoms marked pear branches with white dots
Now came the Feast of Light in the third month
with graveyard rites and junkets on the green.
As merry pilgrims flocked from near and far,

the sisters and their brother went for a stroll.
Fine men and beauteous women on parade:
a crush of clothes, a rush of wheels and steeds.
Folks clambered burial knolls to strew and burn
sham gold or paper coins, and ashes swirled.
Now, as the sun was dipping toward the west,
the youngsters started homeward, hand in hand.
With leisured steps they walked along a brook,
admiring here and there a pretty view.
The rivulet, babbling, curled and wound its course
under a bridge that spanned it farther down.
Beside the road a mound of earth loomed up
where withered weeds, half yellow and half green.
Kieu asked: "Now that the Feast of Light is on,
why is no incense burning for this grave?"
Vuong Quan told her this tale from first to last:
"She was a famous singer once, Dam Tien.
Renowned for looks and talents in her day,
she lacked not lovers jostling at her door.
But fate makes roses fragile—in mid-spring
off broke the flower that breathed forth heaven's scents
From overseas a stranger came to woo
and win a girl whose name spread far and wide.
But when the lover's boat sailed into port,
he found the pin had snapped, the vase had crashed.
A death-still silence filled the void, her room;
all tracks of horse or wheels had blurred to moss.
He wept, full of a grief no words could tell:
'Harsh is the fate that has kept us apart!
Since in this life we are not meant to meet,
let me pledge you my troth for our next life.'
He purchased both a coffin and a hearse
and rested her in dust beneath this mound,
among the grass and flowers. For many moons,
who's come to tend a grave that no one claims?"
A well of pity lay within Kieu's heart:
as soon as she had heard her tears burst forth.
"How sorrowful is women's lot!" she cried.
"We all partake of woe, our common fate.

Creator, why are you so mean and cruel,
blighting green days and fading rose-fresh cheeks?
Alive, she played the wife to all the world,
alas, to end down there without a man!
Where are they now who shared in her embrace?
Where are they now who lusted for her charms?
Since no one else gives her a glance, a thought,
I'll light some incense candles while I'm here.
I'll mark our chance encounter on the road—
perhaps, down by the Yellow Springs, she'll know."
She prayed in mumbled tones, then she knelt down
to make a few low bows before the tomb.
Dusk-gathered on a patch of wilted weeds—
reed tassels swayed as gently blew the breeze.
She pulled a pin out of her hair and graved
four lines of stop-short verse on a tree's bark.
Deeper and deeper sank her soul in trance—
all hushed, she tarried there and would not leave.
The cloud on her fair face grew darker yet:
as sorrow ebbed or flowed, tears dropped or streamed.
Van said: "My sister, you should be laughed at,
lavishing tears on one long dead and gone!"
"Since ages out of mind," retorted Kieu,
"harsh fate has cursed all women, sparing none.
As I see her lie there, it hurts to think
what will become of me in later days."
"A fine speech you just made!" protested Quan.
"It jars the ears to hear you speak of her
and mean yourself. Dank air hangs heavy here—
day's failing, and there's still a long way home."

Kieu said: "When one who shines in talent dies,
the body passes on, the soul remains.
In her, perhaps, I've found a kindred heart:
let's wait and soon enough she may appear."
Before they could respond to what Kieu said,
a whirlwind rose from nowhere, raged and raved.
It blustered, strewing buds and shaking trees
and scattering whiffs of perfume in the air.

They strode along the path the whirlwind took
and plainly saw fresh footprints on the moss.
They stared at one another, terror-struck.
"You've heard the prayer of my pure faith!" Kieu cried.
"As kindred hearts, we've joined each other here—
transcending life and death, soul sisters meet."
Dam Tien had cared to manifest herself:
to what she'd written Kieu now added thanks.
A poet's feelings, rife with anguish, flowed:
she carved an old-style poem on the tree.
To leave or stay—they all were wavering still
when nearby rang the sound of harness bells.
They saw a youthful scholar come their way
astride a colt he rode with slackened rein.
He carried poems packing half his bag,
and tagging at his heels were some page boys.
His frisky horse's coat was dyed with snow.
His gown blent tints of grass and pale blue sky.
He spied them from afar, at once alit
and walked toward them to pay them his respects.
His figured slippers trod the green—the field
now sparkled like some jade-and-ruby grove.
Young Vuong stepped forth and greeted him he knew
while two shy maidens hid behind the flowers.

He came from somewhere not so far away,
Kim Trong, a scion of the noblest stock.
Born into wealth and talent, he'd received
his wit from heaven, a scholar's trade from men.
Manner and mien set him above the crowd:
he studied books indoors, lived high abroad.
Since birth he'd always called this region home—
he and young Vuong were classmates at their school.

His neighbor's fame had spread and reached his ear:
two beauties locked in their Bronze Sparrow Tower!
But, as if hills and streams had barred the way,
he had long sighed and dreamt of them, in vain.
How lucky, in this season of new leaves,

to roam about and find his yearned-for flowers!
He caught a fleeting glimpse of both afar:
spring orchid, autumn mum—a gorgeous pair!
Beautiful girl and talented young man—what stirred their
       hearts their eyes still dared not say.
They hovered, rapture-bound, 'tween wake and dream:
they could not stay, nor would they soon depart.
The dusk of sunset prompted thoughts of gloom—
he left, and longingly she watched him go.
Below, a stream flowed clear, and by the bridge
a twilit willow rustled threads of silk.

Glass Palace Chronicle

~ *1829, Burma* ~

BURMESE COURT HISTORIANS

The *Glass Palace Chronicle* is a nineteenth-century Burmese historical record designed to aggregate and adjudicate among numerous
existing court chronicles to create a definitive version of the royal
past. Its compilation was ordered by King Bagyidaw (r. 1819–1837) in
1829, and it takes its name from the building, the Palace of Glass, in
which its compilers met and carried out their work. It was based on a
substantial body of earlier works, not all of which survive to the present.
The first section of the chronicle is a history of the origins of Buddhism
and of the various Buddhist kings of India, suggesting the ways in which
the Burmese rulers saw themselves as a continuation of this lineage.
The later sections shift to the Burmese royal house itself, and trace the
growth of the first Burmese kingdom and its succession of rulers. Buddhism remains foregrounded in these accounts, as in many Burmese
official texts. This chronicle is in keeping with mainland history writing
traditions, in which courts would periodically compose histories of
their antecedents. The Vietnamese Nguyen dynasty of the nineteenth
century, for example, carried out a chronicle project paralleling that
of the Burmese rulers, as they sought to represent their predecessors
from a particular historical vantage point.

    This excerpt is a description of the reign of King Narathihapati (r.
1256–1287), the last king of the Pagan Empire, when the Burmese pol-
ity was centered upon the plains of Pagan in central Burma along the
Irrawaddy River. The passage is in two parts. The first describes the nature
of King Narathihapati's rule—the palace culture, his ruthless nature, and
the complex interplay among relatives and retainers. It suggests the

complicated dynamics that existed between a ruler and his multiple wives and sons. It also shows elements of the material culture of these rulers—their dining habits, their recreational activities, and their building projects, in this case represented by the famous Mingalazedi pagoda. Indeed, King Narathihapati was noted both for his gluttony and for the forced labor he employed to construct the Mingalazedi pagoda, and this portion of the *Glass Palace Chronicle* reinscribes popular memories of this ruler for future generations. The construction of the Mingalazedi pagoda was undertaken as the ruler's chief contribution to the already temple-strewn plains of Pagan. Like the temple construction projects of those who ruled before him, King Narathihapati's building of Minglazedi was a mark of his piety and a sign of his authority. The selection describes the building of the temple, a prophecy that temporarily delays its completion, and then the ceremony to commemorate the structure, featuring relics of the Buddha, elaborately bejeweled artifacts, and a magical female white elephant.

The second portion of the excerpt describes the circumstances by which Pagan met its fate, for King Narathihapati is also noteworthy for having been on the Burmese throne when Pagan came under threat from the Mongol forces of Kublai Khan in the 1280s. The Mongols menaced various parts of Southeast Asia in the latter half of the thirteenth century, and while they did not ultimately succeed in their military efforts in either Burma or Vietnam (see the selection *Viet Dinh U Linh Tap*), their incursions left a lasting mark on the popular imagination. Moreover, although the Mongols probably did not reach Pagan itself, as this excerpt reveals, the threat they posed caused the Burmese court to relocate southward. Pagan was never restored to its former prominence as a political center. As such, King Narathihapati represented the end of the line for the Pagan Empire, and his story in the *Glass Palace Chronicle* culminates this historical record of the early Burman empires.

Questions

1. What are some of the different elements of Burmese court culture as depicted here? How did family dynamics play out between the different royal relatives?
2. Burmese court histories contain details of supernatural occurrences as well as worldly elements. What are some of the ways

in which the supernatural manifests itself in this account, and how does it shape the direction of events?

3. This court history was written in the nineteenth century about a ruler who lived in the thirteenth century. How might this later historical vantage point affect the ways in which the past was recorded, and what purpose might these stories serve for nineteenth-century or later rulers?

***

Glass Palace Chronicle

> *The Glass Palace Chronicle of the Kings of Burma.* Trans. Pe Maung Tin and G.H. Luce. (London: Oxford University Press, 1923), pp. 167–176.

[The king's rule in the palace.] Because the king had become a man from the state of an ogre, he was great in wrath, haughtiness, and envy, exceedingly covetous and ambitious. He had three thousand concubines and maids of honor. There were thirty chief scribes to examine the lists and registers; they failed not day nor night. The guards of the royal slumbers were staunch and loyal, and guarded day and night at the inner and the outer wall. Thus the king's rule was painful to the palace women, insomuch that none of them dared to challenge him with a single word.

Queen Saw alone was the chief queen. The lesser queens were five: Sawlon, daughter of a master of white magic; Sawnan, daughter of queen Hpwasaw's sister; Shinhpa; Shinmauk; and Shinshwe. These five queens took each their turn to present food before the king.

The king, being one who had received the Lord's prophecy, suffered not from any of the ninety-six diseases, and never so much as sneezed nor yawned; and so none was allowed to sneeze or yawn in his presence. If anyone happened to sneeze or yawn, he beheaded him. One day a young handmaid in the king's presence could feel a sneeze coming on, and because she could not hold it back, she put her face to a great jar and sneezed, hoping that the king would not hear. But alas! the sound was louder than if she had sneezed openly. And the king asked: "What sound is that?" Queen Saw spoke into his ear, saying, "A girl was afraid to sneeze openly, so she put her face to a great jar and sneezed!" And he asked again, "How dared she sneeze?" "O king," replied queen Saw, "sneezing and yawning are even as the ninety-six diseases. Only the king is free from diseases and needs not sneeze or yawn. But all other folk, who are not free from sneezing and yawning, cannot restrain themselves, but must sneeze!" "Is it even so?" said the king. "I did not know this, and so acted with great wrath." And he had great remorse.

Now when the king awoke from slumber his mind was not loosened until he had thrown at and hit his handmaids with anything that was in his reach. So while he was fast asleep queen Saw removed the weapons that were near him and left only *lompani* and other fruits. Once when he awoke from sleep he threw the *lompani* fruit that was near him at a young handmaid; whereby she swelled at the waist. Therefore the *lompani* fruit was called *hkayan*.

In the hot season the king loved to sport at splashing water. He made a great shade from the palace to the river wharf and walled it in so that men might not see, and built a royal lodge for security thereby; and taking his queens, concubines, and all his women, he liked to go along a tunnel of cabins and sport in the water. One day he whispered to a young girl and caused her to drench queen Sawlon with water, so that her eyes and face and hair were wringing wet. Sawlon was chafed at heart, and she put poison in the king's food and said, "Shinmauk, I am not well. I pray thee, take my place and offer the king his food!" And Shinmauk thought no ill but offered the food.

Now, just as the king was about to eat, a dog below the table sneezed. Therefore the king did not eat but gave it to the dog instead; and when the dog ate, that moment he died. "What is this?" cried the king, and Shinmauk spoke into his ear, "Sawlon told me she was ill and begged me to offer the food in her place!" So the king called Sawlon and questioned her and because she could not hide the matter nor jest it away, she cried, "Thou grandson of a turner! I have done thee service and thou hast made me great; and now that I am exalted to this high degree, lo! You have whispered to a young girl and she hath drenched me with water in the eyes of all, so that my clothes and hair were wet! Therefore my heart was warped and I plotted against you."

Then the king called a thousand smiths and caused them to build an iron frame and commanded her to be burnt upon it. But Sawlon gave an abundance of gold and silver to the executioners that they might not finish the iron frame for seven days. Meanwhile she practiced piety and virtue and hearkened to the Law of Abhidhamma night and day for full seven days, and spoke to her (prayer) beads recalling the merits of the Three Gems, beginning each with "Such is He . . . ," with "Well expounded. . . . ," and with "Well accomplished. . . ."

But when the seventh day was come the executioners called her with fair and seemly words: "Wife of a king! The royal anger is terrible! Tarry not, but come!" Then, telling her beads as she recalled the merits of the Three Gems, Sawlon ascended the blazing iron frame. And lo! the fire, they say, was three time extinguished. After the third time she prayed, "May I be burnt and vanish in a moment! And may the boon I ask be granted!" So she died.

Not long after Sawlon died, the king at his hour of sleep raved and shrieked aloud, "Sawlon, come and watch beside me!" Queen Saw spoke into his ear, "O king, did you not put to death your slave Sawlon?" But the king's heart was bruised and broken and he could not sleep. When the elder, the king's chaplain, heard of it he came and admonished him: "Lo! You have put her to death. It ill beseems thee, O king, to be broken and bruised therefor. If other kings, your fellow builders of empire, hear of this, they will laugh you to scorn. It may be that those who visit you hereafter will not revere you. Publish not your heart's remorse, O king, to all the people. Remember the Law of Eight Efforts preached by the Lord Omniscient: "'Strive to avert the spreading of evil that has arisen. Strive to avert the arising of evil that has not arisen. Strive to aid the arising of good that has not arisen. Strive to aid the spreading of good that has arisen.'"

So at last the king was filled with patience and control. From that day forward he commanded his uncle Theimmazi saying, "Though I am angry, you should weigh and examine every matter. Wait for a half month, for a decade of days. Let him die thereafter who deserves to die. Who deserves not to die, let him go free!" Theimmazi was the younger brother of the king's mother. He had been a monk, but when the king came to the throne he turned layman and received the name Theimmazi.

The king's son Uzana was born of Sawnan, a lesser queen, daughter of queen Saw's elder sister. When he came of age the king gave him Bassein town. The king's son Kyawzwa was born of Shinhpa, a lesser queen. When he came of age the king gave him Dala town. The king's son Thihathu was born of Shinmauk, a lesser queen. When he came of age the king gave him the town of Prome. The king's daughter Misaw-u was born of Shinshwe, a lesser queen; and the king loved her. Now the king feared in case his sons should listen to the counsels of those who would destroy him and so make anarchy and rebellion; therefore he prevented them from traveling and ruling in the fiefs whose revenues they enjoyed, but bound them to remain by turn both day and night in his presence.

The king was gluttonous in eating; he hankered after curries of meat. Pig's forelegs and hindlegs he would have as meat for his curries. They were first presented before him, and he would give his son Uzana a foreleg, his son Kyawzwa also a foreleg, and his son Thihathu a hindleg. One day Thihathu's mother thought to herself: "He gives forelegs to the sons of others; to my son he gives only a hindleg!" So she bribed the chief roaster of game and gat for Thihathu, ruler of Prome, the foreleg that was ever given to Kyawzwa of Dala, and for Kyawzwa of Dala the hindleg ever given to Thihathu, ruler of Prome. When the mother of the ruler of Dala knew it, she wove fair words and revealed the matter to the king. And the king said, "I did not know of this. Whose trickery is this?" And he called the chief roaster of game and questioned him, who said, "The mother of the ruler of Prome implored me to give her son the foreleg, and I gave it." So the king punished the chief roaster of game, and would sometimes tease Shinmauk by calling her "Stealer of pig's trotters!" And when his heart was vexed he would also tease Thihathu, saying, "Son of a stealer of pig's trotters!" When he was often teased in this manner, the heart of Thihathu became warped, and he secretly uttered evil words; when Uzana ruler of Bassein heard these words, he took them to heart and said, "These two, mother and son, will certainly attack my lord the king, if the opportunity comes!"

[*The King's curries.*] Whenever the king took of food, there must always be three hundred dishes, salted and spiced, sweet and sour, bitter and hot, luscious and parching. After he had eaten once or twice of these dishes of curry, he would give them to his cousins and sons, to lesser persons of the royal house, and to his councilors and captains. He would give them also to his queens and concubines, excepting none. It was ever the duty of queen Saw to record these curries and note them down in lists with the stewards. Thus she ordered and appointed them.

[*His places of recreation.*] This is how the king made merry during the three seasons. During the rainy season he took his leisure in a garden close to the royal city. In winter he took his leisure wherever there were flowers and fruits in the upper and nether parts of his kingdom. On the coming of the month of Tabaung (the last month of the year) he went each year for sport in fishing at Tonhkaung.

[*Building of Mingalazedi pagoda.*] On Sunday the sixth waxing of the month of Tabaung in the year 636 (1284) he built Mingalazedi pagoda. That was the only year when he failed to go to Tonhkaung. Now in those days a dark prophecy arose: "The pagoda is finished and the great country ruined!" Soothsayers, therefore, and masters of magic said: "When this *zedi* is finished the kingdom of Pagan will be shattered into dust!" Hearing that word, the king delayed the project and built no more for a full six years.

Then Panthagu the reverend elder, filled with piety and virtue, spoke: "O king, you claim to have received the Lord's prophecy, but in fact you have brought about a kingdom of greed, of hate. You have not observed the meditation on Impermanence. Lo! You have built a work of charity and merit, yet now you delay and will not finish it fearing lest the country be ruined. Must this country and you, its king, live forever and not die?" And the king thought, "My reverend master! He has spoken, seeing that I must long be sunk and drowned in *samsara*. He alone has saved me from the four places of evil doom. All the Bodhisats of old gave up their families and kingdoms, their towns and villages, praying only that they might be the Lord. I am a king who has received a prophecy. Who am I that I should delay and not build the Lord's *zedi,* fearing lest the country come to ruin? Perhaps the kings who come hereafter will laugh at and scorn me."

Therefore on a Thursday, the full moon of Kason in the year 636, he built the *zedi*; and having cast in pure gold the images of the eight and twenty [Buddhas], of the seven postures, and of the leading and the great disciples, all richly covered with gems and encased and set with the nine diversely colored jewels, he enshrined them there. Moreover, he cast in pure silver seated images, one cubit high, of the fifty-one kings who reigned of old in the country of Pagan, together with images of his queens and concubines, sons and daughters, ministers and headmen of villages and circles, and placed them around the sacred reliquary. The relics of the Lord's body he set in a gem-embroidered casket fraught with the nine jewels, and, placing them on the ever-victorious white she-elephant, he carried them, accompanied by a mighty gathering, from the royal house to the work of merit (the pagoda).

This was the way in which he carried this out. He housed the white she-elephant in rich harnesses covered all over with jewels. Thereon he set the *pyatthad* and within the *pyatthad* a reliquary richly coated with gems. Within the reliquary were the relics of the sacred body together with a gem-embroidered casket encased and set with rubies and precious stones of inestimable worth. And so he caused the white she-elephant to pass at a soft and easy pace. The king's family, his kindred, and persons of the blood royal, together with the ministers, followed after, eight hundred in all, adorned with ruby earrings, diadems, and pearls. Moreover, he caused his daughters and the daughters of ministers to do their hair in the *suli* knot and to wear apparel gorgeous with ornaments of rubies, emeralds, and pearls; and they followed after, eight hundred in all.

This is how he decked the path on either hand from the royal house to the work of merit. The road was covered with bamboo flooring. Over the bamboo floor were spread hurdles of bamboo chesses. Above the bamboo chesses mats were placed, and above the mats satin, Chinese silks and woolen tissues. When thus the path was spread, one who went along it was not wetted by the rain, which fell ever before him laying the dust. Such was the manner of it. To left and right along the whole way was bamboo latticework, except at the corners, with pots full of lilies, living plantain trees, and living sugar-cane to form a fence. Because the king would have it all designed and built and spread in true and seemly manner, with rigging and hanging of long tapestries and sheets both white and royal, the road was passing fair and pleasant even as the spirits' highway in Sudassana.

After the relics of the sacred body came and were enshrined, the king caused his family and ministers together with the princesses and daughters of ministers, all gorgeously appareled, to unstring and sever all their ornaments and offer them to the sacred relic-chamber. When the *zedi* pagoda was already built, a relic of the sacred body came from the island of Ceylon, and he enshrined it in Pahtotha at the north-west corner of Mingalazedi. And when his work of merit was complete he held a great festival to call down blessing upon it. We have set forth the year and month and day of the building of the pagoda and the enshrining of the relics in accordance with the *thanbaing* of Mingalazedi, offered by king Narathihapate.

[The Mongol Attacks]

[The Tarop ambassadors.]* In the same year the Tarop Utibwa sent ten ministers and a thousand horsemen to demand golden rice-pots, vessels of gold and silver, gold and silver ladles, gold and silver basins, because, he said, they were once offered by King Anawrahta (r. 1044–

---

*The term "Tarop" specifically denotes the Dali kingdom in the mountains of what is today southwestern China. In this instance the term clearly encompasses the Mongol Empire, which was projecting its power through the Dali realm southward toward into the Burmese heartland.

1078). Furthermore, some chronicles say that they came demanding a white elephant. The Tarop ambassadors in making their demands did not show due respect or reverence in the king's presence. Therefore the king commanded: "Slay these ten ministers and thousand horsemen. Let none escape!" Then the minister Anantapyissi spoke into his ear saying, "O lord of glory! Although the ambassadors of the Tarop Utibwa have behaved ill in their ignorance of royal ceremony, it should be noted down, if you approve, and a report sent to the Utibwa. Or again, if you think it appropriate to be patient, speak conciliatory words and so settle the affairs of the villages and kingdom. The kings of old never killed ambassadors. Be advised, therefore, and endure!" But the king commanded saying, "They have affronted me to *my* face! Slay them!" So the ministers feared the king's command and put them to death; they spared not one.

[Tarop invasion.] But when the Tarop Utibwa heard that his ambassadors were slain, his wrath was kindled and he mustered all the parts of his army to the number of six million horsemen and twenty million footmen, and they came marching. Narathihapate, hearing that the Tarop Utibwa's fighting men had marched against him, sent forth his generals Anantapyissi and Rantapyissi with four hundred thousand soldiers and great hosts of elephants and horses saying, "Block the road against the coming of the Tarop warriors, and fight them."

[Fall of Bhamo and Ngahsaunggyon.] So the four generals marched, and coming to Ngahsaunggyan town they made it strong and surrounded it with forts and moats and ditches, and fought in their defense at the river-crossing of Bhamo. For a full three months they killed the enemy and spared not even the feeders of elephants and horses, but killed them all. But when ten myriad men were dead, the Tarop Utibwa sent twenty myriad; when twenty myriad were dead, he sent forty myriad; but because the king's men were weary and exhausted, as soon as the Tarops crossed the river Ngahsaunggyan fell.

[War of Spirits.] Now there was war between the spirits. Tepathin, guardian spirit of the city-gate of Pagan, Wetthakan, guardian spirit of Salin, the Kanshi guardian spirit, and the Ngatinkyeshin spirit were wounded. (The New Chronicle writes, instead of Tepathin spirit, Thanpathin spirit.) And it came to pass, on the same day when the army at Ngahsaunggyan perished, that the spirit who always attended the king's chaplain returned to Pagan and shook him by the foot and roused him from his sleep saying, "This day has Ngahsaunggyan fallen. I have been wounded by an arrow. Likewise the spirits Wetthakan of Salin, Kanshi,

and Ngatinkyeshin, are wounded by arrows." Thus he spoke, it is said; and the monk, chaplain of the king, called a young novice and caused him to tell the king that Ngahsaunggyan was destroyed. But the king asked the novice how he knew this thing. And the novice said, "Tepathin, the guardian spirit of Tharaba gate, has come from Ngahsaunggyan and brought tidings thereof to the chaplain. Therefore I know that today Ngahsaunggyan has perished."

[Despair at Pagan.] Then the king called his ministers and consulted them saying, "Pagan town is now too narrow for us, and its depth is too shallow. It cannot contain the hosts of fighting men, the hosts of elephants and horses. Let us go straightway to the south and establish a strong town from Myitmya Pahtin village in the east, with the town of Ywatha in the west. This is my purpose. And because at this late hour brick and stone cannot be readily obtained, dispatch we all things quickly and pull down pagodas, *gu,* and monasteries, and take their brick!" Thus by the king's order, it is said, these buildings were destroyed: one thousand great *gu,* ten thousand small *gu,* three thousand *Kala-gyaung.*

Now while they were destroying them, Anuraja found a prophecy written on a red copper *parabaik* (a kind of book) and he read the writing, and it said: "In the reign of a king who is father of twins, the country of Pagan will utterly perish at the hands of Tarops." And the king made search among his concubines, and lo! it was found that twins had indeed been born of a young concubine; and they told that matter to the king. Then the king said, "Although I build a town in my defense, I cannot defend it!"

[The king's flight to Bassein.] So he caused them to prepare a thousand boats of war, *sampan,* and great lighting boats, and placed his gold, silver, and all his treasures into them; he stored paddy in a thousand cargo boats. And he set all his ministers on board a thousand *hlawga* and *hjaw* boats. His concubines and maids of honor, his royal guards and tutors, he conveyed in a thousand golden barges. Then because the multitude of slaves, concubines, and maids of honor was too great, and there was no room for all of them to embark, the king commanded saying, "If the people are too many and there is no room, we cannot leave behind us and set free the slave-women of the inner palace, for the Tarops will take them. Tie them up, therefore, hand and foot, and throw them into the water!"

But the elder, chaplain of the king, said, "O king, it is hard indeed for any creature traversing *samsara* to become man. Although he might become a man, it is still very hard for him to be born in the dispensation of the Buddha. There is no need for thee, O king, to suffer the evil that would result if you were to throw them into the water. For if you throw them into the water it will be a theme for future kings hereafter, tempting them to sing thereof forever in frenzied ode and *mawgun* (a type of narrative poem). But if you grant that any slave women of the inner palace who cannot find a place in the boats, be taken at will by any, whether monk or layman, it will be recorded of you as an act of kindness and a giving of life." "It is well," said the king; and he set free three hundred slave women of the inner palace, and men and monks made each their choice and took them away. So the king embarked upon his raft of gold and jewels, and went down to Bassein in the country of the Talaings.

[Death of Anantapyissi at Mt. Mali.] Now when Ngahsaunggyan perished, the generals Anantapyissi and Rantapyissi retreated, and building two towns to the east of Mt. Mali they renewed the defense. The two generals put into their mouths dead quicksilver, and leaping into the sky as high as fifteen or sixteen cubits they made an assault on the Tarops. Thereupon Anantapyissi was smitten by an arrow shot in the war of spirits, and falling from the sky he died. Then because the number of the Tarops was very great, they could not be victorious but were defeated again. And ever the Tarops pursued them.

[Pursuit, and return, of the Tarops.] So the generals gave the order to retreat that they might save the multitude of the army from destruction. And when they reached Pagan, lo! the king and all the inhabitants of the country had departed and fled to the place of refuge; so they followed after him to Bassein. And ever the Tarops pursued them; but when they reached Taropmaw they turned back, for the distance of *la* by land was very great, and with the multitude of warring hosts food and drink were never so scarce.

Babad Dipanagara

~ *1830s, Indonesia* ~

PAGNERAN DIPANAGARA

The *Babad Dipanagara* is an account of the so-called Java War (1825–1830), the last substantial indigenous challenge to Dutch colonial authority on the central island of what had become known as the Dutch East Indies. The Dutch had begun their engagement with peoples of the Indonesian archipelago in the very late sixteenth century, and through a combination of warfare, economic arrangements, and political agreements had become the de facto overlords of Java and some of its adjacent islands. Over the course of the eighteenth and nineteenth centuries the Dutch gradually expanded their authority over more distant island territories from Sumatra to the west, to Sulawesi to the north, and then eastward along the chain of islands that extended from Java through Bali and toward the island of New Guinea.

The Java War, launched by Pagneran Dipanagara (1787–1855) was the last substantive challenge in the core of the Dutch territorial holdings. The origins of the conflict are complicated, but its essential underpinnings lie in a disputed succession in which Dipanagara found himself denied what he considered his rightful position as sultan of Jogjakarta in central Java. He had been in line for the throne before the Dutch interfered with these arrangements. Frustrated by this disappointment, and inspired by religious zeal, Dipanagara mounted an armed a challenge to the Dutch colonial authorities.

This text was composed by Dipanagara himself, in the aftermath of his defeat. Like the earlier texts from the Indonesian archipelago, this history is in an extended verse form, giving it a literary style quite distinct from the prose forms associated with historical chronicles in the

This is a portrait of Pagneran Dipanagara, the instigator of the Java War, and author of the *Babad Dipanagara*. *(Diponegoro, Wikimedia Commons, http://commons. wikimedia.org/wiki/File:Diponegoro.jpg)*

mainland Southeast Asian tradition. The *Babad Dipanagara* captures some of the complex political dynamics found on Java in which multiple and overlapping political authorities engaged in complicated maneuvers. While the Dutch had ostensible political authority over Java and other islands in the region, this authority had often been negotiated in ways that left various local political families in charge of particular regions under overall Dutch supervision. The persistence of these political dynasties left room for challenges both among and within these families, but also between them and Dutch authority. The Java War illustrates one of the basic realities of the nature of Dutch colonial rule, namely that its power was often less than absolute. There were numerous gaps in their control, and while none could shake the overall colonial project, they persisted in forcing the Dutch to recon- figure and rearrange their authority and the balancing act that was their East Indies colony.

The first part of the excerpt below illuminates the ways in which religion influenced the course of religious events. In it, Dipanagara describes his path toward spiritual growth, a path that combined elements of Islamic meditation with local folk practices. It involves religious visions, divine messages, retreat to sacred caves, and even the appearance of Ratu Kidul, the legendary Queen of the Southern Seas, said to live off of the coast of southern Java and to serve as a divine consort of the central Javanese sultans. In essence, this section lays out the divinely appointed course upon which Dipanagara was set. It suggests that Dipanagara's subsequent war against the Dutch was not of his own doing, but rather represented his fulfillment of a predetermined fate that grew out of his religious awakening. In this respect his path toward insurrection was like that of many other figures in earlier Southeast Asian history, for rebellion almost inevitably has at least its claimed roots in the world of the supernatural.

The descriptions of his spiritual pursuits are not unlike those of many who have sought the path of enlightenment. On the one hand, there are echoes of the path taken by the Prophet Muhammad, who had earlier retreated to caves for meditation, where he had encountered God and received the Quran. On the other, the meditation under the tamarind tree and the temptations thrown before him are reminiscent also of the similar encounter of the meditating Buddha, whose period of repose under a Bodhi tree had also been accompanied by chal- lenges and temptations by the demon Mara. In short, this tale, like so many in Southeast Asia, reflects the hybrid cultural, spiritual, and literary forces that have greatly influenced the region and its peoples.

Questions

1. This introduction to the epic contains numerous references to Islam. How does Islam factor into this part of the *Babad Dipanagara*?
2. In what ways are the hero's actions guided by divine forces and divine voices? What does he hear from them, and how does he respond?

3. This selection features a great deal of movement. Where does the central figure travel, for what purpose, and what kinds of natural features does he visit?

***

Babad Dipanagara

Ann Kumar, trans. "Dipanagara (1787?–1855)." *Indonesia*, vol. 13 (April 1972), pp. 72–78. Reprinted with the kind permission of the publisher.

Let the meter of this first part by Sinom,
Serving our purpose of honoring
The work written by the noblest of Men,
famed throughout the land of Java,
that is the exalted Prince Dipanagara,
now departed,
recording his own story,
beginning from the time when he began to give himself up to
the practice of religion.

We tell of his great-grandmother,
The Ratu Ageng.
She lived at Tegalredja
And after the death of his great-grandfather
She remained at that place.
The Prince grew ever more devoted
To matters of religion,
And it was his wish to protect
All his servants and followers, so that their hearts might be at ease.

It seems it was the will of God
That Prince Dipanagara
Desired only to join
His great-grandmother
In devotion to religion,
And so he came to be at variance
With his grandfather, the Sultan,

And seldom visited the capital,
Except at the Garebeg celebrations, when
     his presence was required.

Even though he was forced
To incur such a great sin
Out of fear of his grandfather
And of his father,
Yet in his own heart
He thought only of his religion.
Now at Tegalredja,
During the reign of his grandfather,
There were many who strictly observed the
     commandments of their religion
And many who performed asceticism.
The Prince
Changed his name
When he journeyed through the countryside,
Calling himself Sheik Ngabdurahkim.
At the Capital
He was "Prince Dipanagara,"
So he had two names.
At that time he had reached his twentieth year.

His only pleasure
Was in leading the life of a fakir,
And he was constantly mindful,
Both day and night,
Of how little time we have in this world,
And so his heart served
The First of Souls.
But his human character was an impediment,
And he was often tempted by women.
Whenever he was mindful
Of the purpose of our creation
He would journey through the countryside
Visiting the mosques.
There he would be one with
The multitude of *santri* [devout Muslims],

And lead a life of great asceticism.
He went in disguise,
So that it was seldom that anyone knew him.

If he was recognized
By the teacher of the *santri*
Sheik Ngabdurahkim would leave,
For he desired only
To be one of the ordinary *santri*,
One of the poor and lowly
At the mosque schools,
And so he went from one to another.
When he did not want to be at the mosque schools
       he would go to the jungles,

To the mountains and ravines, cliffs and caves,
Or sometimes follow the coastline.
During the fast month
He would sit in a deserted cave.
Now we tell
That it was beneath a tamarind tree,
Where Sheik Ngabdurahkim
Was sitting in a lonely cave.
When midnight had passed God sent him a trial.

Apparitions in a multitude of shapes
Came to try him.
Now Sheik Ngabdurahkim
Was not distracted from his concentration
And his inner gaze was still upon the All-Disposer.
The apparitions disappeared
And then came
Someone who stood before him,
A man with a radiance like that of the full moon.

His name was Hjang Djatmulja,
And he was Sunan Kali in reality.
Sheik Ngabdurahkim looked at him in amazement.
He said quietly:

"Oh Ngahdurahkim,
God has determined
That in time to come
You will be a king." He gave this warning
And disappeared from sight.

After the disappearance of the revered Pandita
Ngabdurahkim was left uneasy
And exceedingly amazed,
So that he did not continue with his devotions,
Leaving the place in the morning.
He went straight to the mountains,
Thinking nothing of the dangers around him.
He had no concern for his physical body
Thinking only of God's love.

He went deep into the jungle,
Climbed mountains and descended ravines.
He journeyed to no destination,
Being exceedingly perplexed of heart.
When he had traveled far,
He slept wherever he might be.
He arrived at Bengkung,
Sheik Ngabdurahkim,
And stopped there for seven days.

Sheik Ngabdurahkim went down
To the mosque at Imagiri,
Wishing to join the Friday prayer.
He happened to arrive at the same time
As the *djuru kuntji* [guardians of the royal graves]
Who were all coming to the prayer.
They were startled to see
Their lord, and were rendered speechless.
Then they crowded around him and made their greetings.

After the Friday prayer
All the *djuru kuntji*
Paid honor to him by making offerings

Of whatever they were able to give.
He slept one night
In the Djimatan mosque
And in the morning he left.
Sheik Ngabdurahkim set out
Following the river and then went up into the mountains.

He came to a cave, a place of spirits,
And slept there for one night.
In the morning he set out
Following the interior of the mountain.
Then he arrived,
Sheik Ngabdurahkim,
At a cave called Sagala-gala.
He went inside,
And slept two nights there.

On the next morning he set out
Up the steep mountain,
Intending to go to a cave called Langsé,
Heedless of difficulties before him.
He travelled until he reached
The cave called Langsé,
And there Sheik Ngabdurahkim
Stayed to performed asceticism.
He was in the cave for about half a month,

Seeking after enlightenment.
The visible world vanished from his sight:
Sheik Ngadburahkim
Only took care for the Life [within him],
And the Life took care for him.
He had returned to the Life
Which is such
That it cannot be described.
Let us tell of her whose palace was beneath the set:
Ratu Kidul appeared
Before Sheik Ngabdurahkim.
All was light and clear in the cave,

But Ratu Kidul knew
That Sheik Ngabdurahkim
Was as one dead to the world,
And could not be tempted.
So she spoke to give a promise
That she would return in the future when the time came.

Sheik Ngabdurahkim
Heard what she said, though he saw nothing;
Then she disappeared.
Now Sheik Ngabdurahkim
Released his inner gaze
Which returned to the light.
In the morning he went down
To Parangaritis.
Then he bathed in the sea and slept at Parangkusuma.

He was sunk in meditation, leaning against a stone,
Half dozing, when he heard
A voice which spoke thus:
"Oh Sheik Ngadurahkim,
change your name.
You are now Ngabdulkamit.
Further, I say,
In three years will come a time
Of great disturbance in Jogjakarta

It is the will of God
That the beginning of the disturbances in the land of Java
Will be in three years.
And it is determined that you
Will play the chief part.
I give this sign
To you, Ngabdurakim,
It is the arrow of Sarotama. Wear it.

And again I say
To you Ngabdulkamit,
Take care:

For if in future you fail,
Your father will not succeed [to the throne]
But I tell you,
Ngabdulkamit,
You must refuse to be made
The heir-apparent by the Dutch,
For God has determined that this would be a sin.
But as for your father,
Ngabdulkamit, watch over
His succession to the throne,
For there is nothing else
Which can be a means to this but you only.
He will not reign for long,
But will be the ancestor [of Sultans].
Ngabdulkamit, you must return home.

Ngabdulkamit woke with a start.
He looked around but all was clear,
There was no one speaking to him.
Then, high up in the clouds,
Something flashed like lightning,
And fell in front of him.
It was Ki Sarotama.*
When it had found its mark in the stone,
He took it up at once.
Day broke and Sheik Ngabdulkamit set out,

Carrying Ki Sarotama in his girdle.
He followed the water meadows,
And stopped at the river mouth
For a little while, before setting out again.
He came to Lipura
And on a shining stone
He slept overnight.
In the morning he set out again
Until he reached the Setjang cave. Here the Prince stopped,

---

*Ki Sarotama is a powerful arrow belonging to Arjuna, the hero of the *Mahabharata*.

And slept the night.
In the morning he continued his journey,
Back to Tegalredja.
When he arrived there,
He dressed.
Ki Sarotama
He made into a dagger.
Now the subject of the story changes:
In Jogjakarta there was much talk.

Rantjak Dilabueh

~ *Nineteenth Century, Indonesia* ~

Anonymous

Rantjak Dilabueh is a type of traditional literature written by the Minangkabau people of the central and southern parts of the island of Sumatra, the large western island of the Indonesian archipelago. The title of this work refers to a particular individual, one who presents to the world a façade of refinement, while in fact his life is in disarray. *Rantjak Dilabueh* comes from central Sumatra, and is of anonymous authorship. The origins of the tale are probably in the late eighteenth or sometime in the nineteenth century. The entire tale is essentially about the arrangements of a marriage and then lengthy instructions from the elders to the parties to the marriage, both the husband and wife. Thus, the tale is a kind of instructional manual for how to behave in the context of marriage, but also within the context of the larger society, for the marriage described here is that of a local village leader. This excerpt is useful for illustrating the ways in which literature might function directly as a pedagogical device within a community. It serves to reinscribe the traditions and expectations of the community such that any public or family reading of this text would serve to remind listening children of what was expected of them. The term *adat*, which occurs frequently in this passage, might be translated as "customs" or "traditions." It encompasses the practices of a community, and the community's understanding of its inner workings. In modern Indonesia the term *adat* has often been counterpoised with the term *agama*, or religion. The distinction is an artificial one, however, for *adat* can itself contain elements of what scholars consider religion (*agama*), while the reverse is frequently also true.

This excerpt is also significant as an illustration of an important form of what might be called "subnational" literature. This is a type of literature produced in a region somewhat peripheral to the centers of political, and hence cultural, power that emerged with the formation of the modern nation-state. Such texts were frequently written in local languages, dialects, or scripts, ones that were themselves becoming marginalized as national lingua francas were being developed to knit together disparate peoples. In the modern nation-state of Indonesia, Java was the center of power, while outer islands to the east and west were politically and culturally more marginal. Equally, the gradual emergence of a *bahasa Indonesia*—an Indonesian national language—tended to marginalize the spoken languages, and their attendant literatures of outlying islands and peoples. In this particular text, Sumatra represents the outlying region, though one with significant representation in the nationalist politics of the early and middle parts of the twentieth century. Sumatra had an important range of literary traditions, and had a healthy publishing tradition in the late colonial period.

Questions

1. What does this passage tell us about the expectations of a refined individual? What does it tell us about social relations in this community? What does it tell us about gender differentiation in this society and in the family?
2. What benefits accrue from adhering to these admonitions, and what harm might come from failing to adhere to them?
3. How is this set of guidelines similar to or different from ones in other cultures? To what extent is it inflected by religious ideals, and to what extent are secular elements significant? Can the two even be distinguished here?

***

Rantjak Dilabueh

Anthony H. Johns, trans. *Rantjak Dilabueh: A Minangkabau Kaba, A Specimen of the Traditional Literature of Central Sumatra.* (Ithaca, NY: Cornell University Southeast Asia Program, 1958), pp. 138–144. Reprinted with the kind permission of the publisher.

A little while back I said:
Divide the day into three
And divide the night into four
—just as my other said—
join the earth and sky
roll the world up into a small space.
To divide the day into three is:
First, to satisfy one's needs.
Eat and drink to satisfy hunger
And give energy to the body,
So that whatever needs to be done
There will be strength for.
Second to work diligently
In order to earn a living
—enough work to produce a sweat—
to be sure the *adat* is practiced
and also to preserve your health.
Third, in exercising authority
Over the people of the village,
Under the jurisdiction of any *pangulu*
Or in any family group act in every way as you should.
To divide the night into four is:
First, whenever you speak,
To discuss what should be best;
Meditate to find the truth,
Be its aspects a hundred or a thousand.
And all the advice I have given you
Review it again and again.
Second, to study fully sources,
Outer form and inner meaning,
Study the way things are going.
You were of humble birth
With the name Bujueng Géléng
And the title of Rantjak diLabueh.
Now that is nearly all past
But never forget those days.
Never fall into greed or avarice
And always fear to become proud.
Third, to look for happiness

And keep your body healthy,
Have a right amount of sleep,
Just about eight hours.
Fourth, remember our God,
Think of Him and his Apostle,
On the law and its inner meaning
Which we practice while alive
And bear with us after death.
Listen carefully, O, my dear son!
I have been telling you this because
questions of *adat* are settled at the *balai*,
but the world is judged in eternity.
Follow these five rules
Which are the pillars of Islam,
A sign that you have a religion
And are a true servant of God.
Men live by religion
Animals only by their passions.
If you do not live in this way
What sort of people are you from?
To know what people are like
Judge by their religion.
For if we have no religion
In this world, we are of no account
And in eternity, God only knows;

O, my dear son, my own flesh and blood:
If you can practice this,
All will be well with you,
Your family fit and rice crop abundant,
Your health good, and body fit.
Then—if God grants you life—
And it happens you have children,
Recall the advice of long ago:
Don't wait until trouble comes
Take care to avoid it,
—don't neglect their education.
If you have a daughter
Teach her to read and write

Teach her to crochet and spin cloth,
To draw to embroider
To be able to handle a loom
And judge the rise and fall of prices;
To use wisdom and diplomacy,
To know what is cooked and what raw,
What insipid and what salty.
If you neglect this
You will have much to regret later:
It will be difficult to find a son-in-law
Unless you take just anyone.

And if you have a son,
Once he is six,
In the morning send him to school,
The afternoon teach him at home
In the evening send him to the surau (prayer house).
Set two or three traps
So one at least of them will get him.
And even when he comes of age
Go on with your teaching of him;
Teach him well, my dear son
The way a young man should behave.
If he is to attend a feast,
When he arrives at the village
And enters another's home,
He should not choose a place for himself.
He should glance around him to the right and left
Greeting those he should.
He must not push in clumsily
Or step over anyone.
The feast has its host
The guests have their usher.

If the Ampang Limo
Or si Budgjang and Palagan
Move to show him to a place
He should not follow his own whim;
He must do what is right

And follow the arrangements.
He must not be proud, like the people of nowadays;
Once they arrive at a feast
They look for a place to sit
Just anywhere they please
Without any breeding or manners
—they can't even hear a cock crow.
Guest must be shown to their places
—the *adat* has rules for eating—
they must obey the host
and sit as the usher directs.
When one is at a feast,
One may not do as one pleases.

Once he is shown to a place
It is his duty to go there
—and perhaps to demur at first,
and then take his seat there.
Once he is in his place
And the betel bowl comes round
He should reach for it, and smile a little
—that is a sign of good breeding.
Even though I said 'laugh'
There are three kinds of laughter:
The first is 'laughter of the devil,'
Second is 'laughter of amusement,'
And third 'laughter of the prophet,'
The laughter of the devil is
A loud roaring laughter,
A shrieking and giggling
—like a worm touched with salt—
this is something forbidden to us.
The laughter of amusement is
What we hear from groups of friends
Amusing themselves together,
Something they do every day.
The laughter of the Prophet
Is a laugh not expressed aloud;
It is, and it is not.

Checked as a pleasant smile
It is a balance between pleasure and sadness
—this is the laughter we are allowed.
If at a banquet
He should not be too full of jokes
Or always trying to out-do the others.
If he is always making jokes
In the manner of small children
He will only be thought immature.

In addition to all of this
You must plant in his heart
Love for the people of the village,
Love for the guests at the feasts
And love for all of mankind.
And if he gives a feast
Let everything be arranged carefully
Don't let anything be wrong
Or it will be a public disgrace
And everyone will criticize us.

Noli Me Tangere

~ *1887, Philippines* ~

José Rizal

The Spanish arrived to establish a colonial presence in what they called the Philippine Islands early in the sixteenth century, marking the earliest onset of large-scale European colonization in Southeast Asia. This colonial project was distinctive both for its early commencement and for the peculiar alliance of religious and secular institutions that governed the islands. Spanish soldiers had been accompanied in their initial conquest by groups of Augustinian friars whose project to spread their Roman Catholicism became a cornerstone of the Spanish domination of the islands. The rapid spread of the faith by Catholic missionaries from a variety of religious orders not only enabled the process of conquest, but then guaranteed its successful implementation. Parish priests became the de facto leaders of their far-flung communities, making possible what simple military authority could not have achieved. Over the centuries, the strength of the church was central to Spanish control, but at the same time made it the target of growing Filipino resentment over the church's power and wealth, and its reluctance to permit local populations to take on a measure of self-government. The inevitable gap between the priests' message and their actions in a secular context also bred frustration and unhappiness. While some modest increase in access to the priesthood did develop over the course of the nineteenth century, this was slow and only resulted from strong pressure from below. As late as 1871, only 181 out of 792 parishes (22 percent) in the Philippines were under the authority of non-Spanish priests. Popular calls to increase the number of native parish leaders and to require those who administered parishes to learn the local dialect led to a Spanish backlash in the form of a crackdown on the most vocal proponents of this shift, and the execution of one of its foremost advocates. This suppression of Filipino aspirations galvanized a new generation of Filipino elites, among them the author of the novel *Noli Me Tangere*.

José Rizal (1861–1896) represented a new class of educated Filipinos, the *illustrados* (educated ones), who not only acquired education at the institutions of higher learning established in the Philippines but also were increasingly seizing the opportunity to study in Europe during the second half of the nineteenth century. Rizal spent part of the 1880s and early 1890s studying first in Spain and then in Germany, and it was in the latter country that he published his first novel, *Noli Me Tangere*, in 1887. The title, taken from a biblical passage in Latin, can be translated literally as "Do Not Touch Me," but also has been rendered in English as "The Social Cancer." It is extremely significant that this premier work of early Filipino nationalist literature should have been written and first published in Spanish, rather than in an indigenous language such as Tagalog, the primary language of the inhabitants of Luzon (the largest of the Philippine islands). Rizal's decision to write in Spanish reveals both the impact of the Spanish on local culture and the close interpenetration of Spanish colonial culture with that of Filipino elites. Spanish was their literary medium, reflecting very strongly their educational background, which would have been in Spanish-language universities in the Philippines and, for some later, in Spain as well.

The *Noli* (as it is commonly known) is sprawling work of social commentary that skewers the hypocrisies of the Spanish priests who so dominated local life and society, as well as the absurdities of life in the colony more generally. In it, the author provides a rich survey of village life at both popular and elite levels, revealing the central role played by the local church, and the parish priests whose word was all powerful. He unblinkingly criticizes these priests for their heavy-handed domination of village life, and makes them out at times as buffoons as well as figures more concerned with the trappings of power and of the complex conflicts among religious orders than with the exercise of just rule. The economy of religious power is also on display, revealing truths widely understood by the populations of the Philippines. The excerpt reproduced below introduces the center of power in the village of San Diego, showing it to be the parish priest, not the various other secular figures with titles, and not even God himself. The villagers understand precisely where power lies and they adapt themselves to this situation,

This portrait of José Rizal, the author of *Noli Me Tangere*, was made in 1890 during his residence in Spain. *(Last Days of Rizal and His Burial, Republic of the Philippines Presidential Museum and Library, http://malacanang.gov.ph/last-days-of-rizal-and-his-burial/)*

even when the demands of authority figures seem completely absurd, as revealed in the graveyard scene toward the end of the selection.

Questions

1. What impression does the author give of the Catholic Church structure that controls village life in the Spanish colonial Philippines?
2. What is it about the graveyard scene that makes it so absurd? What do you think the author is trying to suggest in this scene?

3. The author of this novel, José Rizal, was a member of the educated elite in the Philippines. What does this excerpt say about his perspective on the long-term impact of the Spanish colonial presence in his country?

***

Noli Me Tangere

José Rizal. *An Eagle Flight; A Filipino Novel,
Adapted from "Noli e tangere."* (New York: McClure,
Phillips, 1900), pp. 32–39.

XI. The Sovereigns

Who was the ruler of the pueblo? Not Don Rafael during his lifetime, though he possessed the most land, and nearly every one owed him. As he was modest, and gave little value to his deeds, no party formed around him, and we have seen how he was deserted and attacked when his fortunes fell.

Was it Captain Tiago? It is true his arrival was always heralded with music, he was given banquets by his debtors, and loaded with presents; but he was laughed at in secret, and called Sacristan Tiago.

Was it by chance the town mayor, the *gobernadorcillo*? Alas! he was an unfortunate, who governed not, but obeyed; did not dispose, but was disposed of. And yet he had to answer to the *alcalde* for all these dispositions, as if they emanated from his own brain. Be it said in his favor that he had neither stolen nor usurped his honors, but that they cost him five thousand pesos and much humiliation.

Perhaps then it was God? But to most of these good people, God seemed one of those poor kings surrounded by favorites to whom their subjects always take their supplications, never to them.

No, San Diego was a sort of modern Rome. The curate was the pope at the Vatican; the *alferez* of the civil guard, the King in the Quirinal. Here as there, difficulties arose from the situation.

The present curate, Brother Bernardo Salvi, was the young and silent Franciscan we have already seen. In mode of life and in appearance he was very unlike his predecessor, Brother Damaso. He seemed ill, was always thoughtful, accomplished strictly his religious duties, and was careful of his reputation. Through his zeal, almost all his parishioners had speedily become members of the Third Order of St. Francis, to the great dismay of the rival order, that of the Holy Rosary. Four or five scapularies were suspended around every neck, knotted cords encircled all the waists, and the innumerable processions of the order were a joy to see. The head sacristan took in a small fortune, selling—or giving as alms, to put it more correctly—all the paraphernalia necessary to save the soul and combat the devil. It is well known that this evil spirit, who once dared attack God face to face, and accuse His divine word, as the book of Job tells us, is now so cowardly and feeble that he flees at sight of a bit of painted cloth, and fears a knotted cord.

Brother Salvi again greatly differed from Brother Damaso—who set everything right with fists or ferrule, believing it the only way to reach the Indian—in that he punished with fines the faults of his subordinates, rarely striking them.

From his struggles with the curate, the *alferez* had a bad reputation among the devout, which he deserved, and shared with his wife, a hideous and vile old Filipino woman named Dona Consolacion. The husband avenged his conjugal woes on himself by drinking like a fish; on his subordinates, by making them exercise in the sun; and most frequently on his wife, by kicks and drubbings. The two fought famously between themselves, but were of one mind when it was a question of the curate. Inspired by his wife, the officer ordered that no one be abroad in the streets after nine at night. The priest, who did not like this restriction, retorted in lengthy sermons, whenever the *alferez* went to church. Like all impenitents, the *alferez* did not mend his ways for that, but went out swearing under his breath, arrested the first sacristan he met, and made him clean the yard of the barracks. So the war went on. All this, however, did not prevent the *alferez* and the curate chatting courteously enough when they met.

And they were the rulers of the pueblo of San Diego.

XII. All Saints' Day

The cemetery of San Diego is in the midst of rice-fields. It is approached by a narrow path, powdery on sunny days, navigable on rainy. A wooden gate and a wall half stone, half bamboo stalks, succeed in keeping out men, but not the curate's goats, nor the pigs of his neighbors. In the middle of the enclosure is a stone pedestal supporting a great wooden cross.

Storms have bent the strip of tin on which were the I.N.R.I.,* and the rain has washed off the letters. At the foot of the cross is a confused heap of bones and skulls thrown out by the grave-digger. Everywhere grow in all their vigor the bitter-sweet and rose-bay. Some tiny flowerets, too, tint the ground—blossoms which, like the mounded bones, are known to their Creator only. They are like little pale smiles, and their odor smells of the tomb. Grass and climbing plants fill the corners, cover the walls, adorning this otherwise bare ugliness; they even penetrate the tombs, through earthquake fissures, and fill their yawning gaps.

At this hour two men are digging near the crumbling wall. One, the grave-digger, works with the utmost indifference, throwing aside a skull as a gardener would a stone. The other is preoccupied; he perspires, he breathes hard.

"Oh!" he says at length in Tagalog. "Hadn't we better dig in some other place? This grave is too recent."

"All the graves are the same, one is as recent as another."

"I can't endure this!"

"What a woman! You should go and be a clerk! If you had dug up, as I did, a body of twenty days, at night, in the rain—"

"Uh-h-h! And why did you do that?"

The grave-digger seemed surprised.

"Why? How do I know, I was ordered to."

"Who ordered you?"

At this question the grave-digger straightened himself, and examined the rash young man from head to foot.

"Come! come! You're curious as a Spaniard. A Spaniard asked me the same question, but in secret. I'm going to say to you what I said to him: the curate ordered it."

"Oh! and what did you do with the body?"

"The devil! if I didn't know you, I should take you for the police. The curate told me to bury it in the Chinese cemetery, but it's a long way there, and the body was heavy. 'Better be drowned,' I said to myself, 'than lie with the Chinese,' and I threw it into the lake."

"No, no, stop digging!" interrupted the younger man, with a cry of horror, and throwing down his spade he sprang out of the grave.

---

*The letters I.N.R.I. abbreviate the Latin phrase "Iesus Nazarenus, Rex Iudaeorum," Jesus of Nazareth, King of the Jews, which had been carved on the cross of Jesus at his crucifixion.

The grave-digger watched him run off crossing himself, laughed, and went to work again.

The cemetery began to fill with men and women in mourning. Some of them came for a moment to the open grave, discussed some matter, seemed not to be agreed, and separated, kneeling here and there. Others were lighting candles; all began to pray devoutly. One heard sighing and sobs, and over all a confused murmur of "*requiem ceternam.*"

A little old man, with piercing eyes, entered uncovered. At sight of him some laughed, others frowned. The old man seemed to take no account of this. He went to the heap of skulls, knelt, and searched with his eyes. Then with the greatest care he lifted the skulls one by one, wrinkling his brows, shaking his head, and looking on all sides. At length he rose and approached the grave-digger.

"Ho!" said he.

The other raised his eyes.

"Did you see a beautiful skull, white as the inside of a coconut?"

The grave-digger shrugged his shoulders.

"Look," said the old man, showing a piece of money; "it's all I have, but I'll give it to you if you find it."

The gleam of silver made the man reflect. He looked toward the heap and said:

"It isn't there? No? Then I don't know where it is."

"You don't know? When those who owe me pay, I'll give you more. 'Twas the skull of my wife, and if you find it—"

"It isn't there? Then I know nothing about it, but I can give you another."

"You are like the grave you dig," cried the old man, furious. "You know not the value of what you destroy! For whom is this grave?"

"How do I know? For a dead man!" replied the other with temper.

"Like the grave, like the grave," the old man repeated with a dry laugh. "You know neither what you cast out nor what you keep. Dig! dig!" And he went toward the gate.

Meanwhile the grave-digger had finished his task, and two mounds of fresh, reddish earth rose beside the grave. Drawing from his pocket some *buyo* (a betel-nut mixture), he regarded dully what was going on around him, sat down, and began to chew.

At that moment a carriage, which had apparently made a long journey, stopped at the entrance to the cemetery. Ibarra got out, followed by an old servant, and silently made his way along the path.

"It is there, behind the great cross, senor," said the servant, as they approached the spot where the grave-digger was sitting.

Arrived at the cross, the old servant looked on all sides, and became greatly confused. "It was there," he muttered; "no, there, but the ground has been broken."

Ibarra looked at him in anguish.

The servant appealed to the grave-digger.

"Where is the grave that was marked with a cross like this?" he demanded; and stooping, he traced a Byzantine cross on the ground.

"Were there flowers growing on it?"

"Yes, jasmine and pansies."

The grave-digger scratched his ear and said with a yawn:

"Well, the cross I burned."

"Burned! and why?"

"Because the curate ordered it."

Ibarra drew his hand across his forehead.

"But at least you can show us the grave."

"The body's no longer there," said the grave-digger calmly.

"What are you saying!"

"Yes," the man went on, with a smile, "I put a woman in its place, eight days ago."

"Are you mad?" cried the servant; "it isn't a year since he was buried."

"Father Damaso ordered it; he told me to take the body to the Chinese cemetery; I—"

He got no farther, and started back in terror at sight of Crisostomo's face. Crisostomo seized his arm. "And you did it?" he demanded, in a terrible voice.

"Don't be angry, señor," replied the grave-digger, pale and trembling. "I didn't bury him with the Chinese. Better be drowned than that, I thought to myself, and I threw him into the water."

Ibarra stared at him like a madman. "You're only a poor fool!" he said at length, and pushing him away, he rushed headlong for the gate, stumbling over graves and bones, and painfully followed by the old servant.

"That's what the dead bring us," grumbled the grave-digger. "The curate orders me to dig the man up, and this fellow breaks my arm for doing it. That's the way with the Spaniards. I shall lose my place!"

Letters of a Javanese Princess

~ *1899, Indonesia* ~

Raden Adjeng Kartini

The engagement with the modern in colonized Southeast Asia took many forms, and was reflected in literature in numerous genres. Among the more poignant of these literary reflections is a series of letters written by a young Javanese woman of high status, Raden Adjeng Kartini (1879–1904). These letters were collected and subsequently published by a Dutchman, J.H. Abendanon, Kartini's friend and champion. The letters' publication in 1911 was met with strong public interest and numerous republications followed.

Kartini's story is that of a young woman struggling with the conflicting feelings brought about by the clash between tradition and modernity. Javanese elites of the late nineteenth and early twentieth centuries lived with one foot in the past and the other in the future. They faced the choice of remaining in the comfortable world of traditions, or of entering the uncertain world of change and modernity. Kartini's life reflected the intensely difficult choices that lay before women in particular, as she struggled to reconcile the possibilities of the modern with the expectations of tradition as represented by her family. Among the core questions she faced was whether one could remain Javanese while taking on new roles and traveling in new directions, and whether in modernizing oneself one also gave up an innate local identity. These struggles took place in the context of a new direction in Dutch colonial governance articulated as the Ethical Policy, in which the colonial overlords sought to encourage certain forms of modernization through educational and cultural opportunities. This policy was made concrete in the form of new schools and access to higher education, potentially even in Holland. Kartini herself debated whether she should leave Java and travel to the Netherlands for a university education, possibly in medicine.

Although Kartini's family was part of the traditional elite, her father was progressive for a man of his rank. He was fluent in Dutch and had close contacts with Dutch officials and their families. Kartini and her two sisters regularly interacted with the Dutch wives of these officials. Thus, Kartini had been exposed, from a young age, to the possibilities that modern education represented. She had also, no doubt, come under pressure from her Western companions to assert herself against tradition and to pursue what they considered a path of individual autonomy appropriate to the modern times in which they lived. Kartini and her sisters were not merely observers of these changing opportunities, but partook of them as well. The three sisters subscribed to Dutch-language magazines and even contributed writings of their own.

Printed below is the first of Kartini's letters, which serves both as a useful self-introduction and as a good general summary of her early aspirations to the modern and all that it entailed. Written in 1899 when she was just twenty years old, the letter already shows the tensions that Kartini faces as she contemplates the allure of the modern and the liberation it promises, and the tug of the traditional, represented chiefly by her obligations to her family, for as she notes rhetorically, "Have I the right to break the hearts of those who have given me nothing but love and kindness my whole life long, and who have surrounded me with the tenderest care?" The letter describes her life to her correspondent, noting the period of seclusion she was forced for a time to endure before once again being freed to engage with the wider world. The letter is noteworthy for reflecting not merely on her own circumstances, but also on the larger consequences of modernity and Westernization, which she recognizes are double-edged swords. Thus, she shows her awareness of the apparent harm of alcoholism in the West (no doubt a result of powerful temperance leagues headed by women), and speculates that the Javanese emulation of Western customs will even-tually bring this evil along with the rest of modernity.

Questions

1. What, in Kartini's view, are the indications of the new, modern era in which she now finds herself?

2. In contrast, what are the elements of her situation that hold her back from committing fully to a pursuit of the possibilities presented by the modern period?

3. What sense of the Dutch colonial presence is revealed in this letter, and how does this contrast with other representations of the European colonial presence in Southeast Asia?

4. How are hierarchies of gender, race, or class depicted in this account? In what ways are there obstacles that prevent movement within these hierarchies?

***

Letters of a Javanese Princess

Raden Adjeng Kartini. *Letters of a Javanese Princess.* Hildred Geertz, ed.; Agnes Louise Symmers, trans. (Lanham, MD: University Press of America, 1985), pp. 31–36.

To Stella Zeehandelaar, Japara, May 25, 1899

I have been longing to make the acquaintance of a "modern girl," that proud, independent girl who has all my sympathy! She who, happy and self-reliant, lightly and alertly steps on her way through life, full of enthusiasm and warm feeling; working not only for her own well-being and happiness, but for the greater good of humanity as a whole.

I glow with enthusiasm toward the new time which has come, and can truly say that in my thoughts and sympathies I do not belong to the Indian world,* but to that of my pale sisters who are struggling forward in the distant West. If the laws of my land permitted it, there is nothing that I had rather do than give myself wholly to the working and striving of the new woman in Europe; but age-long traditions that cannot be broken hold us fast cloistered in their unyielding arms. Some day, those arms will loosen and let us go, but that time lies as yet far from us, infinitely far. It will come, that I know; it may be three, four generations after us. Oh, you do not know what it is to love this young, this new age with heart and soul, and yet to be bound hand and foot, chained by all the laws, customs, and

---

*Until 1949, at the time of independence from the Dutch, Indonesia was known as the Netherlands East Indies, Dutch India, Netherlands India, and often simply India; there were many variations, and Kartini's references to India, the Indian world, and Indian people refer to the multi-island nation and people of Indonesia.

This is a portrait of Kartini, the daughter of a Javanese noble official, and a leading figure in the efforts of colonial-era Javanese women to experience the opportunities afforded by modernity. *(COLLECTIE TROPENMUSEUM Portret van Raden Ajeng Kartini TMnr 10018776, Wikimedia Commons, Tropenmuseum of the Royal Tropical Institute (KIT), http://en.wikipedia.org/wiki/File:COLLECTIE_TROPENMUSEUM_ Portret_van_Raden_Ajeng_Kartini_TMnr_10018776.jpg)*

conventions of one's land. All our institutions are directly opposed to the progress for which I so long for the sake of our people. Day and night I wonder by what means our ancient traditions could be overcome. For myself, I could find a way to shake them off, to break them, were it not that another bond, stronger than any age-old tradition could ever be, binds me to my world; and that is the love which I bear for those to whom I owe my life, and whom I must thank for everything. Have I the right to break the hearts of those who have given me nothing but love and kindness my whole life long, and who have surrounded me with the tenderest care?

But it was not the voices alone which reached me from that distant, that bright, that newborn Europe, which made me long for a change in existing conditions. Even in my childhood, the word "emancipation" enchanted my ears; it had a significance that nothing else had, a meaning that was far beyond my comprehension, and awakened in me an ever growing longing for freedom and independence—a longing to stand alone. Conditions both in my own surroundings and in those of others around me broke my heart, and made me long with a nameless sorrow for the awakening of my country.

Then the voices which penetrated from distant lands grew clearer and clearer, till they reached me, and to the satisfaction of some who loved me, but to the deep grief of others, brought seed which entered my heart, took root, and grew strong and vigorous.

And now I must tell you something of myself so that you can make my acquaintance. I am the eldest of the three unmarried daughters of the Regent of Japara, and have six brothers and sisters. What a world, eh? My grandfather, Pangeran Ario Tjondronegoro of Demak, was a great leader in the progressive movement of his day, and the first regent of middle Java to unlatch his door to that guest from over the Sea—Western civilization. All of his children had European educations; all of them have, or had (several of them are now dead), a love of progress inherited from their father; and these gave to their children the same upbringing which they themselves had received. Many of my cousins and all my older brothers have gone through the Hoogere-Burger School—the highest institution of learning that we have here in India; and the youngest of my three older brothers has been studying for three years in the Netherlands, and two others are in the service of that country. We girls, so far as education goes, fettered by our ancient traditions and conventions, have profited but little by these advantages. It was a great crime against the customs of our land that we should be taught at all, and especially that we should leave the house every day to go to school. For the custom of our country forbade girls in the strongest manner ever to go outside of the house. We were never allowed to go anywhere, however, save to the school, and the only place of instruction of which our city could boast, which was open to us, was a free grammar school for Europeans.

When I reached the age of twelve, I was kept at home—I had to go into the "box." I was locked up, and cut off from all communication with the outside world, toward which I might never turn again save at the side of a bridegroom, a stranger, an unknown man whom my parents would choose for me, and to whom I should be betrothed without my own knowledge. European friends—this I heard later—had tried in every possible way to dissuade my parents from this cruel course toward me, a young and life-loving child; but they were able to do nothing. My parents were inexorable; I went into my prison. Four long years I spent between thick walls, without once seeing the outside world.

How I passed through that time, I do not know. I only know that it was terrible. But there was one great happiness left me: the reading of Dutch books and correspondence with Dutch friends was not forbidden. This—the only gleam of light in that empty, somber time, was my all, without which, I should have fallen, perhaps, into a still more pitiable state. My life, my soul even, would have been starved. But then came my friend and my deliverer—the Spirit of the Age; his footsteps echoed everywhere. Proud, solid ancient structures tottered to their foundation at his approach. Strongly barricaded doors sprang open, some as of themselves, others only painfully half way, but nevertheless they opened, and let in the unwelcome guest.

At last in my sixteenth year, I saw the outside world again. Thank God! Thank God! I could leave my prison as a free human being and not chained to an unwelcome bridegroom. Then events followed quickly that gave back to us girls more and more of our lost freedom.

In the following year, at the time of the investiture of our young Princess,* our parents presented us "officially" with our freedom. For the first time in our lives we were allowed to leave our native town, and to go to the city where the festivities were held in honor of the occasion. What a great and priceless victory it was! That young girls of our position should show themselves in public is here an unheard of occurrence. The "world" stood aghast; tongues were set wagging at the unprecedented crime. Our European friends rejoiced, and as for ourselves, no queen was so rich as we. But I am far from satisfied. I would go still further, always further. I do not desire to go out to feasts, and little frivolous amusements. That has never been the cause of my longing for freedom. I long to be free, to be able to stand alone, to study, not to be subject to any one, and, above all, *never, never* to be obliged to marry.

But we *must* marry, must, must. Not to marry is the greatest sin which the Moslem woman can commit; it is the greatest disgrace which a native girl can bring to her family.

And marriage among us—miserable is too feeble an expression for it. How can it be otherwise, when the laws have made everything for the man and nothing for the woman? When law and convention both are for the man; when everything is allowed to him?

Love! What do we know here of love? How can we love a man whom we have never known? And how could he love us? That in itself would

---

*Queen Wilhelmina of the Netherlands.

not be possible. Young girls and men must be kept rigidly apart, and are never allowed to meet.

I am anxious to know of your occupations. It is all very interesting to me. I wish to know about your studies, I would know something of your Toynbee evenings, and of the society for total abstinence of which you are so zealous a member.

Among our Indian people, we have not the drink demon to fight, thank God!—but I fear, I fear that when once—forgive me—your Western civilization shall have obtained a foothold among us, we shall have that evil to contend with too. Civilization is a blessing, but it has its dark side as well. The tendency to imitate is inborn, I believe. The masses imitate the upper classes, who in turn imitate those of higher rank, and these again follow the Europeans.

Among us there is no marriage feast without drinking. And at the festivals of the natives, where they are not of strong religious convictions, (and usually they are Moslem only because their fathers, grandfathers and remote ancestors were Moslem—in reality, they are little better than heathen), large square bottles are always kept standing, and they are not sparing in the use of these.

But an evil greater than alcohol is here and that is opium. Oh! The misery, the inexpressible horror it has brought to my country! Opium is the pest of Java. Yes, opium is far worse than the pest. The pest does not remain forever; sooner or later, it goes away, but the evil of opium, once established, grows. It spreads more and more, and will never leave us, never grow less—for to speak plainly—it is protected by the Government! The more general the use of opium in Java, the fuller the treasury.

The opium tax is one of the richest sources of income of the Government—what matter if it go well or ill with the people?—the Government prospers. This curse of the people fills the treasury of the Dutch East Indian Government with thousands—nay, with millions. Many say that the use of opium is no evil, but those who say that have never known India, or else they are blind.

What are our daily murders, incendiary fires, robberies, but the direct result of the use of opium? True, the desire for opium is not so great an evil as long as one can get it—when one has money to buy the poison; but when one cannot obtain it—when one has no money with which to buy it, and is a confirmed user of it? Then one is dangerous, then one is lost. Hunger will make a man a thief, but the hunger for opium will make him a murderer. There is a saying here—"At first you eat opium, but in the end it will devour you."

It is terrible to see so much evil and to be powerless to fight against it.

That splendid book by Mevrouw Goekoop I know. I have read it three times. I could never grow tired of it. What would I not give to be able to live in Hilda's environment. Oh, that we in India had gone so far, that a book could cause such violent controversy among us, as *Hilda van Suylenburg* has in your country. I shall never rest till H. v. S. appears in my own language to do good as well as harm to our Indian world. It is a matter of indifference whether good or harm, if it but makes an impression, for that shows that one is no longer sleeping, and Java is still in deep slumber. And how will her people ever be awakened, when those who should serve as examples, themselves love sleep so much. The greater number of European women in India care little or nothing for the work of their sisters in the fatherland.

Will you not tell me something of the labors, the struggles, the sentiments, of the woman of today in the Netherlands? We take deep interest in all that concerns the Woman's Movement.

I do not know the modern languages. Alas! We girls are not allowed by our law to learn languages; it was a great innovation for us to learn Dutch. I long to know languages, not so much to be able to speak them, as for the far greater joy of being able to read the many beautiful works of foreign authors in their own tongue. Is it not true that never mind how good a translation may be, it is never so fine as the original? That is always stronger—more charming.

We have much time for reading, and reading is our greatest pleasure—we, that is, the younger sisters and I. We three have had the same bringing up, and are much with one another. We differ in age, each from the other, by but one year. Among us three there is the greatest harmony. Naturally we sometimes have little differences of opinion, but that does not weaken the tie that binds us together. Our little quarrels are splendid, I find them so: I love the reconciliations which follow. It is the greatest of all lies—do you not think so too?—that any two human beings can think alike in everything. That cannot be; people who say that must be hypocrites.

I have not yet told you how old I am. I was just twenty last month. Strange, that when I was sixteen I felt so frightfully old, and had so many melancholy moods! Now that I can put two crosses behind me, I feel young and full of the joy of life, and the struggle of life, too.

Call me simply Kartini; that is my name. We Javanese have no family names. Kartini is my given name and my family name, both at the same time. As far as "Raden Adjeng" is concerned, those two words are the title. I told Mevrouw van Wermeskerken, when I gave her my address, not to put Kartini alone—that would hardly reach me from Holland, and as for writing *Mejuffrouw*,* or something of that kind, I have no right to it; I am only a Javanese.

Now, for the present, you know enough about me—is it not so? Another time I shall tell you of our Indian life.

If there is any light that you would like thrown upon any of our Indian affairs, please ask me. I am ready to tell you all that I know about my country and my people.

---

*Mejuffrouw is the Dutch equivalent of "Miss."

Dumb Luck

~ *1936, Vietnam* ~

Vu Trong Phung

Over the course of the nineteenth century, France gradually established a colony over the Vietnamese state and the neighboring kingdoms of Cambodia and Laos. The impact of French colonialism was experienced by Vietnamese at many levels: political, economic, social, culture, and educational. The loss of political autonomy was felt acutely among the Vietnamese, and yet Vietnamese elites recognized the significance of the ways in which their society was being transformed by its encounter with the French. Among other things, the French brought with them new literary genres and forms, including the modern novel. The novel, with its many distinctive features of theme, structure, and voice, opened up new possibilities for Vietnamese authors who were beginning to write in the increasingly popular romanized script. The novel offered new ways to engage in social commentary on a world turned upside down by the arrival of the French and the dramatic onset of modernity. The intense transformation of Vietnamese urban society, with new technologies, new social structures, new patterns of culture, and new political hierarchies, provoked a wide range of responses from careful emulation to strong resistance. Novels allowed a new generation of Vietnamese intellectuals to comment on these changes in a variety of ways.

Many of these author-intellectuals were also journalists, among them the author of *Dumb Luck*, Vu Trong Phung (1912–1939). Phung was a prolific writer in a wide range of genres, from social reportage to essays to novels, amassing a staggering literary output before his life was cut short by tuberculosis at the age of 27. *Dumb Luck*, published in 1936, is one of his most popular novels. It is a biting satire of the social climbing and cultural emulation pursued by a particular segment of urban society in Hanoi in what was at the time the French protectorate of Tonkin in northern Indochina. The novel relates a rags-to-riches story of a young street boy who rises from minor tennis partner to national sports champion, passing through brief careers as doctor, journalist, and clothing salesperson.

Vu Trong Phung's satirical barbs are directed at members of Hanoi's Vietnamese society who pursue "modernity" with an intense determination even as they have little grasp of precisely what it means. They mistake form for content, equating provocative clothing and flashy displays of wealth with being modern and hence "civilized." The author provides a sweeping survey of Hanoi urban life in the 1930s, critiquing not the French for their colonial domination, but rather the Vietnamese for their fawning imitation of the French. This form of self-criticism was a common theme among early twentieth-century writers, who saw a degree of complicity in the Vietnamese colonial status, and berated themselves for lacking the moral and physical courage to counter the French presence.

The excerpt below traces an early episode in the story, in which the main character, Red-Haired Xuan (pronounced Swun), has been hired to work in a retail clothing store. The chapter illustrates the obsession with fashion and clothing as critically important markers of modernity, while mocking those who aspire to civilization through clothing. Phung also skewers the general obsession with modernity through his satirical comment on writing forms and art, suggesting that the logical outcome of modernizing scripts is that they become illegible, and that the ultimate modernization of art is that it becomes incomprehensible. The outrageous styles of women's clothing offered in the "Europeanization Tailor Shop," like the "Wait-a-Minute" panties or the "Stop-Those-Hands" bra, reflect the absurdity that Phung sees in the misguided pursuit of modernity. Indeed, here as elsewhere in the novel, Phung portrays an urban society in which the modern is understood chiefly as the inverse of the traditional. Conservative dress is replaced with see-through clothing. Filial piety is replaced with plots and schemes to kill one's elders to inherit their money. In short, he depicts a world turned on its head. *Dumb Luck* reflects a radically transformed world in which life will never be the same, particularly for those living in fast-moving and fast-changing urban centers. The novel does not reject this transformation (though its author is clearly ambivalent about it), but rather questions the ways in which Vietnamese are responding to it.

These colonial-era buildings in Hanoi reflect the low-slung architectural style of the French era, and the trees and wide street were also typical of the colonial approach to urban planning. *(Author's collection)*

Questions

1. What, as the author depicts it here, are some of the key elements of modernity? How does the author use absurdity to express his views of modernity?
2. What role does clothing play in this excerpt? What can it do for people and how can it affect their lives?
3. How does this story depict changing gender roles and family dynamics, and what is the threat posed by modernity to traditional relationships between men and women?

***

Dumb Luck

> Vu Trong Phung. *Dumb Luck*. Trans. Nguyen Nguyet
> Cam and Peter Zinoman. (Ann Arbor: University of
> Michigan Press, 2002), pp. 57–64. Reprinted with the kind
> permission of the publisher.

Chapter 4

The Anger of Hoan Thu
Art for Life's Sake
The Products of Europeanization

Following the instructions he had from Mrs. Deputy Customs Officer, Red-Haired Xuan arrived in front of a modern-looking tailor shop for women at precisely eight the next morning. He dared not enter immediately, however, for he could not be sure if this was, in fact, the Europeanization Tailor Shop of Mrs. Civilization. Red-Haired Xuan's limited education had endowed him with the capacity to make out a laundry list but not to understand the ultramodern and largely illegible lettering favored by today's advertising designers. As Xuan looked on, workers were putting up a new storefront sign. Five bizarre-looking pieces of newly painted red wood lay frying on the pavement. One worker had propped a ladder up against the wall. A younger man, whose rolled-up shirtsleeves indicated that he meant business, barked out orders and issued occasional rebukes. The tailor shop was remarkably swank. Three wooden *ma no canh* (mannequins) imported from Europe stood poised behind its large plate-glass window. Although they had been made to resemble beautiful European women, the shop owner had skillfully arranged turbans and strands of black hair on their heads so as to make them look more Vietnamese. Each mannequin displayed a different article of clothing. One sported a swallow-tailed coat, the kind that girls and young women often wear to go out. Another wore a swimming suit, the kind that girls and young women wear on the beach in order to display the art of their bodies. A third wore lingerie, the kind worn by powerful women so as to remind their husbands and lovers not to forget their most sacred of masculine duties.

Xuan inched toward the five wooden letters on the pavement. Try as he might, he was unable to make out the specific letter that each was supposed to symbolize. There was a round one with a hole in the middle and a strange square one with two round holes in the middle. Even more bizarre were three triangle-shaped ones with holes in the middle! Ever since he was six, Red-Haired Xuan's coarse mind knew that a triangular shape with a hole in the middle could only signify one thing—one very dirty thing. He smiled to himself.

The young man with the rolled-up sleeves began shouting at his workers. "No! No! This one goes first! The triangle, damn it!"

"What is a triangle?" asked the worker, confusedly.

The young man scolded him again. "A triangle . . . with a hole, damn it! And the triangular shape here is supposed to be the letter A."

"But, Sir," the worker protested, "you just said that the triangular shape is the letter U."

"You idiot! The right-side up triangle is a U. The upside-down one is an A. What kind of craftsman are you? Don't you know anything about art? Nail the upside-down triangle first, then put the right-side-up one after it. That's A followed by U—giving us AU—Europe in other words. Then put up the square piece with the two holes—that's an H. Then the round piece with a hole in the middle—that's an O. Then another upside-down triangle—I mean another A. That spells HOA-ization. Together, it all means Europeanization! Get it? You guys are dumber than pigs!"

Despite the insult, Xuan was happy to have found the shop.

"Screw those god-damned letters!" he murmured to himself.

A moment later a young man appeared wearing a European hiking outfit. He approached the young man overseeing the design of the storefront sign. They shook hands and greeted each other noisily in French.

"My God! The Vietnamese common people are so backward, artistically speaking."

"Yes, yes, it's simply a waste of breath to talk about art with the common people."

"Of course, but remember that you are a journalist. Your duty is to help enhance the knowledge of the common people so that one day they too may understand art. I, on the other hand, am an artist. I am much too busy devoting myself to art to explain my work to them."

"Yes, but your influence is already quite widespread, even among ordinary folk."

"Still not enough. There is much work to be done. Ours are a lazy people. They do not want to think deeply; they rarely try to comprehend the vast, complicated problems that those of us in the fine arts must confront. Of course, the more difficult a work of art is to understand, the more valuable it is. For example, in Italy and in Germany, I hear, those painters whose works are completely incomprehensible are worshiped as saints. When the dictators Hitler and Mussolini took power, they were so jealous of these artists that they threw them in jail. I only pray that someday our artists will be good enough to be thrown in jail as well!"

"Indeed!"

"Due to the low level of our society, we artists must take responsibility for the reform of women's fashions—by far the easiest genre of fine arts to understand. Only when our society learns to enjoy the beauty of . . . women's thighs, will it be able to appreciate the value of nude paintings and thus appreciate fine art at the highest level."

"Quite right!"

"How do you like these ultramodern letters? They are my latest creation! Aren't they unusual? The fact that the most common people cannot understand this style of lettering only confirms its sophistication. Someday I hope to craft letters that are so very, very modern that even intellectuals cannot read them. What a victory for art!"

While eavesdropping on this conversation, Xuan caught a glimpse of Mrs. Civilization through the storefront window. He gingerly entered the shop. The two young men followed him inside, still engrossed in conversation.

"Good morning, Madame," Xuan said politely.

Mrs. Civilization nodded to Xuan and shook hands with the other two. "Please sit down, Monsieurs. To what do we owe this visit?" she asked the journalist. "Are subscriptions up or down these days?"

"I've come for an important reason. Our sales are up to fifty copies . . ."

She cut him off briskly and turned to Xuan.

"And what about you? What can I do for you?"

Xuan blushed and rubbed his hands together.

"If you please . . . please . . . Yesterday, the great Madame Deputy Customs Officer . . ."

Mrs. Civilization interrupted him.

"Quiet! You must refer to her as Madame Senior Clerk; otherwise, she will be annoyed."

"Yes, Ma'am! Madame Senior Clerk told me to come here . . . she said . . . to meet you . . ."

"Fine. Wait here for a moment."

Mrs. Civilization gestured to the journalist to enter the salon inside the shop. Xuan sat down on an upholstered chair near the door. Despite his nervousness, he took advantage of the rare opportunity to admire those secret aspects of the gentler sex that only the Europeanization movement dares to display openly. It was truly a party for his eyes—provocative breasts cupped in brassieres of silk and lace, thighs cased in sheer silk stockings and all manner of slips and panties, each capable of provoking lust in men well into their seventies. Huge colorful rolls of solid and floral-patterned silk gave the shop an especially lively ambiance. There was also a dressing room covered on three sides by velvet drapes and another room in which male and female tailors worked, busy as bees, before a row of sewing machines.

A poorly made-up middle-aged woman appeared outside the glass window. She gazed inside for several minutes before entering the shop. The shop owner greeted her warmly.

"Can I help you, Madame? Would you like to buy clothes or perhaps have something made?"

The customer thought for a long while. "I want . . . a custom-made modern outfit."

"Of course you do," Mrs. Civilization replied glibly. "Today we must all reform our wardrobes to keep up with fashion. The conventional trends in makeup, for example, tend to make people look older. We must replace them! As you know, Madame, one can no longer remain ignorant of the latest fads in beauty maintenance and hope to maintain family happiness. Nowadays, all young girls dress in a modern way—the competition is increasingly brutal."

The woman nodded and opened her eyes wide in agreement. "Yes! Yes! You are absolutely right! Young girls today dress even more provocatively than wives of Westerners in the past! So modern! So slutty! My god! They are so beautiful compared to me, and my husband is obsessed by them. What am I to do?"

Her voice rose to an almost hysterical pitch. Mrs. Civilization tried to calm her down. "Now, now! Don't get so worked up!"

"But my husband spends every night chasing after those modern sluts! What, for Heaven's sake, can I do?"

"The answer is simple, Madame. If you can't beat them, you must join them. You must try to dress just like them."

"Yes! Yes! I can dress like that too, of course! Who cares if people call me an old whore! It's all your doing anyway. It all starts with you tailors!"

Mrs. Civilization shrugged her shoulders.

"Madame, our society progresses according to the basic laws of evolution. During this deeply reformist era everything conservative will be eliminated! Since we opened this tailor shop, countless wives have saved their marriages, recaptured the love of their husbands, and reestablished the happiness of their families."

"In that case, Madame, I would like to order a custom-made outfit right away, the most modern possible! Only, please do not charge me too much!"

"Of course! I will be happy to suggest several new and different styles for you . . ."

Mrs. Civilization drew the attention of her customer to a row of mannequins. "See . . . here . . . The many innovative styles displayed in our shop were all designed by well-known art students. If you please, Madame, the sign under each mannequin explains the meaning of the outfit it displays. For example, this one is called 'Promise.' A girl may wear this outfit to reassure her boyfriend that she promises to show up for their appointment that evening. This one is called 'Win His Heart.' Men are like putty in the hands of girls who wear this outfit. And here, of course, we have 'Innocence.' This one is 'Puberty'—appropriate for teenage girls. Clothes in this section are for 'Commanders of Internal Affairs'— housewives, in other words. This one is called 'Women's Rights,' for wives whose husbands are afraid of them. This one, 'Resolute Faithfulness,' is for widows determined to honor their late husbands and remain unmarried. This one, 'Hesitation,' is for widows who are somewhat less determined. And here we have our newest model, finished several days ago. We have not named it formally yet, but we are planning to call it 'Conquest.' In this outfit you should be able to stoke the passions of any man, even your own husband!"

Conquest consisted of a transparent black blouse and pair of pants over a set of black panties and a black *cooc xe* (corset). It also exposed the arms, deep cleavage, thighs, and legs of the beautiful wooden woman that exhibited it. Mrs. Civilization stared at the outfit with a look of utter satisfaction.

The customer, however, appeared unconvinced. "To wear this outfit . . . well, it's just unsightly!"

At that moment the journalist and artist joined the conversation.

"It's very sightly indeed, Madame!" the journalist said. "If you wear this outfit, men will pursue you, just as they pursue innocent young girls!"

"Ah, Conquest!" the artist chimed in. "I chose the name, you know."

"But such clothing barely covers anything at all," the customer protested.

"Madame," the artist retorted, "the very concept of clothing has changed. We developed this particular style following the conceptual lead of famous European designers. Clothing should enhance and embellish one's natural beauty, not cover it up. Soon clothing will progress to that extreme, exquisite, perfect point where it will no longer cover up anything at all."

Mrs. Civilization peered uneasily at the doubtful expression on the face of her customer.

"It may seem too modern for you now, but just wait until the next time your husband plans to go on one of his evening outings. As soon as you put it on and stand before the mirror, your husband will desire no one but you."

"Yes! Yes!" the customer nodded. "Perhaps I ought to give that one a try."

"Madame, what is family happiness if not the happiness of husbands and wives? What else can be done when love begins to fade?"

"You're right! You're absolutely right!"

"We have designed new styles of undergarments for this same reason. Never mind what those old-fashioned moralists say about us. We do not simply reform the outside. A slip or a pair of panties from our shop may be thought of as a secret weapon in the fight to retain one's husband."

"Where are they? How can I order one?"

Mrs. Civilization turned around and gestured toward a glass case. She reached in and pulled out a pile of panties, brassieres, long slips, and mini-slips.

"I call this one 'Coquette.' And these are known as 'Wait-a-Minute' panties. This is the 'Happiness' slip. Here is what we call the 'Stop-Those-Hands' brassiere. Feel free to look them over. Only the Europeanization Shop cares so much about the satisfaction of the fair sex."

The female customer nodded her head vigorously. "Yes, I will do as you say! I will Europeanize myself and follow the ways of civilization! I vow to dress progressively! Call your tailors and show me the changing room!"

Mrs. Civilization pointed to the artist. "Here, Madame, is your tailor! He was originally a student at the Indochinese Fine Art College. Your beauty is now his responsibility!"

The artist bowed his head very low. "Please follow me, Madame. I am deeply honored to serve you."

They disappeared behind the velvet drapes of the changing room. Xuan remained in his chair. Mrs. Civilization turned to address the journalist.

"Monsieur, your newspaper cannot possibly propose to charge more for advertising. The cost is excessive already."

"You are wrong, Madame. Our newspaper has more and more readers every day. Our prestige is constantly under attack by conservative forces—another clear benefit to you. More people are following the news than ever before."

"That is only natural, Monsieur. But, of course, it benefits your business much more than mine."

"No! It benefits you and your kind as well, maybe even more!"

"It is you who calls for renovation. Hence, you benefit most when people heed the call!"

"No! You benefit most!"

"So says you!"

"It's not true! Haven't you noticed the recent progressive evolution of our society? It's all over the daily papers! So many divorces! So many cases of adultery! Girls chasing boys, men getting bored with their wives, officials leaving their posts to pursue modern girls . . . It's great for your business. Newspapers clearly have a huge influence. New dancing halls are popping up every day . . ."

At that moment Mrs. Deputy Customs Officer entered the shop. Red-Haired Xuan stood up. Mrs. Civilization left the journalist alone to contemplate the influence of his newspaper.

"My niece! My niece! . . ."

"Auntie . . . Over here . . . I need to ask you something."

Aunt and niece huddled together in the far corner of the room. As the journalist put on his hat and walked angrily out of the shop, he grasped one of life's basic truths: journalism is a wretched profession. Red-Haired Xuan continued to wait.

"Why did you send this guy here, Auntie?"

"I need you to hire him. I want to keep him around while they are building the tennis court at my house. We can use him for practice."

"But the court won't be finished for a while. Why hire him now and waste all that money?"

"You have a point. But he may starve if we don't do it now!"

She paused a moment and then whispered to her niece: "How about this . . . before the tennis court is finished, we could . . . in that way, we won't waste all that much. What do you think?"

Just like that, Red-Haired Xuan became a member of the movement for social reform.

Oil

~ *1938, Burma* ~

THEIN PE MYINT

While the French were imposing colonial domination over the In-dochinese Peninsula to the east, the British were doing the same toward the west in Burma. In the course of three Anglo-Burmese wars (1824–1886), the British overthrew the traditional monarchy and brought the Burmese realm into their larger colony on the Indian Subcontinent. Like the French, the British introduced two significant literary forms to their colony in Burma, the novel and the short story. Both forms became extremely popular among Burmese writers, with the first novel in Burmese appearing in 1904. Many novels followed in subsequent decades, though some still straddled the line between traditional tales and modern fiction, with many focusing on Burmese historical figures. Among the masters of both short story and novel was Thein Pe Myint (1914–1978), a writer with a strong educational background who had studied English and Burmese literature, re-ceived a BA, and had begun to study law. His involvement with the young Burmese nationalists, particularly the We Burmans Society, however, disqualified him from work in the legal profession, and he devoted himself to writing full time. He also belonged to a Marxist group and helped to found the Red Dragon Book Club, which was committed to publishing Burmese translations of Marxist texts as well as original writings by its members. Myint was among the club's most prolific members, writing three novels and a biography in the brief period between 1936 and 1938. Perhaps his most famous and most controversial work was *Modern Monks* (1937), a novel that attacked the corrupt elements of the Buddhist monastic system and provoked a powerful backlash from the *sangha*, the institutionalized community of Buddhist monks. Myint's writings reflect his strong involvement in the nationalist movement and his Marxist orientation and contain thinly veiled criticisms of the British for their domination of a proud people and their unfair and oppressive economic policies.

The selection included here is one of his 1938 short stories, one that in remarkably spare form explores the attitudes of the ordinary Burman toward the colonial rulers. It illustrates the peculiar circumstances in which Burmans found themselves, and clearly betrays its author's Marxist leanings. The story is centered on a family confronted with the simple challenge of acquiring enough fuel to keep their lamps lit at night so that their children may study. The story neatly reveals some of what its author viewed as the absurdities confronting the Burmese subjects of the British. On the one hand it reflects on the peculiarity of being nominally ruled by a king so remote that the Burmese are unsure of his precise status, while on the other offering a strong critique of an absurdity much closer to home, namely, the fact of impoverished Burmese workers living in the midst of the British oil field while being unable to afford to buy even a little oil for their lamps. The story reveals the moral dilemma confronting the central character, who is forced to compromise his integrity to provide basic needs for his family, and subsequently witnesses the consequences of his actions, including rifts within his family and unjust punishment for his friends. In this fashion, Myint illustrates the untenable position into which the British colonial arrangements forced the Burman people.

Questions

1. What are some indications of the impact of the British colonial presence on the Burmese, both in terms of their material and their intellectual lives? In what ways is it a daily reality, and in what ways a remote abstraction?
2. What evidence of poverty is depicted in this story?
3. How do the consequences of colonial exploitation affect the sorts of choices his characters make, and what is the author saying about the colonial situation?
4. How does Burmese Buddhism affect the rhythms of this story?

***

Oil

Thein Pe Myint "Oil." In *Selected Short Stories of Thein Pe Myint*. Trans. Patricia M. Milne. (Ithaca, NY: Cornell University Southeast Asia Program, 1973), pp. 36–42. Reprinted with the kind permission of the publisher.

I

Away in the distance the B.O.C. (British Oil Company) buildings were brightly lit by electric lights, but in the small village where the workers lived, everything was in darkness except for the headman's house and the house of the master carpenter who earned seventy *kyats* a month. Up in the sky, a few stars appeared momentarily among the scattering clouds.

Just then . . . "God save our gracious King, long live our noble King, God save the King. Send him victorious, happy and glorious, long to reign over us, God save the King." The words of the British national anthem rendered into the Burmese issued plaintively from the workers' quarters which were hidden in the darkness.

"Kyaw Yin, that's a good song but we don't understand it. What does it say?" said Ko Lu Dok to Kyaw Yin, his nine-year-old son. Kyaw Yin was lying on his back, propping his feet against the wooden wall; he was reciting as much as he could remember from what he had been taught at the B.O.C. school.

"That song you're singing—what does it mean?"

"Oh, really, Father! It's not a song; it's a prayer. Our teacher taught it to us," he answered, looking sidelong at his father who could not see his face.

"I've heard it before. So it's a prayer, then? Tell us what it means . . . Ow! . . . now there's a wretched bed bug biting—that's going too far." Ko Lu Dok sat up in bed as he spoke. His wife, Ma Hsin, struck a light for him and together they looked for the bug.

"I'm not sure, Father. It prays to the Lord that the glory of our king should be great, and that his lands and seas should greatly increase," said Kyaw Yin, reaching out with his fist and hitting his twelve-year-old sister, Mya Nyun.

"Oh, you! You are too big for your boots. I was nearly asleep."

"Big . . . big," said Kyaw Yin, pounding Mya Nyun even harder with his fist.

"Hey, you, Kyaw, do you want a taste of my slipper? Let her go to sleep," said Ma Hsin, intervening.

"You used the words 'our king' just now. Who's that? We haven't got a king. Our king went away a long time ago."

"Really, Father, you've got it all wrong. Of course we have a king, we still do, we really do."

"Who is he, then?"

"He's called King George. He lives a long way away in that place, England or whatever it's called."

"Who taught you that?"

"Teacher."

"He's wrong."

"He isn't."

"He is completely and utterly wrong. I've got a book. You have a look at it. Oh well, never mind. And about those prayers, haven't you ever heard a prayer?"

"That was a prayer just now, Father."

"That was a song. Don't you know any proper Buddhist prayers?"

"No, I don't," he said, kicking at the wall with his foot.

"If you don't know any, you must learn some. A man must know how to pray." Ko Lu Dok laid his hand on his son's forehead and stroked it.

Like a hungry person who pricks up his ears at the sound of spoons and plates, Kyaw Yin accepted the suggestion and asked eagerly, "Where is the book. I want to learn some then."

"Ma Hsin, would you light the lamp, please."

"We haven't any oil," said Ma Hsin, in complaining tones.

"Oh, woman, there's plenty of oil."

"Certainly, if you buy it; but you don't get it for nothing. Come on now, just go to sleep, all of you. There isn't any oil." Ma Hsin turned over on her side and closed her eyes firmly.

"We used to get it for nothing, but we don't now. Very well then . . . we'll buy some on pay-day."

"It won't be possible. Your daily wages won't stretch that far. We've got to pay our debts and buy rice, and Mya Nyun needs a new blouse too."

Since Ma Hsin had forestalled him with these sound arguments, he just gave a deep sigh.

II

It seemed to Kyaw Yin that what his father said and what his teacher taught him were as diametrically opposed as north and south.

"Are you sure that's right, Father?"

"Of course I am. We haven't got a king in Burma. Your prayer isn't one of our Buddhist prayers. I'll give you the right ones to read."

"It's difficult when there isn't any oil, Father."

There were five families altogether in the quarters where they lived. A newly married couple lived in the next room on the south side; ever since they were married, they hadn't dared to enjoy themselves happily in bed for fear of the embarrassment of being overheard in the next room. The poor young wife pleaded with her husband to speak quietly, pointing out that everything could be heard next door.

"I'll find a way to get some oil. You must read, my son, and not waste your time." Ko Lu Dok's voice sounded from the adjoining room.

"Let's go to bed," said the young husband.

"Wait a moment, they haven't gone to sleep yet next door." When the young man heard his wife's answer, he heaved a sigh and retired abashed.

"Hey, Ko Lu Dok!"

"What is it?"

"What's the time? I think it's getting late, isn't it?"

"Yes," agreed Ko Lu Dok patiently, and lay still.

Ko Lu Dok couldn't sleep. He kept thinking about his young son. "My son is learning all the wrong things. Even at his age he doesn't know how to say a prayer. It's a good thing that he can read, but not when he has to read wrong things and bad things," he pondered, stretching his arms above his head. The noise of the pump machinery penetrated the village with a dull roar. "I can't buy paraffin oil so my son can read . . . my fate must be very bad. Even though I work as hard as I do, I shall never get out of debt, and I shall never be free of the consequences of past sin, shall I?" As he muttered complainingly to himself, the sound of giggling, like the clucking of a house lizard, sounded loudly from the next room, and Ko Lu Dok's train of thought was broken.

Ko Lu Dok was sitting with his knees drawn up and his head buried in his hands, thinking about it again. "What can I do to get paraffin oil for my son? It's like being thirsty in the middle of the ocean." As this thought occurred to him, he pictured in his mind the tins of oil stacked up at the B.O.C. shop. He often had to go to the B.O.C. shop with a lorry which he stopped in front of the storage godown (warehouse).

It would not be difficult for him to enter the godown alone. Because the watchman trusted him, he did not usually watch closely while he was unloading the lorry. Here was the answer . . . this was his chance. While no one was looking, he could load a tin of oil onto the lorry. "No, that's not right . . . the punishment is severe for stealing, for taking what is not one's own. I would really suffer the torments of hell for that." He dropped his knee and stretched out his leg as he thought about it again. He sighed deeply.

"This oil is produced by our own work; it is our digging that gets it out of the ground." The excuse made itself heard again. In his mind he could see the workers digging the wells. He heard the night watchman striking the gong for ten o'clock. He folded his arms across his chest.

"After all, don't they say that this land belongs to us Burmans; we have owned it from the beginning of history. So we must own the oil which comes from our land. Why should I suffer the torments of hell? I am only taking back what belongs to us. I'll steal it, yes, I'll steal it."

As he came to this decision, he became aware of the sound of his own heavy breathing.

III

And so it was that a few evenings later a small lamp was burning in Ko Lu Dok's room, and the shrill sound of Kyaw Yin reading aloud could be heard. In the quarters where the five families lived, the old man furthest away on the left rejoiced when he heard Kyaw Yin reading prayers. In the room immediately to their left, they remarked crossly that they were fed up with the sound. To the young couple on the other side who were waiting to retire to bed, his reading sounded just like a funeral dirge, while the family in the room beyond said unkindly, "He's awfully fond of reading, that young chap over there. I suppose it's because his father used to be a monk!"

However, Kyaw Yin's elder sister, Mya Nyun, was feeling cross with her brother because the light was shining in her eyes and stopping her getting to sleep. Mya Nyun was wearing a gilt ring which gave off a reddish glow in the light of the lamp, and which was conspicuous on her hand.

Ko Lu Dok was like a violinist delighted by the sound of his own playing; he was overjoyed when he heard his young son reading and learning to say his prayers.

"My son is fine; as well as being able to read and write properly, he will know what is right and he will know how to pray. He will be a true man. When I compare him with other children, none of them are half so clever as my son. My son is among the best." And his pride in his son grew.

IV

Thus for several days he remained jubilantly happy for his son . . .

Mya Nyun was asleep with her face buried in her pillow. Kyaw Yin was so tired from reading that he had fallen asleep with his book open on his chest. Ma Hsin was rolling up cheroots by the foot of the bed, and Ko Lu Dok was sitting cross-legged in the doorway.

The light of the lamp lit up the whole room clearly. The room was only about ten feet square with a low roof. The floor planks were laid down with an inch gap between each one. Their shoes were placed in a row at the head end of the family bed, right next to the upturned cooking pots and the dishes and plates. At the foot of the bed was a six-inch-high bag of rice on top of which had been placed the folded *htamein-skirts*. At the southern end of the room there was a *thanat-hka* grinding stone on which Ma Hsin had put the basket of cheroots.

Ma Hsin took a cheroot and lit it. She tucked her left foot under her and stretched out the other leg, puffing away at her cheroot.

"Ku Lu Dok . . . have you heard?"

"What?" asked Ko Lu Dok, glancing up briefly.

"TT Mon, the watchman at the Company godown, has been fined."

Ko Lu Dok showed rather more interest after Ma Hsin had explained what had happened.

"They say a tin of oil is missing from the warehouse," she said in reply to his question.

"Oh dear, I'm sorry to hear that," muttered Ko Lu Dok in an unsteady voice.

He looked towards the electric lights which seemed to blossom luxuriantly like the magic *padei-tha* tree. As he stared each light grew into two before his eyes. His mind was in a turmoil; all that he could think of was the unhappy look there would be on U Mon's face; in his mind's eye he saw first U Mon's face, and then the way he had stealthily loaded the tin of oil onto the lorry. His heart was pounding.

"Here's a cheroot," said Ma Hsin, passing one over. Ko Lu Dok shook his head.

As he realized what he had done, he began to hate himself, thinking, "I am a thief, I am a thief; and because of this, poor Ko Mon has been fined." He was disgusted with himself. "Someone else has landed in trouble because of my wickedness. Ko Mon, you don't know this, but it is I persecuting you, I am the beast doing it."

Ko Lu Dok stood up. He could not hold his head high; his shoulders drooped, and he felt weak. He hung his head and went outside.

"Ko Lu Dok, where are you going? It's late," said Ma Hsin, putting down her cheroot.

"Just out here," he said as he walked slowly up and down in front of the house.

"I have done a stupid thing. I have never stolen like this before. I have never done anything wicked before. But now, because I've done wrong, another person has got into trouble. I'm not a man; I'm a dog. I'm not worthy to live the life of a human being. These rich men aren't willing to dismiss even a trifling loss lightly, and here they are persecuting someone who had nothing to do with it. When they get millions of tons of oil a day, why do they have to hand out punishment to one man for the loss of a mere gallon or so? Have they no pity? This oil is our oil. Tell me how they can punish us for the disappearance of our own oil."

He looked into the room. Ma Hsin was asleep on her side. The small lamp filled the room with light. He went back inside again.

"Ko Mon has had to pay a fine, and he's been fined because of me. It's I who ought to be paying the fine; it's nothing to do with him. I'll make it up to him. I'll find the money somehow."

He tried to think of a way to get the money for the fine. He thought of this and that, pondering on a way to do it. Mya Nyun was sleeping on her back with her left arm folded across her chest. In the light of the lamp, her small gilt ring shone brightly, and Ko Lu Dok caught its beckoning gleam.

"I've got it . . . I will take this ring and send it secretly to Ko Mon. That's the answer . . . everything will be alright. When he sells this ring, he should be able to get at least three *kyats* for it; I'll send it off to him. He won't know who sent it. Yes, yes, that's it."

He went over to his small daughter and took hold of her small hand. When he saw how well the ring looked on her small slender fingers, he remained gazing at it and could hardly find the heart to slip it off.

When it became light in the morning and Mya Nyun woke up, she couldn't see her father nearby. She washed her face, and as she was wiping it, she noticed that her ring was missing.

Mya Nyun shook out her blankets, but it wasn't there. She repeatedly moved her pillow, grimy and thick with dirt, as she searched, but she couldn't find it anywhere. She looked all over the floor but it was nowhere to be found. She then shook her mother to waken her.

"Mother, mother, my ring has disappeared," she cried out. Ma Hsin sat bolt upright like one of those push-down-pop-up toys, rubbing her eyes with her hand.

"What's that? Your ring's disappeared?"

"Yes, it has."

"Hey, Kyaw Yin, wake up!" Mya Nyun shook Kyaw Yin to waken him.

"Ow, who is it? Go away . . . let me sleep." Although Kyaw Yin muttered grumpily, Mya Nyun persisted in arousing him.

"What is it?"

"My ring has disappeared. Have you taken it?"

"For goodness sake, why should I take your ring?"

"You must have taken it . . . give it back, you!"

"I didn't take it. Go away . . . and don't spoil my sleep. I'll hit you if you don't go. I said, go away!"

"I won't. You took it."

Kyaw Yin couldn't bear to be wrongly accused of being a thief for no reason at all, so he kicked her with his foot.

Mya Nyun punched her young brother on the head with her fist.

"Huh! . . . hit me again, would you?" shouted Kyaw Yin, grabbing Mya Nyun and pulling her down by the hair.

"If you didn't take it, then it was because of your lamp that someone must have seen it and stolen it. Ow!" She kept on hitting Kyaw Yin.

At that moment Ko Lu Dok arrived. "What's the matter?" he asked as he came hurrying in.

Ma Hsin had been looking on helplessly, making no effort to separate her fighting son and daughter. "They are quarrelling because her ring is lost."

"Stop it, or I'll give you both a beating, now!"

The fighting stopped. Dazed Ko Lu Dok looked at his children. He felt as if his heart would break as he watched the tears streaming down his daughter's face as she wept for her lost ring. In the silence he stood there, thinking bitterly about the oil.

After a while, he took the tin of oil, went outside, unscrewed the lid, and tipped the oil away.

"Accursed oil; it has caused my son and daughter to quarrel; it has got my friend into trouble; and it has made me into a despicable creature. Away with it, ill-fated stuff!" he muttered as he solemnly poured it away onto the earth.

Return

~ *1950s, Malaysia* ~

Miao Hsiou

Often overlooked in the history of modern Southeast Asian literature are the contributions of Sinophone authors, those writing in Chinese rather than an indigenous or national language. The literary canons of modern Southeast Asian nations have tended to valorize works in what had emerged as "national" languages over the course of struggles for independence. Texts produced by Southeast Asian authors in other languages, whether those of the colonizers or those of minority populations, were frequently ignored. Given the dispersion of Chinese across the region, it is hardly surprising that literary production in Chinese would represent an important element of Southeast Asian culture. In some places, most notably Singapore, where the Chinese are a strong majority, Chinese language literature is given a prominent place in the national culture. Elsewhere in the region, however, writing in Chinese is not given the same accord.

This particular example of Sinophone literature, a short story by the author Miao Hsiou, is from Malaysia, a country in which the modern Malay language was valorized from a literary perspective, and writings in the languages and scripts of the other prominent minority populations—Indian and Chinese—were not recognized as part of the national literature. Despite this lack of official recognition, Malaysia has a very strong Sinophone literary tradition, with numerous prominent authors producing significant shorter works and full-length novels reflecting on the complexities of life in Malaysia as it made the transition from British colonialism to a fraught multi-ethnic independence in which ethnic Chinese made up nearly a quarter of the country's population.

Miao Hsiou was part of a generation that wrote under colonialism, continued to write through the Japanese occupation and then into the period of Malaysia's independence in the late 1950s. He was a journalist and teacher in addition to writing novels and short stories. This story, *Return*, tells of lost love, of the directions in which people are pulled—between city and *kampong* (village), between Malaysia and China. The central character, Ching Tze, sees her lover being drawn back to China and being forced to give up his love for her. In the same way, she had earlier given her up her love for the young teacher in her village to go to the big city. It is a simple yet compelling story that traces universal themes of love and loss, of travel and return, as the title suggests.

Questions

1. The title of this short story is simply "Return." What does this refer to? Is there more than one way to interpret this title?
2. In many respects this story is a somber one in which the characters face difficult choices or unhappy partings. What devices and word choices does the author use to invoke this mood?
3. What is the nature of the dynamic between city and village in this story? What allure does each have for the main character?
4. What gives this story a sense of place? In other words, how does the author evoke Malaysia as the setting for the story?

***

Return

Miao Hsiou. "Return." In *An Anthology of Modern Malaysian Chinese Stories*. Trans. Ly Singko. (Singapore: Heinemann Educational Books, 1976), pp. 53–62.

It was early in the morning. The sky was grey and overcast, and it had started to drizzle. The train was about to depart. The passengers were few, and the people seeing them off were fewer still. As the rain started falling, it caused a slight stir here and there among the thin crowd standing on the platform. But Ching Tze did not notice it at all; she was almost motionless in her seat. She was looking out of the window, aimlessly, one hand resting under her slim pointed chin, the lightly powdered face tilted upwards, the long hair which had been dressed some hours ago spreading over her shoulders. Her eyes looked disproportionately large in her small, thin, oval face. She was staring vaguely at the grey sky overhead.

Sitting as though in a trance, she did not even bother to turn her head when someone crossed in front of her or sat down next to her. Only when the rain dropped on her face and arm and the chilly feeling made her realize the change of weather, did she change her position; then she opened her little suitcase, took out a light blue woolen cardigan and covered her shoulders with it.

It was drizzling heavily. The glistening rails were shining with a cold luster in the early morning darkness.

The damp air, mixed with the coal dust from locomotives, spread a dull mist over the whole station.

Outside the massive iron gates, the buildings of the colonial city could still be seen through the screen of drizzling raindrops, towering over the low shaky *atap* huts all around, a familiar picture which one always sees without really seeing at all.

Yes, it was a familiar picture. She knew almost everything about the city; uncaringly she had spent ten full years there; the impression etched on her memory could not be erased easily.

Ten years—not such a long time really. When she had left the country all that time ago to settle in the city, she was still a young girl full of life and without fear. Now, she was twenty-eight. To a woman like her, twenty-eight years of age sounded like a warning; she had then to think about her future.

Thinking about the future was something which had troubled her like a chronic disease every time she had been together with that nineteen-year-old boy. When his young, firm flesh had touched hers, she had felt as though she was drinking very potent wine. She felt then that she was exhausted, physically and emotionally. She had liked that moment of contact, for he seemed to pour into her the vigor of life and the energy of youth which she had lost and was so eager to retrieve . . .

Perhaps this was happiness. She had tried to believe it, to grasp it firmly, to enjoy it as much as she could, never to let it slip away and never to lose it, but she had failed miserably.

There was a shrill whistle, the train moved and was chugging noisily along the track. The city was left behind under a blanket of greyness, and as it slowly receded into the distance so also the last familiar landmarks disappeared, obscured by a red mound of rock as the train rounded a hill.

She cast a quick final look at the city, not without a certain amount of sorrow. She did not regret her departure from it; no, she had nothing to regret in bidding it goodbye. But the moment of departure made her remember her arrival. It had been in the spring ten years ago; the war had just ended. She was like all young people of that time, seeing the promise of a bright future stretching ahead, and wanting to plunge into the torrent of life, her heart bursting with the warm blood of youth. So she came to the city, full of hope and ambition. She wanted to do something and, because of this, she did not hesitate to make great sacrifices, among them her primary-schoolmaster lover and her old-fashioned family, in order to start a new life of her own in the brighter and busier bustle of the city. That was ten years ago, when she had not had the slightest idea that she might fail and would have to return to where she had come from, broken in heart and spirit and physically spent.

She sighed involuntarily, deciding not to think about it any more. She would have liked to have all recollections of the past washed away by the drizzling rain falling on the city she had left behind. But, no, the past clung to her tenaciously, haunting her with its bitter poignant memories.

Yesterday morning, on the eve of her departure, she had once more strolled down that dark quarter of the city alone. It was far away from the busy center, a long road; on the left there was a small hill, on the right a dirty river. She had strolled down there, on lonely nights, who knows how many times, during the past three months. She had become well acquainted with the block of two-storied shophouses built at the foot of the hill, which were in a state of utter disrepair; acquainted too with some of the faces in those shops, with the little *sampans* along the river bank near the stone steps, and with the stench from the dirty, black, sluggish stream.

She would never forget the night when she had slipped out from a coffee-shop near the ferry landing, hanging on to the arm of the nineteen-year-old boy with broad shoulders. They had strolled towards the dark lane farther down the river. A full moon such as is only seen in the tropics had just risen, throwing a lustrous cloak over the everlasting filth of the river, in which here and there floated the carcass of some rotting animal. Cows, late on their way home, mooing ceaselessly, were hurrying towards the dark bush on the hill behind a block of houses. But at the time, everything had a sentimental touch, bore a special meaning, enough to make her head reel as though she had been taking strong drink.

At the end of the road, beyond a narrow bridge, the amusement park had shone with its neon lights, painting a crimson glow over half the sky. She had walked shoulder to shoulder with him, chatting and laughing like all youngsters. They had tried the "Underground Paradise" tunnel ride; the ride in the dark was fascinating; the sudden appearance of a monster with a threatening sword looked to her more funny than terrifying; she had felt her companion's boyish stubble rough against her neck, she had not been able to help throwing herself into his arms and letting him hold her as tightly as he liked. She had thought then that maybe there was still a chance for some happiness in her empty life. . . .

The train was speeding along the sea-shore. The sea was dark green, and here and there appeared a brown warehouse or a clump of trees. One could see the white foam on the sea, the boats in the distance, all of them but vague indeterminate shapes because of the rainy mist.

She hated the sea and the ships. It was the sea and a ship which had carried away the happiness she had hoped for.

As far as she could remember, it had happened in the durian season— the strange smell, disgusting to newcomers and so saliva-enticing to the locals, had filled the air—when she had sensed a dark shadow falling on her relationship with her nineteen-year-old boyfriend.

The hitherto happy young man had begun to turn silent. They kissed and embraced each other as usual, but he seemed absent-minded, looking into empty space. His broad forehead, usually so smooth and carefree, was furrowed and perplexed.

What was happening to him, she wondered, uneasily.

But he had not been willing to tell, except with his frowning eyebrows. Under pressure, he had spoken at last:

"I was thinking about quitting this place, but I cannot leave you."

"Go away? But what on earth has given you such an idea?" She had pulled away from his embrace, shocked. "Don't you feel happy here?"

"No, I don't belong to this country. It is good for you, but not for me. I don't know why, but I always feel that I have no roots in this land. I can't drag on any longer; life here is killing me."

"If it must be so, I'll go with you. As you know, I am prepared to make any sacrifice for you."

But he had shaken his head, with a sad look in his eyes.

"Don't you believe me, darling?" She had shaken his arms.

But he dropped his eyes and there was no answer. A sudden light
flashed through her mind; she understood: she was twenty-eight while
he was only nineteen; there was an insurmountable wall between them.
They could never make a life for themselves together.

"Yes, I understand. You go, go away. I won't stop you."

She could not continue, in a hurry to hide her feelings she had buried
her face in her hands, crying bitterly.

He did not turn up to see her for two days, then there was the letter
handed to her by the postman. She had trembled when she had opened
the envelope.

"Darling,

I am sorry but I cannot help going away. When you read this letter,
we shall already be separated by the sea. Please forget about everything. . . ."

She put aside the letter and could not finish it.

The train conductor opened the compartment door and the chilly air
from the corridor rushed in. She was awakened from her dream by the
sudden chill and felt something cold on her face; she put her hand up
and discovered that there were tears running down her cheeks. She threw
a sidelong glance at her fellow-travellers; fortunately they were either
sleeping or reading; those travelling with children were occupied with
their offspring, and nobody seemed to have noticed her.

The train entered a small station and came to a stop. She looked out
from the window: it was a *kampong* station, a very old and small one,
with a row of dilapidated tiled roofs; she immediately recognized it as a
place she had once passed through ten years ago on her way to the city.
It hadn't changed much since then, but the heavily clouded sky made it
look still gloomier.

As it was raining, the station was deserted. There were very few passengers getting either on or off the train. A twelve- or thirteen-year-old
kampong boy came over to her with a basket of salted eggs; he stood in
front of her with a look which was almost begging. She heaved a sigh.
Ten years ago, when she passed through this very station, there had been
a similar boy trying to sell salted eggs to her. She opened her handbag,
took out some money and bought one, not because she really needed it
but only to remind her that ten years ago she bought a salted egg at the
same station.

How would her own *kampong* look now? It had not changed very much
either, until recently. But, according to a letter from her aunt, it seemed

that it had been much modernized and developed since the arrival of a garrison of British soldiers. The price of land had gone up; her aunt told her that some people were offering an attractive price for the vegetable garden owned by her father, who had died in January last year. She had still been with her boyfriend when she received the letter, and as she had had no intention at all of returning to the country, she had not thought very much about it.

Now, with a broken heart, she was going back. In the first place, she hated to stay any longer in that city which had made her so happy as well as unhappy. Secondly, whether she would admit it or not, she was eager to see an old acquaintance. Her aunt had told her something about him in the last letter. The schoolmaster who used to visit her was now separated from his wife. "She's a terrible woman," her aunt said. This seemingly casual information in her aunt's letter had brought back a flood of sad memories, and she was now more sensitive to them while licking her own fresh wounds.

She recalled his long oval face and sad bright eyes so easily prone to tears. Yes, he was too emotional and not as mature as a man should be; he found it so easy to weep that he had very often burst into tears before her just like a child. She used to pity him. But pity is not love, neither is it a substitute for it; and finally she had decided to leave him, leave for the city, for a far bigger goal. Then, as time went on, the picture of him, her first love, had faded away and become buried in vague memories.

She had accidentally learnt from her aunt's correspondence something about him, her schoolteacher, her first love; and recalling that miserable look of his stirred up many things in her mind, dim and remote recollections which became brighter and brighter. . . .

But the train was drawing nearer and nearer her *kampong*. The closer the destination became, the more she doubted the real object of her return. What was it truly for? She felt ashamed. But she was something of an optimist: "I still have a chance to start again," she thought.

This hope persisted throughout her journey. When the train stopped at the little wooden station she felt confused. Was it happiness, or sorrow, or happiness-cum-sorrow? She couldn't tell.

Looking into a mirror which she took from her handbag, she rearranged her hair. Then, carrying her small suitcase, she went down the corridor with the other passengers.

The little wooden *kampong* station looked the same as it had been ten years ago, nothing had changed, even the stationmaster was still the same Indian fellow; the only change in him was that his hair was turning white.

Beyond the platform, there were many trishaws with Malay riders waiting for fares; one of those joyful brown faces came up to her. But she preferred to walk on her native soil.

Once out of the station, she did not direct herself towards the main street, but turned in the other direction, towards the countryside. After walking past a white-domed mosque, she went through a small coconut plantation; then there was the little river with its ever-rushing yellow torrent from the hills.

Coming out of the coconut plantation, she immediately caught sight of it. She stopped in surprise: it used to be a no-man's land, with wild-growing vegetation and grass on both sides of the river. She used to meet her schoolteacher lover there. There, they had kissed, embraced and fondled each other. But it had all changed; on the no-man's land on the river bank now stood a whole market with brick dwelling-houses and shops.

She was deeply stirred and her heart was heavy. She moved along the sandy river bank step by step—the sand which she had walked on God knows how many times. Yes, here lay her childhood, her youth, her happy moments, her first lover, in every grain of sand. The midday sun was shining over the river. She stood there, staring at the ceaselessly flowing stream and recollecting her carefree teenage. She used to come here to collect those small egg-shaped stones, but that was ten years ago. The evening when the schoolteacher learnt that she had decided to leave, he had almost collapsed on the river bank in a flood of tears. Hadn't she perhaps been too cruel to him?

"But does he still hate me?" she earnestly asked herself.

Perhaps he could never love me as much as before.

She would have stayed there, unwilling to move at all, but for the scorching sun which burnt the tender skin at the back of her neck.

She retraced her steps to the main street, but instead of making for her own home, she turned towards the Chinese temple. There she stopped for a moment: the old building still had all those variously shaped name-plates, but it was quiet inside; not even a single child was in sight. Was the class over? She glanced at her wristwatch: it was only quarter past twelve; and, besides, she knew for a fact that there was an afternoon class. Was the school closed down for good?

Opposite the primary school was the stage for theatrical shows. She remembered that during her childhood, the temple had been very prosperous; there were festival celebrations at least twice a year and every time there would be theatrical troupes coming up from Singapore to stage open-air shows. It would be *hari raya* for the whole *kampong*, and she would insist on her aunt bringing her to see the shows.* Now the stage was there no more; in its place a two-storeyed shop had been built. There was a coffee-shop just opposite the primary school. She felt tired out and thirsty, and went over to it and ordered a black coffee.

An old attendant came over respectfully and put a cup of coffee in front of her.

"What day is it today? Why is the school not open?" she asked him.

"Well, the school is closed because the teacher passed away yesterday. All the children have gone to the funeral."

"What? Which teacher has passed away?" She put down the cup clumsily.

"Which one? There was but one teacher here, the late Mr. Chang, a jolly good fellow who died young. It's deplorable, but life is just like that."

"Was he ill?"

"Something wrong with his lungs for quite some time," said the old man, shaking his head. "But the worst thing was that he was divorced recently—that finally killed him. Oh, look, that's the funeral procession coming up this way."

She looked in the direction he indicated; there came slowly an open lorry with a narrow white coffin on it, followed by some middle-aged men on foot carrying oilpaper parasols, and a crowd of schoolchildren in their white shirts and yellow shorts.

She stood up, feeling dizzy. She heard vaguely the old man murmuring: " . . . that hard-hearted woman, she does not even turn up for the funeral . . ."

She paid for the coffee, took her suitcase and joined the crowd of schoolchildren, still feeling dazed. She tried to hold back her tears but couldn't; and she found she was hardly able to stand up. For some distance she followed the funeral procession but stopped suddenly when she noticed that she had become the focal point of curious eyes.

She stood there motionless for a while; then abruptly she turned away and hurried back to the railway station.

Hari raya is the Malay term for the feast that marks the end of Ramadan, the Islamic month of fasting.

Not Out of Hate

~ *1955, Burma* ~

Ma Ma Lay

In the period after Burma gained its independence in 1948, the literary scene there flourished even as the country's future remained uncertain. Among the prominent writers of this period was Ma Tin Hlaing, more commonly known by her pen name Ma Ma Lay (1917–1982). She was a noted journalist, short story writer, and novelist whose career spanned the later colonial period and the first decades of independence. She had come of age in the 1930s and had experienced colonial life in Rangoon at the height of British domination. She ran several newspapers in Burma from the late 1930s and into the latter 1940s, first with her husband and after his death by herself. She not only coordinated production of the papers, but also regularly contributed articles. She also continued to write short stories and books, and *Not Out of Hate* (published in 1955) was her fifth novel. She won several national literary awards and her works were extremely popular among the Burmese people. Her writings have been translated into numerous languages, and *Not Out of Hate* is among the very few modern Burmese novels available in English translation.

Not Out of Hate was set in the waning years of the colonial period of the late 1930s, not long before World War II irreversibly changed Burma's trajectory. As several commentators have pointed out, the author's decision to set it in the recent past rather than the Burmese present of the mid-1950s was perhaps to recapture a time in which the Burmese people were united in purpose against British colonialism. The post-war, post-independence period had become one of social and political upheaval, and the novel evoked memories of greater harmony. And yet, *Not Out of Hate* is a novel full of tensions, ones that play out primarily within the family. The family in the novel becomes a microcosm of the complexities introduced by British colonialism. The plot is centered on the young protagonist, Way Way, and her growing attraction and eventual marriage to a highly Westernized older man, U Saw Han. The story's complex familial dynamics also include a mother who has gone off to a life of seclusion as a Buddhist nun, a father slowly dying of tuberculosis, a brother who is a member of the anti-colonial student movement, and a sister (Hta Hta) who is skeptical about Way Way's potential for happiness with her new husband.

The excerpt included here takes place on the first day after Way Way's wedding, and it foreshadows her growing unhappiness in a marriage apparently doomed from its outset. Previous chapters had introduced Way Way and her initial infatuation with the Anglicized U Saw Han, and had suggested his powerful charm but also his domineering personality. While Way Way had been cautioned by her siblings, she was swept off her feet by the new arrival, and pulled in his wake toward marriage. The rest of the story traces the trajectory of her marriage, which is complicated by her father's growing health issues and her husband's great fear that she might have contracted tuberculosis in the course of caring for her father. He pursues ever more aggressive regimens of preventive medications for his young wife, and becomes protective to the point of suffocation.

While a story about family tensions and illusions and disillusionment, Not Out of Hate is also clearly a commentary on the complicated Burmese relationship with the British. There was both bitter unhappiness at the oppressive and smothering nature of British colonial domination, and a fascination with elements of British culture and society. Some Burmese came to adopt British social customs, emulating them in dress, foods, and behavior. Even those who rejected British colonial authority and sought to shore up traditional Burmese practices had often been educated in English at colonial schools, and adopted elements of British politics, law, and literature in their campaigns for independence. In short, the story in Not Out of Hate explores the nuances of the encounter between the British and the Burmese, one that was marked by a range of emotions as suggested by the novel's characters.

Questions

1. What are the sources of tension between the characters in this story?

2. How do Burmese and English customs clash in this excerpt? To what extent does the author describe a conflict between customs, and to what extent is the conflict perhaps influenced by class issues?
3. Way Way's first day as a married woman gets off to an unhappy start. Why is this, and what pressures does she feel from her husband and her new situation more generally?
4. How does the Burmese experience of British colonialism by these upper middle-class characters contrast with that of the impoverished working class seen in the short story *Oil*?

***

Not Out of Hate

Ma Ma Lay. *Not Out of Hate*. Maureen Aung-Thwin, trans.; William H. Frederick, ed. (Athens: Ohio University Center for International Studies, 1993), pp. 82–89. © Ohio University Center for International Studies. This material is used by permission of Ohio University Press, www.ohioswallow.com.

Half awake, Way Way squinted in the darkness. A cold draft from the window had awakened her. She reached for the velvet blanket at her feet. Her eyes opened wide in astonishment as she heard a faint but steady breathing beside her. Puzzled, she focused on the sound, clutching the blanket. Only when she felt the breath on her skin did she become completely conscious of where she was. She pulled the blanket over her head, clasped her hands over her chest, and shut her eyes tight.

Closing her eyes she sees a pretty dancer, slender and supple, dancing in the lamplight as pleasant sounds from musical instruments wafted through air. The dancer's gossamer green scarf loosens from her shoulders, falling gradually to the floor. As she twirls around, the scarf drags behind. A tall, thin, dark-complexioned man dressed in a green royal sarong, a short-sleeved tee shirt, and a pink *gaung-baung* appears on the scene. He picks up the scarf, winds it around her shoulders, and pulls her down with him in time to the music, which ends with a clash of cymbals as they both fall to the ground. She hears a great roar of laughter from the spectators. Before it subsides, she pushes away the blanket, and with heart pounding, opens her eyes. She turns her head on the pillow to look next to her. She sees U Saw Han facing her, sleeping on his side.

Her heart beat hard as she remembered. She was married to U Saw Han that day. It seemed like a dream. Thoroughly awake by now, she began to recall the wedding. It brought back to her mind the scene of U Saw Han participating in the dressing of the bride. She could see him rearranging the sprig of gold *mahur* flowers that Hta Hta had fastened to the side of her headdress. He had chosen the color and style of the bridal outfit and had gone along to Rangoon when the bride's trousseau had been purchased. He had insisted that her outfit be according to English tastes. Instead of covering the bride with jewels, the customary Burmese way, he had her dress with restraint.

There he was, among the group of women dressing the bride, standing with folded hands watching Hta Hta fix the bride's hair, and giving his opinion about the *samei,* the tassel of hair that hangs down fetchingly to one side. He did not just look on quietly, but joined in to help. He watched Way Way as she was being made up as though he could not get enough of the sight of her, and he watched her reflection in the mirror as well. When the time came to get into her outfit, she threw him an imploring look but he said, "Put it on, Way Way. I won't watch. I'll turn my back," and he went to the window and looked out.

"Gosh, he's sure a persistent one," whispered Hta Hta into Way Way's ear. Smiling, Daw Thet mockingly thrust out her chin at him. The bridegroom did not change his clothes until the bride was almost ready. His outfit, the *gaung-baung*, the elaborate *longyi*, and silk jacket were laid out on the bed of the bridal chamber.

"Hey, young lady! Take a look at me," he said after putting them on. Way Way did not know how to take this in front of everybody. She blushed furiously and looked up at him timidly. "Hta Hta, isn't the diamond comb a little lopsided?" he asked, looking at Way Way's coiffure.

"Oh, no, it isn't," Hta Hta replied.

"Isn't it too heavy on your head, Way Way?" he asked. "Are you cramped from sitting too long? Aren't you going to eat anything?" One could hear him constantly saying something or other as he kneeled by her stool in front of the dressing table mirror.

She was ready. The ceremony began. They descended the stairs together. She did not want to hold the large bunch of flowers in the English style. The wedding bouquet was of expensive imitation English flowers tied with a white satin ribbon, specially ordered from Rangoon.

She felt ill at ease carrying it in front of all the people, but she did it to please him. She had her eyes down and did not look at anyone in the assembled audience, but glanced up at her father. She saw him dressed in fine clothes, his face thoughtful and reflective. She was so moved at the sight of him that she missed a step.

She and U Saw Han sat together as bride and groom on ceremonial cushions, heads bowed in the traditional manner. Her controlled outward demeanor belied her inner thoughts, which were coming and going as they pleased. She seemed to have little control over them. Irrelevant thoughts darted about, quite unconnected with what was happening. As the welcome address was being read, Way Way looked across to the paddy fields, where she saw swarms of tiny crabs coming up from holes in the ground. Her neck ached as she sat with her head down. She felt dizzy and her head felt heavy with the hairdo and the ornaments in it.

Hta Hta sat behind, fanning her. Way Way's eyes fell on the pattern on U Saw Han's sarong. She noticed the interlinking of pink threads with blue and brown in the traditional *cheik* pattern. Having nothing else to look at, she stared at the design. As she sat she recalled, above the sounds of the speeches and the music, Ko Nay U's voice three months ago. They had just seen Hta Hta off at the wharf. "I don't want to come between you two, Way Way, but I must let you know how I feel," he had blurted out when they were alone. "I don't approve of the match at all. Do you really think you will be happy married to him?" This conversation could hardly bear recalling, and she quickly turned her mind to other things. She thought of the huge wedding cake that U Saw Han had ordered from Rangoon; it would have to be cut. Then she thought of Hta Hta's wedding and compared it with this one. It seemed to her that she did not mind her own wedding, half-English and half-Burmese as it was. She then thought of U Saw Han's agreeing to stay in the bride's house for seven days after the ceremony, as was the traditional Burmese custom. She did not want to think about her moving into the groom's house after that, so she forced herself to listen to the gift list, which was being read aloud.

Her mind had been in a flurry all day, and now as she lay awake in bed she still could not quiet her thoughts. The fact that she was really and truly married could not escape her. She thought with sadness and remorse of her lost virginity. She felt trapped under the velvet blanket. She had married because of U Saw Han's importunity. In surrendering to U Saw Han's burning ardor, she had not considered her own feelings, nor had she let him know how she felt. In the period after the betrothal had been settled upon, she had stayed close to her father and spent as much time with him as possible. U Po Thein had been more cheerful than ever and planned a big wedding for his little daughter. He sat daily with Daw Thet discussing details. It had taken a month to construct a wedding pavilion in front of the house to accommodate all the guests. It had been decorated with flowers and looked like a veritable bower. Her father had said that expenses were not to get in the way, and had gone on expanding his plans till Way Way had to step in and curb him.

She also kept a strict watch to see if he had shown any signs of brooding over her imminent departure, but she could find none. It seemed as if he had forgotten his illness and did not act like an invalid. He was hiding his real feelings and so was she. Neither of them had talked about the future and what would happen to the family business after her marriage. Her impending departure seemed to make her more and more attached to the old house and its pots and pans as she realized that she was not going to be living there anymore. In this mood she reflected to herself that, after all the pain and hurt of parting with her mother, she was now going to part with her father. She knew that the pain she felt at this moment would only get worse.

For them all to live under one roof was what she wanted most, but she knew that it was not possible because of U Saw Han. She realized that it would be an ordeal for him to put up with them even for the seven days. Way Way wiped away the welling tears with the palm of her hand and looked out of the window and saw only darkness. Her thoughts, over which she had no control, drifted away into the dark.

U Saw Han had been quite intoxicated as he watched the dance performance in the wedding pavilion that evening. When the star lady dancer of the performing troupe had wished the bridal pair "a hundred years of married life," U Saw Han had stood up unsteadily, taken a wad of banknotes from his pocket, and given it to the dancer. Way Way had known that he was too drunk to realize how much he gave, and she did not know how to hide her shame in front of all the people. She had always told herself that he held his liquor well and was not like others who lost control, but she had never seen him like this, all bleary-eyed and unsteady.

He had gone over to his house after the ceremony to entertain a group of Englishmen from his company who had come up for the day from Rangoon. She did not know how much he had had to drink, but when he returned after his friends left he smelled of liquor, and it frightened her. She watched the dancing without enthusiasm, her eyes glistening with unshed tears. The smell of intoxicants made her dizzy, but she had to bear it. It seemed that she could not escape from it that night.

Way Way closed her eyes, which had been staring out into the dark all this time. She shut them tight and knit her eyebrows in an effort to blot out her thoughts. Then she quietly put the blanket aside and got out of the bed. She made her way down the stairs, feeling her way quietly in the dark. She switched on the light in the sitting room and looked at the time. It was four o'clock.

Later, upstairs, Daw Thet rose hurriedly from her bed. The dawn was lighting the sky with many hues of red. A new day had begun. She heard the sound of the monastery bell in the early morning. Last night she had stayed up past midnight watching the dance performance to the very end. She was late getting up. She had not cooked the food for the monks. She hurried down the stairs and stopped halfway. Goodness me! It isn't light yet and breakfast is ready! she exclaimed to herself. The round marble table was laid. A fine display of china and silverware gleamed under the light above it. Way Way had set a splendid table. She had tried her best to set a table just as good as they did at U Saw Han's. She was worried that in the seven days he was here, things would not be as nice as they were in his own house.

Daw Thet was taken aback, but she soon began to admire Way Way for her diligence and industry. She smiled as she continued down the stairs. Daw Thet came into the kitchen as Way Way was slicing the bread into very thin slices. Way Way spoke first. "Auntie, your rice for the monks is already cooked—there on the stove."

"My goodness, young lady, you needn't have cooked the monks' food as well as our breakfast!"

Way Way was embarrassed. She said shyly, "Oh it was nothing. Just the rice. And I only set the table."

"Tsk, tsk . . . , this early in the morning!" Daw Thet declared wonderingly in a mildly disapproving voice as Way Way set off to wash her face.

"Just getting things started early. I had qualms about leaving it to Meh Aye," Way Way replied as she left.

Outside, the sun was coming up and the world was awakening. The birds were singing little pleasant morning tunes, enjoying themselves in the early sunlight. The cool morning breeze revived the flowers. The air was redolent with the fragrance of flowers. To see these sights made one's heart overflow with a feeling of well-being. To hear the sounds brought peace and harmony to the senses. Way Way went to U Saw Han upstairs.

"Time to get up. Time to wash your face!" She pulled him up by his hands and took him to the table on which stood a white enamel water pitcher and basin. She poured some water for him and waited nearby.

Not getting on with his ablutions, he held Way Way by both shoulders and, speaking in the same wheedling tones one might use with a child, he hugged her and said, "Young lady, what time did you get up and leave me all to myself? It was odd getting up with you not there. From now on, we get up at the same time. Do you hear? Promise?"

She winced inwardly when she heard his words, but nodded in agreement, trying to be pleasant. She poured more water so that he would begin, and only then did he start.

Aware that U Saw Han was awakening, Hta Hta had come downstairs to prepare an English breakfast. Soon the aroma of coffee permeated the house. The thin slices of toast were ready, brown and crisp, and a very special bunch of Nathapyu bananas, wonderfully fragrant from ripening to perfection in an earthen-ware crock, sat on the table. The smell of crisp bacon filled the air. The Variety Biscuit tin, the jam, and the butter were on the table. Seeing that the salt and pepper were missing, Hta Hta opened the sideboard to look for them. As she did so, she heard a voice behind her.

"Miss, may I go upstairs?" Hta Hta recognized the voice of Maung Mya, the servant, and turned around. She saw him, dressed in a spotless jacket and pink *gaung-baung*, a clean starched napkin on his left shoulder, and a large tray held over his right shoulder. A teapot, creamer, sugar bowl, two cups and saucers, bread, butter, eggs, grapes, cake, and toffee and boiled sweets were on the tray.

Oh my God! she thought in stunned silence, her heart beating fast. To her it was the proverbial situation of the black elephant not daring to look at the magnificence of the white elephant. The grand dining table was not worthy of comparison with the tray on Maung Mya's shoulder; it seemed to withdraw into itself as though not wanting to confront the magnificent tray. Everything on the table seemed to fade and diminish, everything except for the delightful and pleasing bunch of bananas which were prominently displayed. Hta Hta's eyes flashed with fire. She had to try to control herself as she glowered at Maung

Mya. She calmed herself and gradually let out a long breath and said, "Yes. You may go up."

Maung Mya, very circumspect, with a deportment befitting a butler in an English household, went soundlessly up the steps.

"Oh, it's all been prepared downstairs!" Way Way let out a loud startled voice. Very upset, her lips quivering, not looking directly at him, her eyes brimmed over.

At this, U Saw Han took her face in his hands, pulled her to him and blew on her face till her bangs were wafted about. He then laughed aloud and said, "I ordered it because I wanted to have breakfast alone with you, just the two of us." He sat Way Way on the edge of the bed, put the table in front of her, and drawing up a chair, sat down facing her. Maung Mya set the tray on the table, retreated a few paces, and stood.

Way Way sat all bunched up with her head bowed. U Saw Han had no inkling of the upheaval going on inside her. He was so delighted to be having a meal with her, all to himself, that he was dizzy with happiness. He went on talking non-stop; she did not utter a word.

"First, you are to have two eggs. You will have to have two eggs every morning from now on. Only when you have two eggs will I let you have coffee and toast . . . now remember that . . . do you hear?"

She gazed at him as he cracked the egg with a teaspoon while continuing to talk. Her thoughts were downstairs with Hta Hta and her father having breakfast without them. She could picture them in her mind and wanted to cry her heart out.

"There you are, young lady!" he said as he handed her an egg. He fixed her coffee for her, buttered her toast, and peeled grapes and put them into her mouth, one at a time. U Saw Han was solicitous and very busy, as though looking after a doll he had come to own, a doll which, in his mind, required his care. As to how the doll was feeling inside. . . .

When they were done eating, and before Maung Mya left, she heard him order lunch for twelve noon, so she came to understand that he was not eating at their house. He did not seem to have the least compunction about what he was doing. That he was a guest in their home yet was having his meals next door did not seem outrageous to him at all, neither did he seem to feel the need to inform the family of his plans.

Maung Mya left with the tray. Way Way went cold as she thought, Now they are seeing him downstairs. She was so tense and upset that she could hardly breathe or let out her sobs. She waited a long time, unable to go downstairs after U Saw Han had left for the office. She could not face her family. It upset and embarrassed her that she could not eat with the rest of her family, that she was kept separate from them. It felt as if someone had thrown sand in her eyes. She fell on the bed and sobbed with her face flat on the pillow. The whole pillow was wet with her weeping.

While Way Way lay sobbing, Hta Hta came into the room softly and tenderly patted her on her shoulder and said soothingly, "Don't cry, little sister, don't cry." Hearing that, Way Way cried even harder.

Letters from Thailand

~ *1969, Thailand* ~

Botan

Communities of ethnic Chinese people can be found across all parts of modern Southeast Asia. At times, ethnic Chinese communities find themselves in complicated relationships with the national state or with native populations, a function of their socioeconomic status and distinctive cultural patterns. Many Chinese migrants to Southeast Asia, however, have been so fully integrated into their communities that they are virtually indistinguishable from those of other ethnic backgrounds. Chinese have been engaged with Southeast Asia for well over 2,000 years, but until the middle of the second millennium, such encounters were generally of limited duration, with the exception of the roughly 1,000 years during which the Vietnamese realm was dominated by Chinese political forces. Chinese travelers to the region tended to engage in short-term commercial activities before returning to their homeland.

This began to change in the seventeenth century, however, as increasing numbers of Chinese settled in Southeast Asia permanently. They formed small and then growing communities in the island region, including the Philippines and parts of the Indonesian archipelago, but also on the mainland, noticeably in Vietnam and Thailand. Chinese immigrants often retained their ethnic identity, language, religious practices, and customs, even as they learned local languages and in various ways connected themselves to their new homes, including, increasingly, by marrying local women. The number of Chinese grew rapidly over the course of the nineteenth century, when laborers streamed into the region to work in plantations and mines established under colonial regimes. Many worked in the tin mines of Malaysia, or in the tobacco plantations of the Dutch East Indies. Most intended to return to their homeland after making their fortunes, but few actually did so. Instead, they remained in the region and began to put down roots. In Thailand, the Chinese arrivals experienced considerable early success, primarily in commercial undertakings, but also in politics. In 1767, a man of Sino-Thai ethnicity was even elevated to the throne of Thailand as King Taksin, a position he held for fifteen years. Although he was later ousted in a coup, the story suggests the degree to which Chinese could take important roles in national affairs transcending their ethnic origins.

Botan's *Letters from Thailand* is a fictionalized account of a much more recent episode in the history of ethnic Chinese immigration to and then slow settlement in Thailand. Published in 1969, this epistolary novel was awarded the SEATO (Southeast Asia Treaty Organization) international prize for literature in 1970. The story is told through a series of letters written between 1945 and 1966 by a new Chinese arrival in Thailand back to his mother, who remained behind in China. In his letters, the protagonist, Tan Suang U, describes the process by which he begins to settle into his new life in Thailand. He writes of the many challenges that he faces in the course of a difficult journey of adaptation, one in which he slowly becomes assimilated to elements of Thai culture and society, even as he retained significant elements of his own Chinese identity. The two letters below illustrate precisely this tension between assimilating and maintaining an ethnic identity. They also show the generational divide that frequently separates first-generation immigrants from those of the second generation. The latter are often reluctant to yield to the wishes of their parents to study their heritage, when such lessons are seen as unwelcome or a waste of time.

Questions

1. Both letters below deal in some form with education, but while the father learns Thai, he insists that his son study Chinese. What are the benefits of being able to read Thai for the narrator, and what benefits does he see his son gaining from studying Chinese?
2. In what ways does the main character continue to hold to his Chinese roots? What are the manifestations of his Chinese identity, even as he settles himself into a new society?

3. What are some of the generational tensions in this story? How is
   the second letter and its description of the young schoolboy's
   complaints and observations characteristic of a seemingly
   universal perspective?

***

Letters from Thailand

Botan. *Letters from Thailand*. Trans. Susan F. Kepner. (Chiang
Mai: Silkwork Books, 2002), pp. 215–222. Reprinted with the
kind permission of the translator and publisher.

Letter 41

First Day of the Waxing Moon
Sixth Lunar Month
Year of the Hare
(July 3, 1951)

I *can* read Thai, and even write a bit! You will be amazed after I have written that I have no time for anything but work, even to read the newspaper
after dinner. Well, that remains so: but this I must do. Dealing with the
government, especially, we depend too much on their dubious largesse
even with some knowledge of their language.

To be more than averagely successful here, a Chinese must read Thai,
write reasonably well, and speak with a decent accent. There are a few
Thai sounds which trip on Chinese tongues; even though Mui Eng was
born here, I am aware that her Thai sounds different from that spoken
by a real Thai.

I can practice speaking anytime with our employees, but take care to
do so only when W'eng Kim is at school and Chuey Gim napping. To
learn reading and writing, I went out and bought the books myself and
pulled one of our more literate bakery workers off his job for an hour a
day to help me get started. The major difference between written Chinese
and Thai is that Thai is written with an alphabet: 64 symbols, each with
its own sound. When you put them together, they make "words;" there
are no characters. That makes it rather easier than Chinese, for in Thai,
if you know how a word ought to sound, you can read it when you see

it. Writing is not so easy, for the letters must be combined in a particular manner, and for some sounds there are several possible letters; I do not know why this is so. Still, a man can study on his own, with the book as teacher. I know enough of the language to learn in this way because I have been listening to it for years. To learn this way when I first came here would not have been possible. Before long, I shall be able to read and write fluently; if only the Thai wouldn't write their words all run together in a string! That is what they do; there are no spaces between the words. But I shall get used to that in time; what is far more irritating is my handwriting. Why, when my calligraphy is so graceful and controlled, is my Thai handwriting so awkward? I do not understand. It has occurred to me lately that the concept of calligraphy will certainly change because of the new pens we use. For the thickness and shape of a line made with an automatic pen depends entirely on the pen, not on the skill of the calligrapher, and our life is too busy to spend time contemplating style as men used to do; the world I live in has far more respect for speed than for style and subtlety. Another sign of the times: the costumes of opera players, which used to be gorgeous. Now, they are put together with any inferior stuff which can be had cheaply and studded with tarnished sequins, acceptable under electric lights.

Now I can read contracts and newspapers (I read the financial page every day), no longer shall I fear being duped with paper and pen because I am Chinese. The newspapers often carry stories of illiterate Thai farmers (even their own, they cheat) who are tricked into signing away their land on the assumption that they are signing a loan agreement.

And I can read street signs. The first time I recognized, with pride, the name of our street, I thought of Ang Bui's plea, so many years ago, that she be allowed to study Thai. (She has taken care of that, by the way, long since.) How nice, not to have to embarrass myself asking strangers for directions. In short, I no longer need to borrow another man's nose in order to breathe. Before, whenever we received a letter written in Thai, we had to call on one of our Thai workers, most of whom would read with ponderous inaccuracy, guessing half the words—a dangerous nuisance at worst and boring at best, and I would always end by losing my temper and demanding to know why they didn't practice reading at home. To which the answer was always that they "didn't need to read in order to make a living." One fellow remarked sullenly that "books don't fill an empty belly;" what a fool. Work, get paid, run out, and spend everything, that is the extent of their imagination.

When I had mastered the newspapers, I began to look around for something more satisfying. The newspapers, after all, are mainly concerned with lurid murders and other unwholesome events, beyond the financial page, they do not interest me. I want to learn something of Thai literature, but I don't know where to go. I do not believe that the opinions of my cookie stampers represent the summit of Thai thought; they too, must have their fine books.

I picked up a few of Weng Kim's schoolbooks other day. They're for children, of course, but I found admirable the tales encouraging kindness to animals (and it is gratifying to be able to read anything when one is beginning). But I am a grown man, and talking animals could not keep me amused for very long. Yesterday, I bought a novel in the small book shop down the street. He loves her, the parents disapprove, and after several hundred pages the parents see that they were wrong after all, especially when it turns out that he was the long lost son of a rich prince. These are called "ten *satang* tales," describing both price and literary value.

Chinese novels are expensive and difficult to come by, so this morning I picked up the newspaper again, resulting in my learning more disturbing facts about my homeland. So China is divided now, this news saddens me. History repeats itself, and if there is yet another division we may see Three Kingdoms return in our own lifetime. Why? With wits and skill in abundance, why do we allow our greedy stubbornness to drag us down to civil war? And still China remains behind the rest of the world, so poor that its sons must desert it in order to survive.

I tend to my business and do not encumber my mind with politics. If only all men could put aside this obsession with power, and work sincerely toward their nation's progress; what do these people imagine politics can do for them? Thailand is no better. No one has gone so far as to divide the nation, but unity? No, it would be easier to find a needle in the ocean, as the Thai say. I wonder if it is much different in the countries of the red-haired ones, the *farang*, my reason tells me that it is not, except for differences in local customs, the details of treachery. (Do they kill the losers? Exile them? What fine-sounding name do they give to victory over the weak?) Power and money blind men to the things that matter most in life. More than enough is more than I want.

As for family news I am resolved to send Chuey Gim, first daughter, to the school too. Nowadays, boys and girls go to school together. Ang Bui says it is "a matter of equal rights." A lot of good that will do them, when they go out to take men's jobs and gain only the right to come home at night dead tired. It is nothing more than another case of grabbing power toward a dubious goal. I cannot be pleased with this business of sending boys and girls to school together, but I must go along with the times, for I am given no choice. You will be shocked, no doubt, for when I was a boy no girl saw a man's face outside her own family. Here they see everyone, anyone, even sit next to each other in the school from their earliest years. But I have been thinking, dear Mother, that such familiarity may not give them any ideas about the differences between the sexes. They may never notice any.

Letter 42

Third Day of the Waxing Moon
Tenth Lunar Month
Year of the Hare
(October 2, 1951)

I have taken Chuey Cim to school, the "nursery class" where children do little but play and sing rhymes. Oh, they learn a word here, a simple number problem there, nothing worthwhile. It doesn't matter for her, of course, but if I were the father of a boy in that class I wouldn't much like it.

I do everything possible to supplement Weng Kim's schooling, for the teachers are terribly lax. He cannot even read a newspaper yet! The only books he knows well are those I have taught him in the early mornings. Why should the school do less? They waste time on all kinds of foolishness and encourage the natural laziness of the pupils. I am more concerned about his Chinese studies than the nonsense they expose him to, but what do you think? He cares less for Chinese than for anything!

"It's so hard. Papa! So hard to remember all those—those lines and things, how to draw the characters just so."

"But you have been drawing characters for a long time, Weng Kim."

"Yes, but now that I have learned so many, they—they all seem to jumble together in my head!"

"It is simply a matter of discipline, that is why we write our characters every day, son. Why do you not whine like this about your Thai studies? Or mathematics? Why must it only be Chinese that is so 'hard?'"

"Thai is easier," he said, averting his eyes and drawing a little man in the corner of his practice paper. "You know that is true, Papa. And the stories in the Thai books are funny. Our Chinese master yells all the time, and it's impossible to please him. One line too short or too long changes the whole meaning of the character, Papa, and who can remember every line all the time?"

He is quite right, but shall I let him think his own language is too difficult to be mastered? It is not true, surely, he must realize that millions of other Chinese boys have learnt to write their characters accurately.

He is so good with figures, such a quick mind; why shouldn't he be as quick at Chinese? When he's working in the store with Mui Eng, what a joy it is to watch him. He will scoop up a kilo of dried shrimps, toss it on the scale, and the arrow leaps precisely to the mark; by the time a customer has finished ordering, Weng Kim already has the total in his head. It is a fine sight, yes; but he doesn't seem to enjoy it, and I want him to love work, not endure it! Do you know, I love this business more than I used to love the soil. The bakery, hot, steaming, and bustling all day; the dry goods shop, full of chattering people, and the good smells of spices and tea, dried shrimp and squid; the import business, which challenges me in some new way every day. These are my "trees," bringing forth fruit in due season in return for faithful tending.

What of the day when Weng Kim must take my place? Will he follow in my footsteps, do things as I do them? I wonder . . . all that time he spends with Ang Bui, all the things he is learning in school, and the ideas he gets from other boys. Of these, the last worries me most. Last night, he dared to criticize the Chinese master to his face!

"He makes his face look—like this see? A tiger! And he is always angry, Papa; when anyone makes a mistake, he strikes the boy with his ruler, or throws a blackboard eraser at him!"

I disapprove of his lack of respect, as any father would, though this teacher sounds unfit to instruct small children. What if he should cause a real injury? Nevertheless, I cannot allow Weng Kim to see my doubts about the man.

"Sometimes he pinches us, Papa . . . oh, it's not at all like Thai class. The Thai teacher smiles and uses polite words with the children, and she never yells. Sometimes she wears a blue dress the color of the sky . . . she's beautiful."

"A woman teacher? A Thai woman?"

"Oh, no! Her parents are Chinese people born in Thailand. She's even prettier than Mama. She has short hair and short skirts and red lips; who wouldn't love to learn Thai, with her as a teacher!" He laughed at his own joke, as he often does.

Mui Eng's eyes flashed dangerously. "So. We like Thai because the teacher is pretty!"

Jealous! That is how Mui Eng shows interest in her son's education. But she is absorbed in her precious Meng Ju, who grows only more unattractive. She is not a likeable child, I am sorry to say, plain, puny, and fussy. Bak Lee, second daughter, has been handed over to a servant so that her mother may give every possible moment to her favorite.

"The Chinese master should be fired!" Weng Kim continued, looking immediately terrified at his own daring. "That—that's what we think, my friends and me . . ."

"Enough! You must at least show respect for the man. If a teacher is strict, it is only because he wants his students to succeed."

His earnest face puckered into a righteous scowl. "Our parents pay him, and they aren't getting their money's worth!"

"What nonsense this is! Who is putting these thoughts into your head?"

He wilted visibly; swallowed, then persevered. "Well, he's hired by the school to teach us, that's what my friend Lim says. That makes him an employee, not some kind of god, to pinch and hit us whenever he feels like it."

Ah, so it is young Lim who has brought my gullible son to doubt and defy his elders. The boy's father is a wealthy gold merchant, and the mother indulges him ridiculously. He takes expensive imported toys to school to impress his classmates and according to Weng Kim, "Lim has a motor car that runs like a real one, Papa!"

"The Chinese master is not to be thought of as an 'employee,' Weng Kim. Of course he must eat like other men, but the money we pay him is given out of respect and gratitude. He teaches because it is the work he likes best; don't you realize that he could earn far more in another job? He cares about you boys, and how do you think you would learn Chinese without him?"

"You could teach me!"

"I could not. I haven't enough time, and many of the other fathers cannot even read Chinese. They want their sons to be better educated than they were. You should be glad of the opportunity, all of you."

"Nothing can make me like him, Papa. I don't like our mathematics teacher either, but at least I like the subject, and I don't get hit because I never make a mistake. Lim doesn't even like the Thai teacher, and she's the nicest one!"

"This is the boy you choose to call your friend."

"His desk is beside mine. I can't not talk to him, can I?"

"You sit in the rear of the classroom, don't you? Well, then, tell the Thai teacher that you can't see from back there—you seem to have her wrapped around your finger."

"What if the boy who sits in that desk doesn't want to trade places?"

"What if he doesn't," I exclaimed angrily. "You seem to care more for the opinion of a lot of ill-mannered boys than for the opinion of your father!"

He promised to try, but before many days had passed there was an unexpected and, for the boy, disastrous development. The young Chinese girl who taught Weng Kim Thai left the school to be married, and she will not return. Since then, he has moped about the house, inconsolable, and his school work grows worse with each passing day. But children forget their little sorrows easily, and I am sure he will soon attach his affections to another teacher. He has been avoiding me, no doubt because he is afraid I will quiz him about his lessons. Well, no matter. I am trying to raise him as you raised me, and I haven't turned out so badly, do you think? Your son's dearest wish is that you will feel pride in his achievements.

Sacrifice

~ *1980s, Laos* ~

OUTHINE BOUNYAVONG

Outhine Bounyavong (1942–2000) was among the most significant authors of contemporary Laos, one who wrote through the numerous calamities and changes that beset his homeland during his lifetime. Born in the waning years of the colonial period, Outhine learned French, and later English in the 1960s, when there was a substantial American presence in Laos as the United States waged a secret war against the communist insurgency there. Outhine thus became exposed to two literary traditions, and in the mid-1960s began to write and self-publish his own short stories. The war in Laos finally ended in 1975 with the defeat of the American-backed royalist Lao government at the hands of the Pathet Lao communist forces. The change of regime had significant consequences for the country, as the Communist Party imposed rigid controls on the Lao people. The nature of the new regime also had a strong impact on Lao writers, including Outhine, for many found themselves compelled to work for state-controlled cultural institutions of various types. He worked for the State Publishing House, and then for a time in Moscow, translating Russian works into Lao. But, like other authors now working for the state, Outhine continued to write his own stories, which were published in newspapers and in *Vannasin*, a literary magazine that he founded, and that remains a prominent literary outlet in Laos.

While the political landscape changed after 1975, many aspects of life remained the same, including long-standing problems with poverty and the kinds of social solidarity this brought with it. This is reflected in Outhine's writings from the 1980s, including this story—pieces that sought

The Pha That Luang Buddhist stupa, today the most prominent national architectural symbol, looms over the center of the modern Lao capital of Vientiane. In the foreground a motorcyclist and his passenger illustrate a common mode of transportation, one featured in the short story, *The Sacrifice*. *(Author's collection)*

to capture basic elements of the human condition in such circumstances. Outhine's stories reflect on how people interact with one another, their virtues and flaws. They have a simple elegance that reveals basic elements of daily life. In "Sacrifice" we do not find a strong narrative line taking the reader from a definitive starting point to a conclusion. Rather, we have a narrator who interacts with a variety of members of Lao society as he passes them along the side of the road, first on a bicycle, and later on a borrowed motorcycle. The story is about how the people he meets respond to his presence and to his offers of a lift.

Some accept, others decline, and the narrator ponders the reasons for each. At a basic level, the story illustrates a virtue, the willingness to help strangers out of a simple sense of being helpful. At another level, the story speaks to a collective sense of a Lao society in which such acts are to be encouraged, and yet do not always materialize. The epilogue extends this sense of collective solidarity; there, a character speaks of donating blood to strangers simply because the need is one that they can meet. At the end we see the narrator reflecting with satisfaction on a society in which such acts of kindness continue to take place.

Questions

1. Why does the narrator offer people rides? What kinds of reactions does he get when he does so? How does he reflect upon the people he encounters along the roadside?
2. What does this story tell us about human nature? Is Lao society of the 1980s very different from your own, or are there important similarities?
3. How is the earlier experience of riding the bicycle different from the later one of driving the motorcycle, and how does it impact the narrator's engagement with the people in the story?
4. What does this story suggest about Laos, the rhythms of life there, and the challenges that its populations faced in the 1980s?

***

Sacrifice

Bounyavong, Outhine. "Sacrifice." In *Mother's Beloved: Stories from Laos*. Ed. Bounheng Inversin and Daniel Duffy. (Seattle: University of Washington Press, 1999), pp. 45–55. Reprinted with the kind permission of the publisher.

Bicycle riding—it's cool when the wind blows . . . I comforted myself with this thought regularly, but riding on a bicycle, although comfortable, was certainly less glamorous than riding on a motorcycle or in a car, especially in the soaking rain or under the hot sun. In any case, if there was a gentle breeze after a hot and exhausting ride, I liked to repeat the same sentence to myself over and over again.

Bicycle riding—it's cool when the wind blows . . .

Although pedaling a bicycle was exhausting in this heat, I felt sorry for those who had to wait along the road. I thought of offering one of them a ride because I felt that they must be more miserable standing in the hot sun than I was riding a bicycle. However, I did not dare offer my help because I didn't know anybody, and besides, I was in a fairly difficult situation myself. To reach out and offer comfort, one should be in a superior position: offering a ride on a motorcycle or in a car would be more appropriate.

Then one day, somebody did end up riding on the bicycle with me unexpectedly.

"Hi mate, how are things? I haven't seen you in a long time. Can I get a ride?" He waved his hands for me to stop and greeted me in a very familiar and informal manner. I was stunned. I had no idea where I had met this person before, but since he approached me in such a friendly way, I had to reciprocate in kind. Therefore, a weight of more than fifty kilograms was added onto the back of my bicycle. I had to pedal harder to make it move.

"So, how far are you going?" I asked.

"Oh, not far! I'll get off soon."

"I won't be able to take you farther than two kilometers, OK? That's where I live," I warned him.

"Oh, I'll get off way before that," he assured me.

Throughout the entire trip, he kept talking about why he was walking to work today. It seemed there were two bicycles in his family, but one was broken and his wife was using the other one to get travel documents for a visit to her home village. Then he exclaimed over the qualities of my bicycle, that it was strong, easy to pedal, and almost effortless for a rider to board. . . . Most of this time, as I listened, I wondered over and over again: Who was he? What was his name? It would be embarrassing to bluntly ask his identity. I was afraid he would reply, "Gee, can't you remember old friends?" Perhaps he was one of my many past acquaintances. Satisfied with that, I pedaled on quietly.

Soon he exclaimed, "We're here, we're here! I'm getting off, OK?" I did not have to stop to let him off. I turned to have a good look at him before we parted. He thanked me and waved to show his camaraderie. I nodded in acceptance and continued on my way.

Because I doubted my memory, I didn't want to condemn him as a bold stranger. Well, what if he was a stranger? There had been no harm done. In fact, I felt happy to have been able to help a total stranger by getting him to his destination faster than if he had walked. At least the ride might have done something to alleviate his exhaustion. Helping others was a joy. However, human beings have their dignity, their pride, and a well-defined plan for social interaction, which has to be observed when approaching others, especially in large cities. Some people need assistance, but do not dare ask for fear of being humbled and looked down upon. Others want to offer help, but hesitate because they're afraid people might interpret the gesture in the wrong way. This is why the person who needs help and the one who wants to offer it do not meet each other at the same level, even though they travel the same road.

Many days later, on my way home in the hot sun of May, I saw an old man standing by the roadside. His eyes clung anxiously to each passing vehicle. When I came closer I met his eyes. His face and eyes cried out for help. I stopped my bicycle and approached him.

"Where are you going, Uncle?" I asked.

"I'm going home to Sikhay."

"Would you care for a ride? I'll take you home."

"Oh, yes. Please."

So I let another complete stranger ride with me. The man lived beyond my home, but I decided to take him all the way, then I made a U-turn back to my house. I felt good as I mumbled to myself: "Bicycle riding—it's cool when the wind blows. . . ."

On another occasion, I was left in charge of a motorcycle. A friend had asked me to look after his green Honda while he went on an assignment in a rural area. Since he was single, he lived in the workers' dormitory and allowed me to use the bike while he was gone. So the Honda became my mode of transportation to work every day, and I meant to treat it with the utmost care so it would not be stolen or break down. During those two weeks that I was in charge of that bike, many funny incidents occurred because of my carelessness, or rather because I wanted to show off.

I saw a woman of about thirty, maybe four or five years older than I, waiting for a taxi in the hot sun. She was waving her hand to stop a car. I thought at first she was waving at me until I noticed a cab slowing down. It did not stop, however, because it was already full of passengers. So I pulled up close to her and said, "The cab was already full, that's why it didn't stop. Would you like a ride with me? I'll take you home."

"What's the idea? Why should I go with you?" she shot back, displeased.

"You don't have to pay. I'll just give you a free ride," I assured her sincerely.

"Free or not, I won't ride with you even if you pay me!"

"I saw you in the hot sun and, really, I mean well!"

"Yeah, right. You mean well, but don't expect something else. Thanks, but no thanks!"

I didn't linger, but rode off immediately and did not look back. My gesture had been misunderstood. I didn't want to judge that woman. She was right to refuse a ride from a stranger. She was being alert and careful. Why would a decent woman go off with a stranger? I pondered her words along the way: "Thanks, but no thanks!"

No, I wasn't upset that I had been seen in the wrong light. Instead, I felt amused and had to smother an outburst of laughter as I rode away.

But I did not give up on helping others, especially when I believed my intentions were honorable. If I was not successful in the beginning, I would try a second time to see how it went. If, again, I was not well received, I wouldn't make another attempt.

One morning I was on my way to work as usual. As I approached Hua Muong district on my motorbike, I spotted a young woman standing by the roadway, holding a *pinto* with one hand.* I slowed down by easing up on the throttle, and the bike soon coasted to a halt very close to where the young woman was standing. I got off the bike and pretended to tinker with it here and there for a while. Then I tried to start it up again. And since there was nothing wrong with it, of course, it started right away. I turned to look at the woman, who appeared very anxious and in a hurry to reach her destination quickly. So I asked, "Excuse me, are you waiting for someone?"

"Well, uh . . . I'm waiting for a cab," she answered uneasily.

"If you're in a hurry, can I take you there?"

"Well, sort of . . . uh . . . I'm taking this food to my mother in the hospital."

"Would it be all right if I gave you a ride?"

Overjoyed by my offer, she accepted gratefully. I gave her a ride to the entrance of the hospital. She got off, mumbled her thanks once more, and we went our separate ways. I arrived at work five minutes early.

*A stack of small interlocking metal pots arranged vertically in a carrier, convenient for carrying foods of different consistency, taste, and temperature.

After two weeks had passed, my friend came back to reclaim his motorcycle. The bike was still in good shape, as it had been when he entrusted it to me. He said he'd be more than happy to let me borrow it whenever I needed it. We've been good friends since high school.

So I returned to riding my bicycle once again. When I saw older people waiting by the roadside, I sometimes invited them to ride with me, especially if they were heading in the same direction and the distance was not too great. Some people refused the offer, probably because they felt that riding on the back of a bicycle was not that comfortable. However, I never again offered a ride to any woman who had not requested one.

Epilogue

One Saturday evening, I went to the hospital to visit a nephew who was sick with hemorrhagic dengue fever. The epidemic had entered its third month in the Viengchan municipality. This particular outbreak, which had begun in May 1987 and spread throughout the country, was the most serious of all. Physicians suggested various preventive measures as well as methods of caring for the sick. One recommendation was to give the children lots of fluid, such as coconut, citrus, and other fruit juices.

There were a few people gathering next to the children's ward. Some of them were with their sick children and others carried needed items for the sick. All sorts of discussions were heard. There were questions about traditional remedies, about the pharmacy, about transportation. . . .

"If my child had received immediate attention, he probably wouldn't have gotten this sick. It's so hard without transportation. You see, he had a fever the evening before, but we couldn't get him to the hospital until the next day!" lamented one person, full of anxiety.

"I didn't take any chances. When my baby had a slight temperature, I rushed him here right away. It is such a blessing to have a neighbor with a car. Whenever a child is sick, we can ask him for help. He is so kind and has brought us here so quickly and so often!" said another with gratitude.

" . . . Who? Me? Oh, I'm here to give blood to my nephew, but unfortunately we don't have the same type, so I decided to donate mine to the child in the next bed. Everyone needs blood. I wish I had plenty of it to go around."

Then a woman's voice spoke: "Me, too, I have trouble with transportation. I can't afford too many taxi rides, especially now with two children sick at the same time. The other day, my eldest daughter was on her way here and was waiting for a cab a long time. Then a motorcyclist stopped and offered her a ride so she could get here real fast. You know, it's so nice to know that kind people still exist. . . ."

It was hard to believe I was the motorcyclist she was praising, because the incident had occurred many months ago. Maybe that woman simply needed to talk and kept repeating the same story over and over again, making it sound as if the event had just happened yesterday or the day before. I really didn't want to think it was me she was talking about. In any case, there really might be someone else who offered a ride to her daughter. And yet, I couldn't help feeling very happy hearing stories about people who were kind and generous.

So whenever I ride my bicycle, even sometimes when a breeze isn't blowing, I still feel very cool in my heart.

Tales of the Demon Folk

Thotsakan and Sida

~ *1984, Thailand* ~

Sri Daoruang

This story is testament to the enduring appeal and cultural influence of the great South Asian epic, the *Ramayana*. This tale, which made its way into Southeast Asia at some point in the first millennium, has an amazing capacity to inspire retelling and retransmission. Like the *Mahabharata*, which holds immense appeal in Indonesia, the *Ramayana's* hold on the mainland world is powerful. The story has been reconceptualized numerous times in Thai literary history, from the tales of Prince Samuttakote contained in this volume, to the later *Ramakian*, which was rewritten by the Thai monarch, to this latest incarnation. In this version, the up-dating and localization of the story is complete, for it situates the main characters in later twentieth-century Bangkok, and transforms what had traditionally been a primarily rural tale into an urban one.

Sri Daoruang (1943–) is a prize-winning Thai writer of short stories and short novels, whose writings sometimes reflect her experiences as a woman in modern Thai society. Among such writings is the following excerpt, which is the first of six episodes written as a series of separately published short stories. In it, we meet the two main characters, Sida (recognizable as Sita, the heroine of the *Ramayana* story), and her husband, Thotsakan. Rather than pairing Sita with the heroic Rama, Sri Daoruang's tales assign as her spouse Thotsakan, who in the original tale was the demon king who kidnapped her. While the original *Ramayana* story is one of grand adventures, epic battles, and struggles for kingdoms, Sri Daoruang has here emphasized the other dimension of that tale, namely its more intimate and personal side. In the original, this is the marriage between Sita and Rama, and the complexities it entails. Seen as a tale of marital challenges, it includes a fall from grace and wealth and the struggles of life during a time of exile in the forests. It features a stay-at-home wife whose husband leaves the hearth on a daily basis to fight demons (literally) and to support his family. It includes a marriage disrupted by Sita's kidnapping, and her eventual rescue by a determined husband. In some tellings, however, it ends with a marriage that cannot be saved, beset by jealousy and suspicions of infidelity.

This modernized version explores the challenges faced by its two main characters as it reimagines them against a contemporary Thai urban backdrop. These are people barely getting by, living paycheck to paycheck. In this episode, Thotsakan faces the humiliation of his wife wanting to work to supplement their family income. Sri Daoruang's version of the tale also gives Sita and her spouse an offspring, not found in the original story. In this case, the story diverges yet further from the original by naming their son Hanuman. In the original *Ramayana* tale, and its later Thai retelling as the *Ramakian*, Hanuman is the monkey king who allies with Rama in his battles against the demon king Thotsakan (Ravana in the original), who has kidnapped Sita. Moreover, as the tale's English translator, Susan Kepner, has pointed out, this Hanuman is not the energetic, magical, and indestructible monkey king, but rather a fragile young boy. What these characters share is their support for the Sita character, whom Hanuman helps rescue in the original, and in this version assists around the house with her sewing projects.

Questions

1. Although this story's characters are named for heroes and demons, their lives are far from epic, but rather experience the rhythms of a much more mundane existence. What are some of the daily routines and the elements of their lives?
2. What are the sources of tension between husband and wife, and how does each propose to resolve them?
3. What is the dynamic between the two parents and their son? What is his role in holding the family together, and does he side with one or another parent, or neither?

***

Tales of the Demon Folk: Thotsakan and Sida

Sri Daoruang, *Married to the Demon King*.
Trans. Susan Kepner (Chiang Mai: Silkworm
Books, 2004), pp. 31–43. Reprinted with the kind
permission of the translator and publisher.

When Thotsakan and Sida exchanged words of anger for the first time, their son Hanuman was stricken with confusion and sorrow. He sat midway between his father and mother, holding an old picture album he had picked up from the shelf beside the chest, turning it over in his hands before opening it. In the album, Sida had arranged photographs in careful order, from long ago to the present. Hanuman opened the album to the first page and let his gaze move slowly over the pictures, but his heart was not in it.

Thotsakan, leaning against the wall with his arms crossed, could not help glancing at the open page, could not look away from the image of himself as a young fellow. And in that moment, he was seized with regret—for his lost youth, and for the past. Thotsakan felt that those years ought to stand as some sort of—well, some sort of assurance, in his wife's eyes. He also felt that she ought to accept his status as the head of this family more than she did. There he was, on the album page, a strapping lad, dark complected, with strong features. Beneath heavy brows, his large eyes looked half-lidded, as if he were winking—that is, winking on one side of his face. If one looked carefully, one could see that Thotsakan's gaze projected one sort of nature from the left eye, and another sort of nature from the right eye; he looked to be all temper and ferocity on the one side—and softness, kindness, and understanding on the other.

At the time this picture was taken, Thotsakan was a young man who had cherished his single state for thirty years. He had been an eager if unparticular lover about whom it was said, "*Ai* Thot, eh? If he feels around and doesn't find a tail, she'll do." But he had competed with many young men to win, at last, the heart of the young woman named Sida, a fatherless orphan, a seamstress in the largest dressmaking establishment in the market and younger than himself by one cycle. Once he had established a household with Sida, Thotsakan had forsaken his bachelor ways absolutely; but then, as the legend tells us, Sida was utterly lovely, so lovely that *Ai Khaek* "Ramalak" had spent a fortune and even gone to battle, not once but many times, because of her.

These days, however, Thotsakan and Sida shared their lives without obstacles of any kind to hinder them. In fact, the two of them had become a veritable model of husband and wife, a couple to whom their neighbors invariably referred when they spoke of honesty, endurance, hard work, thrift, and high principles. Both of them came of poor families. No jewels had they, nor a single revealing birthmark. Their loving hearts were the only dowry they brought to their marriage.

Yes, once he had taken upon himself the duties and obligations of father and husband, head of the family, Thotsakan had forsaken the pursuit of selfish pleasures, whether that meant playing *mak-ruk* (chess), or *takhro lot huang* (a game with a wicker ball), or riding his bicycle past the movie theater to flirt with the attractive young females who stood out front. The drinking of liquor, the tossing of tasty bits of grilled fish into his mouth, all such pleasures he gladly eschewed upon the birth of his son. He was content to live quietly with his wife and his boy, and work ever harder to keep up with the soaring cost of living. Both husband and wife were determined not to owe anything to anyone, or to give in to the desire for luxuries and buy on credit. Thotsakan's monthly salary of four thousand baht provided no modern conveniences or dinners in fancy restaurants, but they did not feel at all poor—for did they not have hot rice to eat and a soft bed to sleep on? Every day when Thotsakan came home from work, Sida met him at the door with a glass of cool water. Life, in his opinion, was excellent, and he felt contentment and a sense of quiet pride when he thought of himself as the "shade of the po tree, shade of the banyan tree," under which his little family was able to live a contented and happy life.

Time passed . . . Life was happy some of the time, sad some of the time, as it is for all human creatures. When Hanuman, their only child, completed *mathayom* 3 (grade 9), Sida expressed the opinion that he ought to leave school for awhile, and work; and it was this opinion that led to harsh words between his father, who insisted that Hanuman continue his education immediately, and his mother, who pointed out that he could return to school easily enough, after a season of work. Moreover, Sida was thinking of going to work herself!

Truly, Thotsakan loved Sida and their son very much, even if Thotsakan was sometimes grumpy when he came home from work, exhausted at the end of the day. Why, he wondered, was she doing this? Why had she begun this campaign of rebellion, this stubbornness? When she had first brought up the matter, uncomfortable suspicions had begun to invade his mind.

"Are you feeling ill?" Sida had asked.

"No. There's nothing wrong with me," he had replied hastily. "Why do you ask?"

"I noticed that you look pale, that's all. *Khun* . . . er . . . I thought—well, what I want to say is that I have been thinking of looking for work myself."

At those words, Thotsakan's heart had dropped. What was this? His own Sida, telling him his health was not good, his body not strong! She thought that he looked pale, and sick, and weak—such a poor fellow that she must go and work outside their home. Eh . . . Sida had never been like this before, no, never.

"Why do you want to go out and work? Don't you have enough to eat, from one day to the next?" His temper was rising fast.

Sida gently laid her arm across his shoulder. "It is only that I have watched you coming home so tired, for so long. When our son was small, I thought only about caring for him. Now he is grown, and I have free time—why shouldn't I help out? Rice grows more expensive by the day, and everything else too. Our son will have opportunities to study further, just as you wish . . . But for now, if you are the only one working, before you know it you will make yourself ill from working too much, and then whole family will suffer."

The conversation on that day made Thotsakan feel quite distant from Sida. That her words were reasonable did not make him want to listen to them. He did not want to hear that he could not provide for his family. No doubt the monthly budget, which had never interested him, was now going to be dragged before his eyes, whether he would look at it or not.

"And where do you think you would find a job?" he continued. "What do you know? Let me assure you that ones doing the hiring don't want people your age. They only want to hire young women."

"I thought . . . sewing," Sida said softly.

"Aw-w . . . You want to go out of your home and sew in some shop, is that it?" His fury was increasing by the moment. "Where they can all say, 'Well, now we see that Thotsakan can't support his family!' And where will you get the money to dress yourself to go to this shop? Or to pay the bus fare? Where will you find the money for something to eat with your rice, at lunch time? And another thing—if you go out of our home early in the morning, and the both of us return at night quite exhausted, then what? When I return home in a foul mood, and you are in a foul mood as well from your sewing job, I ask you—in such a situ-

ation, where is the comfort and happiness of the home to come from?
Answer me that!"

Sida continued to sit quietly, gazing out the window and thinking, "He
thinks that I will give in to him, as usual . . ."

"The fact is that we simply do not have enough money," she said, in that
maddeningly reasonable, cool tone of voice she liked to use during arguments. "You know very well how much everything costs nowadays."

"Then why don't you economize?" Thotsakan asked, as if this were
a solution. "Other men bring home less money every month, and their
families seem to survive. Perhaps it isn't necessary to go upcountry quite
so often . . ."

At this reference to the few trips she made to visit her very own mother,
Sida lowered her head, and felt the tears well up hotly in her eyes. Oh,
how she hated having to depend upon him! Her thoughts drifted to the
past, and she was struck with wonder: in those days, when they were first
together, everything had been so—different from the way it was now,
everything had seemed so easy then, so clear . . .

Ten years before, there had been only the two of them. Thotsakan's
salary was a little over two thousand baht. Over the years, it had gone
up steadily, until today it was double that amount. But the cost of living
had much more than doubled, while Thotsakan's strength had steadily,
naturally declined. Oh, the stubbornness of the man! He would not think
of accepting his wife's sympathy—oh, no! He would continue to go into
battle with the "Ramalaks" of the marketplace, again and again, all by
himself!

The wind was changing direction . . . Thotsakan considered how to
escape from the problem that faced him. But his view of the situation
was entirely different from Sida's. Each considered what to do next, but
it did not occur to either of them that they might sit down together, and
find a compromise. Sida thought only of working as a seamstress, and
bringing more money into the family; Thotsakan thought only of how
he might recapture the former warmth and happiness of his home, and
make things exactly as they had been before. Thotsakan fought hard—
and then, he made a momentous decision.

Here it is, look! A color television set—see? A fourteeninch screen!
And there—look! A gas stove with four burners, and an oven besides.
These were the machines that supplied convenience, and also modern
happiness, and they were the first of their kind to enter the household
of Thotsakan and Sida. A catalog displaying the newest refrigerators

from Japan lay enticingly on one piece of the new suite of living room furniture. You choose, Sida! Which refrigerator do you want? Whatever you want, they have it!

The sulky look on Thotsakan's face had been replaced by a merry grin. Up-to-date clothes in the latest styles and more or less splendid household accessories began to proliferate in the home of Thotsakan and Sida. In other words, they had become like their neighbors. Despite his modest salary, Thotsakan had been able to buy a houseful of conveniences and luxuries in return for a lifetime of debt. Thus did the modern family increase the happiness and quality of life, along with the monthly payments. But Sida did not grin merrily; no, she looked sad, and was very quiet.

"Kan, how much longer will you have to make payments on these things from *Ai Khaek* Ramalak? Now he wants to bring in a wi-dee-oh, and let us use it to see how we like it. I don't want a wi-dee-oh! I want only the things we need."

Thotsakan's face clouded with an expression somewhere between confusion, melancholy, and anger. He expelled a great sigh, and lowered himself to the floor heavily.

"Oh dear, I can't do anything right," Sida said, her voice full of both sorrow and exasperation. "I don't know what you want, Kan. You don't like this, you don't want that—and look at all of these things! I can't keep up with you—"

"No, you can't—and do you want to know why? Because I'm old, that's why!" And then he roared at her: "Ta-a-a-a-w-w-w!" and the wrathful side of his face overwhelmed the cool, sweet side so that it seemed that everything upon which his gaze fell must surely burst into flame. "Ta-a-a-a-w-w-w! But I am not so old that I can't handle a few other women—how would you like that, eh?" She feared that his rage would burn out of control altogether, but she too was angry.

"Go ahead, then—go find your 'few other women,'" she snapped. But as soon as the harsh words had left her lips she regretted them, and said, "Oh, Kan—how can I talk to you? As for the matter of my going to work—I don't have to work outside our home, you know. We live in a row house, and we're near the main road. Maybe we're not so close to the market, but we live on a busy lane. All I need to do is put up a sign that I take in sewing,—and I could sell sweets, too. Hanuman could help me. It would bring in enough money to make a difference with the household expenses. We are both growing older every day, Kan, not only you, and we don't even own this house. I am not going to argue with you about this anymore. I'm going to do what I need to do."

Sida wanted to add, "I love you," but the words would not come.

***

Thotsakan lay awake nearly all night after his beloved wife had told him that she did not want to go to work only to be away from their home. No, it was only the money she cared about! What was he, in his wife's eyes? He felt that his status, his role as head of the household was shrinking away to nothing. He lay with one arm over his forehead, deep in thought.

***

"Hanuman . . . bring that fabric and stack it over here. Then you can go out with this sweet—I have it all wrapped and ready. Oh, we forgot to buy that thread I wanted this morning. Now I shall have to finish the dress tonight. You know whose dress I'm talking about—while you're out, be sure to stop by and tell her it will be ready by tomorrow evening."

***

Nearly six months passed, during which Sida was strong and resourceful. She sewed, she made sweets to sell. She and Hanuman worked hard together. In the little time she had, she tried to please her demon in every way she could, but there were times when Sida had to allow Thotsakan to return to something of the life he had known in his youth . . . As for Thotsakan, he was not a little annoyed to find the home which once had been quite tidy littered with scraps of cloth from the sewing of dresses, and scraps of paper and banana leaf from the making of sweets. And yet, he felt himself to be at something of a loss for words when, returning from work or from a few beers he had consumed along the way, his wife and son were clearly happy to see him, and took pains to make him comfortable. True, when the two of them were busily rushing about, he scarcely knew where to put himself, or whether it would be a good idea to offer his help, or not. (Certainly, he could not use a sewing machine!) But Sida seemed to understand, and would make some thoughtful comment such as, "Kan, why don't you go watch the Muppets on TV, and I'll be finished with this sewing in a few minutes." Or, "Are you hungry. Kan? There's some nice tapioca with pork tripe in the cupboard. Hanuman, go fix a nice bowl for your papa . . ."

Thotsakan had had no experience with such a level of activity and confusion. He knew that his wife and son were tired from their labors, and that sewing all day and night was not something anyone did for fun. But he did not know what to do about any of these goings-on. What he found most irksome were the times when his own wife's name sometimes came up, when he was at the bar with the other demons.

"*Ai* Yak—your wife is not only beautiful but hard-working, and I am jealous as hell! Why do you think I sit here drinking? Because my wife stands around doing nothing all day, with her bare hands open and waiting to be filled, that's why."

"But it's a nuisance, I tell you," Thotsakan replied irritably. "I used to have a quiet home, and now it's nothing but work, work all day. It isn't good enough for her, keeping a nice home—no, she has to show off how tired she is, from working all day."

"Eh? Listen, my friend, I tell you that she's right," his demon companion offered. "If my own wife had the same idea, would I complain? Not with two of us spending—and two of us earning!"

Not long after, on another evening in the tavern, someone remarked that *Ai Yak* Thotsakan hadn't been around, lately.

***

"What color thread do you need?" Thotsakan asked. "Why can't I go and pick it up?"

Mother and son sat staring at each other.

"And I don't know why you can't show me how to wrap those sweets," he added, with a sheepish grin.

"Oh, you don't have to do that. You're already tired from working all day. Really, we can do these things ourselves. It isn't hard, working the way Hanuman and I do here at home. We work some, then we rest some. It's easy." Sida looked down as she spoke so that Thotsakan could not see the expression in her eyes, and therefore he was not sure how to answer her.

"See, Mama?" Hanuman asked brightly. "Our hero has come to help us! Now, I'll be able to go to the Adult School."

"So, you think you have saved enough already?" Sida asked him.

"Yes! You give me money every day," he said proudly.

His mother beamed, but his father's face fell. "What about the money I give you, son?"

Sida replied for Hanuman. "He uses the money you give him, and he saves the money he earns working with me—all of it. He's a smart boy, your son is," she added, glancing proudly at Hanuman from the corner of her eye.

The boy grinned at his papa. "Don't you think it's the right thing to do, Papa? After all, one has to have a present before one can have a future!"

This was a favorite slogan from a television commercial much admired by Hanuman, only son of Mr. Thotsakan and his wife Sida.

***

And now, you have seen a beginning, taken from somewhere in the middle of a legend, the legend of Thotsakan and Sida, and some other folks, a legend which appears to be unfinished. Who, one wonders, will be waiting to see the next act?

An Umbrella

~ *1990, Burma* ~

Ma Sandar

Ma Sandar is a noted Burmese writer of both long and short literary forms. She has written twelve novels and dozens of short stories. Ma Sandar wrote her first novel, *Innocence of Youth*, while still an under-graduate student, and it was released to acclaim in 1972. She has continued to write since then, balancing a career in architecture with one in literature. She has won several Burmese literary prizes, includ-ing the 1999 Myanmar National Literature Award for Collected Short Stories.

Ma Sandar's short story "An Umbrella" is a bittersweet and realistic tale reflecting on gender dynamics in Burma and the challenges that women face within the family and in relation to men. As with some of the other stories contained in this volume, we see here not an ideal-ized representation of romantic love, but a depiction of the more mundane realities of the lives of the underclass. Since this is a story by a female author focused on the plight of women in the family, it is perhaps unsurprising that the narrative focuses almost entirely on female characters. There are men, but we only meet them through descriptions by the narrator or one of the main characters, and are not privy to their thoughts. This is a story about resignation in the face of betrayal, of grim self-reflection upon love that has given way to dreary day–to-day life. It contains reflections upon changing bodies, upon male desire, and on the many challenges faced by women as wives, providers, and mothers. Financial hardships also loom large as the characters make do with limited resources, try to meet the demands of daily life, and lament their misfortune. At one level the story suggests its particular place and time. The foods, the clothing, the names, the cultural practices all point to Burma in the second half of the twentieth century. And yet, as one views the story from a certain remove, a distinctly universal element comes into focus. It would not take much of a leap to replace the Burmese characters, names, and cultural elements with those of many other societies. Thus, as with many modern tales, the comment of the author is on the general, through the means of the particular.

Questions

1. This story, while set in Burma, addresses a number of seemingly universal themes in the relationships between men and women, husbands and wives. What are some of these themes and how do they play out in this story?
2. What, on the other hand, are the distinctively Burmese elements of this story that give it its distinctively local quality?
3. How do the lives of women and men in Burmese society differ, as recounted in this story? What are their responsibilities and how do their burdens differ?

An Umbrella

> Ma Sandar. "An Umbrella." Trans. Than Than Win. In *Virtual Lotus: Modern Fiction of Southeast Asia*, Teri Shaffer Yamada, ed. (Ann Arbor: University of Michigan Press, 2002), pp. 18–24. Reprinted with the kind permission of the translator.

Ko Yay Geh was dozing off, leaning against the wall. He had a short cheroot that had gone out and was being lightly held in the corner of his lips. Every time Ma Sein Mya saw him like this, she got a feeling of uneasiness in her mind. Then she remembered the words her mother often used to say: "A woman who has no husband to lean on is like a person walking in the rain without an umbrella. There is no one to shield her from the rain and wind."

Even though she married him out of love and by her own choice, Ma Sein Mya was not quite satisfied with her husband Ko Yay Geh. It is true that he gave her all of his small salary without keeping even one *pya* to himself. However, she became very irritated when she could not hold onto it, for the money diminished gradually until there was nothing left. By the middle of the month, Ma Sein Mya repeated the following words twice a day: "Since we have a bunch of kids, it's not enough to depend only on your salary, Ko Yay Geh. We need to plan for some extra income."

To this, the snoozing Ko Yay Geh agreed by straining to open his eyes and saying, "Um . . . of course! You plan that. Plan. Plan." Then he tried to close his half-open eyes.

"I'm asking you to do it because I don't know how to. I'm asking you!" May Sein Mya curtly retorted. Ko Yay Geh's eyes became a little wider and he sighed unobtrusively.

"Okay. In that case I will have to do it."

"How are you going to plan it?"

"Oh! Do I have to do it right away?"

"All you have to do is to say it. What's so difficult. Say it. Say it now!"

"Oh! Do you think it is easy to say it? If I'm that good why am I working as a clerk? I'd be working as a director general or a managing director."

Ma Sein Mya gave Ko Yay Geh a big dirty look. She muttered. She banged things around. At that moment, bad luck fell upon the eldest and the middle sons, who happened to be messing around in front of their mother and got a good spanking from her.

Ko Yay Geh heaved a big sigh. He took the short cheroot out of his mouth. Then he put it back. He reached for the matches and lit it again. He ignored everything as if he did not see nor hear any of it. He puffed on his short cheroot until there was a lot of smoke. About ten minutes later he leaned back on the wall again. He puffed on the cheroot absentmindedly. After ten more minutes he narrowed his eyes and dozed off again.

"Whenever I talk to him it always ends like this. You don't know how fed up I am." Ma Sein Mya poured her heart out to her elder sister Daw Sein Kyi, whose husband, Ko Yu Swan, was part Chinese.

Even though he had the same habit of sitting and leaning against the wall like Ko Yay Geh in the evenings, Daw Sein Kyi's husband did not doze off. He constantly used his abacus. It seemed like he was always calculating in his small head which commodity he should sell, which commodity he should be buying at a reduced price, and which commodity he should be storing. He was someone who could contrive to increase his monthly income in accordance with the ever-rising prices of food and commodities. That is why even though there were five children in both of the families, Daw Sein Kyi's family was able to have elegant meals with the good white Nga Kyweh rice, meat and fish curries with enough oil.

Ma Sein Mya, on the other hand, was rather fed up with life. She told her sister, "We never make ends meet each month. We have to borrow, or pawn, and it's always a vicious circle."

Even if Indra, king of the gods, showed up in his headdress and said, "Ask for anything you desire," it was unlikely that she would even make a wish to reach Nirvana within a few days. It was more likely that her prayer would be: "Dear Lord, may my husband Ko Yay Geh be a good provider like my sister Daw Sein Kyi's husband." However, it did not seem that the magic emerald slab in the world of the thirty-three gods hardened to remind Indra that a good person was in trouble. The king of the gods did not show up. And so, while Ko Yu Swan was diligently using his abacus, Ko Yay Geh kept snoozing.

"Ko Yay Geh is a good man." Even though her sister had never responded to Ma Sein Mya's complaints before, this time she defended Ko Yay Geh. Her daughter brought them a plate of *lahpet thouq,* pickled tea-leaf salad. "He doesn't drink, gamble, and have affairs," continued her sister while pushing the salad plate toward Ma Sein Mya. "When you become husband and wife, loyalty is more important than financial matters, Sein Mya. How can you have a happy marriage if you can't trust each other?"

Ma Sein Mya gave her sister a quick glance. She immediately noticed a gloomy pair of eyes full of hurt. "What's wrong sister? Is Ko Yu Swan . . ."

"Yes, your brother Ko Yu Swan has a mistress," said her sister curtly, turning her head away from Ma Sein Mya. "The girl is young. She's also beautiful. About the same age as your elder niece Mi Tu."

"Wow! His own daughter's age!" muttered Ma Sein Mya in shock. She thought that Ko Yu Swan was only devoted to doing business. She never thought that he would be interested in seeking other pleasures.

"As for me, I'm over forty, close to fifty. I'm fat. My stomach is bulging. My waist is thick. There's no way I can compete with a young mistress in good shape, Ma Sein Mya."

"Oh God! . . . Oh God!" Looking at her sister's protruding stomach, Ma Sein Mya secretly called out to God. Even though it was not as bad as her sister's, her stomach was also protruding. Her abdomen was thick;

the waist was also thick. She noticed that her stomach and waist were in a straight line. She remembered how once in a while Ko Yay Geh jokingly called her "Miss Turtle Waist" or "Miss Frog's Butt" instead of her real name "Ma Sein Mya."

Besides, it had been a long time since she wore a shapely bodice. And so, not only was her body below the waist ugly, it was certain that her body above the waist was not a pretty sight either. As for her face, even before she got married it was only mediocre. Now without powder and lipstick . . .

"Oh God! . . . Oh God! I wonder if Ko Yay Geh also would like to have a mistress if he could afford it." This unhappy thought came to Ma Sein Mya while she put a spoonful of pickled tea-leaf salad into her mouth in a delirium.

"Has it been long since you found out?"

"Uh huh. About two months, I think." Ma Sein Kyi wiped her tears. "Of course he tries to cover it up. Since he looked suspicious to me, I followed him without his knowledge. I found them right away."

"What did you do then?"

"Me?" Elder Sister Sein Kyi clenched her teeth tightly. Then as if to swallow something, she gulped laboriously and gave Ma Sein Mya a weak smile.

"I left that place quietly so that he wouldn't know."

"Oh no!"

"Think about it. What would he do if he knows that I know? He would move forward boldly since it's no use hiding from me anymore. From supporting her secretly, he'll support her openly. I have five children. I'm just sitting and eating what he earns. I have no skills . . . If we divorce, how will I get an income? Since there's no divorce yet, I think it's better to pretend that I don't know anything about it."

This time Ma Sein Mya really admired her sister. But she also felt a deep sorrow for her. It was certain that if Ko Yay Geh behaved this way her reaction would not be the same as that of her sister.

"You are angry with Ko Yay Geh for not earning enough money. He can't find a lot of money, but everything he earns goes into your hand. Shouldn't you be satisfied with that?"

"Should I be satisfied?" Ma Sein Mya asked herself and became very sad. How could she be satisfied with a head of the household who was always sitting and dozing off whenever there was free time—in a poor household like theirs.

"You know Ma Shu Kyi, don't you? Ko Yu Swan's sister."

"Yeah. I know."

Ma Sein Mya recalled that Ma Shu Ky was fair-skinned, and very pretty before she was married. She got married to an officer who worked in a department that brought in a lot of extra income. Ma Sein Mya heard that they lived quite elegantly and had saved quite a bit of money.

"Her husband is very nice if he doesn't drink. But as soon as some alcohol gets into his body, he picks fights with her. He'll try to find any old reason to scold and beat her."

"Oh, really?"

"When he's sober, of course he'll say, 'Ko Ko made a mistake.' Of course he will pacify her. But this Ko Ko keeps making mistakes again and again. So poor Ma Shu Kyi is always in tears . . . She came yesterday. One cheek was swollen. Ko Yu Swan was so angry that he was even saying, 'Why don't you divorce this animal?' and so on and so forth."

"Yes, of course. Divorce him."

"But they've already got two children. Will it be easy to divorce him? And in our culture, a widow might get respect from people. As for a divorcee, even the neighbors don't respect her," said Elder Sister Sein Kyi reflectively. Her lifeless eyes looked grim and dark. The colors were dim and faded. "Nowadays I meditate at night when I'm free."

"You do?" Ma Sein Mya knew that even though her sister had a tender heart, she was not a very religious person.

"Earlier of course, I thought of all kinds of things—whether I should cut my hair, or perm it, take an aerobic dance class, or go on a diet to become slender. But whatever I do, a person over forty is over forty. I'll never be pretty again like a twenty-year-old. When I realized all this, I gave up. Now I read prayer books. Meditate. I'll only try to have peace of mind this way."

Ma Sein Mya heaved a deep sigh. She thought, "Why are there so many unpleasant marriages in this world? If there is money, there is no loyalty. When there is money and loyalty, there is no compassion. For those marriages with compassion, money is lacking. Since basic needs are not met, people become short-tempered and have fights."

"This is depressing. I'd better go home." Ma Sein Mya got up and readjusted her long Burmese skirt. She saw a reflection of a not-so-pleasant-looking body with a loose bodice, a protruding stomach, and a thick waist in the cupboard mirror.

"Hmmm. It's worse because there are no pretty new clothes to decorate this body and turn it into a bearable sight," thought Ma Sein Mya bitterly, while looking at the reflection in the mirror with a frown.

"Hey, are you leaving already?"

"Yeah. I haven't prepared dinner yet."

"Here. Here. Take some snacks for the kids," *Ama* Sein Kyi gave her a packet of biscuits and twenty-five *kyat*. "It's so cloudy and dark. Did you bring an umbrella with you?"

"Yes, I did. Here it is." Ma Sein Mya reached for her big umbrella which was full of holes and patches and put it under her arm. The black color of the umbrella had faded due to its old age. You wouldn't need an umbrella this big for a little drizzle. Her sister gazed at the umbrella under Ma Sein Mya's arm for a while and gave a forced laugh.

"Ma Sein Mya, do you remember what mother used to say often?"

"What?"

"That a woman without a husband is like someone walking in the rain without an umbrella."

"If only mother were here I would like to tell her that I'm using an umbrella; but if that umbrella is a ragged one, I still get soaking wet from the raindrops that keep dripping."

This time both of them looked at each other and laughed heartily. Then *Ama* Sein Kyi quite loudly said, "The good folding umbrellas and the ones with steel handles are not reliable either. When there's strong wind and rain they turn inside out."

On the way home it rained heavily. So, Ma Sein Mya had to use her old umbrella. Since it was a locally made cloth umbrella, it did not turn inside out like the folding ones.

"It should be enough that it does not turn inside out. Tolerate the leakage. Tolerate it," said Ma Sein Mya to herself.

The rain got to her from the side. It also beat her from the front. On top of that, the umbrella cloth could not keep the rain from dripping on her. By the time Ma Sein Mya got home, her whole body was soaking wet. Also the biscuits in the plastic bag that *Ama* Sein Kyi gave were moist and soggy.

"*Ama* Sein Mya, were you caught in the rain?" asked Than Than Khin from next door. Her little face, full of *thanakha* powder with thick circles on her two checks, lit up the gloomy room like a little lightbulb. "The rain is really heavy. It never rains but pours. I'm lucky that I didn't go out today."

(Than Than Khin owned a treadle sewing machine. She was a seam-stress. However, since the blouses she made were not so shapely, there were not many customers. Every afternoon, she dressed up and went out. Even though she said she did some buying and selling, Ma Sein Mya did not know for sure what she sold and what she bought. Ma Kyawt from the front house gossiped: "How much income will she get from sewing? Will it be enough for the mother and daughter to eat? You don't know what she is up to going out in the afternoons." Sometimes young mischief makers from the neighborhood sang out from the dark some lyrics from a well-known romantic song: "Ma Than Khin. Oh, Than Khin. I'd only like to see you beautiful like a flower. I'm also concerned that like a little flower you will wither away. I'm concerned." And they giggled.)

"I did take my umbrella along, but I still got wet."

"Hmmm. When the rain gets really heavy, how can you remain dry with an umbrella of this size?"

"Oh, it's also because the umbrella is ragged. It would have been better had I walked in the rain without it."

Ma Sein Mya handed the biscuit packet to her middle son with her left hand and with her right hand forcefully threw the umbrella down on the floor of the front room. She was irritated with the ragged old umbrella as well as with Than Than Khin, who was smelling sweet and looking beautiful.

"Daughter, bring me a kimono from my cupboard. I'm going use it as a bathing garment," she yelled out sarcastically while gathering the lower end of her long Burmese skirt and squeezing out the water from it. The older son, however, not realizing that it was only a sarcastic remark, muttered with surprise, "You have a kimono? Do you?" With wide eyes he looked at the faded Chinese print garment that the middle daughter brought to her mother.

"You stupid ass," swore Ma Sein Mya in her mind at her son while changing. She picked up the wet skirt that fell near her feet and squeezed out the water. Even though she had not glanced at Than Khin he could hear her whisper: "When the rain is really heavy you get wet no matter what kind of umbrella you are using. At least this one makes you look dignified."

The Water Nymph

~ *1992, Vietnam* ~

Nguyen Huy Thiep

Nguyen Huy Thiep (b. 1950) is among the best known Vietnamese writers of the post-war period. He began to publish his short stories in 1986, the same year that the Vietnamese Communist Party embarked on a new economic-political policy which it labeled "doi moi," or renovation. This was a shift away from a centrally controlled economy toward greater privatization and emphasis on individual enterprise. The new policy also brought with it a loosening of cultural controls and restrictions, paving the way for new forms of cultural production in the realms of literature and film. Authors began to use this opening to engage not only in more critical assessments of problems in con-temporary Vietnamese society, but also in critiques of past policies, including those that contributed to the many hardships of the long war. Some of these criticisms were quite blunt, while others were made in more oblique fashion. Nguyen Huy Thiep's works belong to the latter tradition, for he frequently used the past, whether the early nineteenth century or the middle of the twentieth, to offer commentary on what he regarded as failings of the current regime and society. His training as a historian and years as a history teacher clearly shaped his approach to literature and his choice of subjects. His historically inflected works are particularly notable for their reinterpretations of major figures of the past, depictions that often attracted intense criticism of his writings. At the same time, as critic Peter Zinoman has pointed out, his literary output belongs in some respects to the realm of post-modern fiction, with its narrative complexity and the uncertainties it raises about what is real and what imagined.

Nguyen Huy Thiep's short story "The Water Nymph" manifests some of these post-modern elements, as it mixes apparently straightforward narration of everyday village life with surreal scenes in which the narrator encounters a figure that may or may not be a supernatural water nymph. The story is set in the Vietnamese countryside during and after the protracted Vietnamese-American war (1960–1975), and evokes the hardships of rural life that are to be found in its many daily tasks, from tending rice fields, to plowing the earth, to carving stone from quarries. At the same time, it captures other elements of village life: entertainment such as wrestling, the importance of family, and the dynamics of inter-village rivalries. Like many of Nguyen Huy Thiep's stories, this one ends in uncertainty. Is the water nymph whom the narrator has dreamed about, and apparently encountered, a genuinely supernatural phenomenon? Or is she, as another character claims, a fabrication? Here Thiep plays with Vietnamese belief systems, in which spirits of the water and soil hold a prominent place. It is also a story about social and interpersonal dynamics, illustrating the relationship between the individual and village leaders, between village boys from different hamlets, that between a mother and her son, and that between teachers and their pupils. The narrator lies at the center of these relationships, which are fraught with tension. Thiep's story suggests the difficulties of Vietnamese life in wartime and post-war years. Winning the war did not bring prosperity or even substantive improvements in most people's lives. Rather it left them with troubling questions about whether it had been worth so many sacrifices. Was it, like the fantasy of the water nymph who could rescue the people, merely a scheme concocted by a bygone generation?

Questions

1. What devices and images does the author use to convey elements of rural Vietnamese life?
2. What kind of a character is the narrator? What are his strengths, his weaknesses, his aspirations?
3. What do we learn about village social dynamics from this story? Who is in charge? How are responsibilities shared? What are the factors from outside the village that affect village life?
4. What might the water nymph represent? How does her presence, or tales about her, affect the course of this story and the narrator's life?

The Water Nymph

Nguyen Huy Thiep. *The General Retires and Other Stories.* Trans. Greg Lockhart. (Oxford University Press, 1992), pp. 39–55. Reprinted with the kind permission of the publisher.

Many people are sure to remember the typhoon in the winter of 1956. During that storm, thunderbolts cut the tops off the giant mango trees in Noi Fields near Cai River. I can't remember who said they saw a pair of dragons coiled tightly around each other, thrashing up the mud in an entire section of the river; but, when the rain stopped, there was a newborn baby girl lying at the foot of one of those trees. This was the Water Nymph.

People in the area called the girl 'Me Ca' and, although I don't know who raised her, I heard that a man from Tia Temple did. There was also a story that Aunt Mong from the market took her home and looked after her. According to yet another story, the nuns at the convent in town took her in and gave her the religious name Johanna Doan Thi Phuong.

During my youth, I kept hearing stories about Me Ca. Once, my mother returned from Xuoi Market and told the story of how she saved a Mr. Hoi and his eight-year-old daughter at Doai Ha. Mr. Hoi was building a house and took his daughter along when he went out to get some sand. Apparently, as he dug the sandpit, it caved in, burying the two people. Me Ca, who was swimming in the river, saw the cave-in and, using magical powers, turned herself into ten otters that dug the two out with a fast flurry of paws.

On another occasion, Mr. Chung, who had been digging a well, reported that he had dug up a bronze drum. People from the District Cultural Office came down and asked him if they could take the drum away. As they crossed the river, thunder and lightning suddenly crashed in the sky. Without warning, the waves rose and the wind blew up in a gale. "Throw the drum down here," called Me Ca, who was swimming in the river. With their boat rolling dangerously, the people from the Cultural Office threw the drum down to Me Ca who sat on it and proceeded to beat it: "Tung, tung." With that, the storm subsided. Me Ca took the drum in her arms and dived to the bottom of the river.

These were the kind of stories—half myth, half reality—that multiplied about Me Ca. But since my childhood was such a somber routine of back-breaking work, I did not have time to pay attention to all of them.

My family worked the fields, dug laterite, and also made bamboo hats. As everyone knows, there is nothing easy about working the fields. At fourteen I was the main ploughman in the cooperative. I remember one morning at 4 a.m. when Mr. Hai Thin, the head of the ploughing unit, called at the gate: "Hey, Chuong, plough the field down at the foot of Ma Nguy Hill, OK!"

I crawled out of bed, ate a quick bowl of cold rice, and left. It was still dark. Bronze rats rustled in the strip of maize along the edge of the field. I was half asleep, stumbling along behind the buffalo which I drove towards the shining disc of electric light that hovered like a halo over the town.

The bottom of Ma Nguy Hill loomed up. Leached white and rocky, this was the worst piece of ground in the area. I ploughed a furrow until late morning. Feeling the midday sun, I released the buffalo and went home. My mother said: "Hey, Chuong, Mr. Nhieu has advised me that he hasn't received all the laterite he ordered from us this month. He's eighty basket loads short; the other day your father delivered only just over 400."

I took the shovel and went up to Say Hill. Here, the laterite can only be dug for a few meters before you reach clay, and it's only possible to dig on sunny days. When it's raining, the mud turns red and sticky, and the laterite crumbles. In an afternoon of very hard work, I can dig twenty loads. Mr. Nhieu came by and praised me: "That's very good work," he said. "In the old days when I was digging, I cut off my big toe." He held out a foot in a rubber sandal for me to see where his big toe was missing. Nhieu's foot was what we call a *Giao Chi* foot; one that's completely splayed and that no shoe can ever fit.

In the evening, I sat down at home to strip bamboo which I had bought from some raftsmen on the river. First, I peeled it. Then, I chopped off the notches, cut it into sections, and put these into the boiler. Next, I steamed the sections in sulphur and put them out to dry, after which I tied them into bundles and stacked them under the roof of the house. I finally left the bamboo to absorb the sulphur for a few days, before I took out the stripping knife. I should say here that you have to be very careful stripping bamboo, because it requires the use of a special knife made by a blacksmith. It has a very thin sharp blade that will take off your hand in a flash. When you strip the bamboo, the hard outer skin is separated from the soft inner one. The outer skin is then split into regular strips, and children are hired to weave it. Each roll is twenty meters long and is sold to people with sewing machines to make hats. "This business is not a very profitable one," my mother said, "but it occupies the youngsters and keeps them out of mischief." In fact, my younger brothers and sisters knew how to weave by the time they were four years old. They keep their hands moving all day, and wherever they go they have got a bunch of splints under each arm. When the cock crows at the third watch, I go to bed. After a day crammed with work, sleep overtakes me quickly. And, at very long intervals, the image of Me Ca comes into my dreams through some small crack in my consciousness. I am not sure that I see her even once a year.

Once, when Mr. Hai Thin had become the director of the co-operative, he said to me: "Chuong, all the strong men in the village have joined the army; you're the only one we've got left. You're honest, and I counted on turning you into a bookkeeper. But you haven't got the education, so you can work on the Control Committee or as a watchman." "What does someone on the Control Committee do?" I asked. "What does a watchman do?" Mr. Hai Thin replied: "The Control Committee checks on graft and reports it to Mr. Phuong, the village secretary. The watchmen protect the cooperative's cane fields from the gang that comes over from Noi Fields to steal our cane. You carry a gun, and when you see one of the thieves you just fire into the air to frighten them off!" "I won't work on the Control Committee or become an informer," I said. "I'll work as a watchman."

The cane field along the side of the river was about twenty acres in area and a difficult one to keep watch over. As a result, I built a watch-tower, although, once in it, I usually lay down to read. I would doze off for I do not know how long. There were times when I dreamt I was ploughing. Once I had ploughed from the bottom of Ma Nguy Hill all the way to town, and continued ploughing up the town until its people fled in terror. There were times when I dreamt I was digging laterite. I cut off my big toe with a spade, and a moment later it grew back. I cut it off again and it grew back again. 1 had this nightmare dozens of times, and each time the loss of the toe caused greater pain. There were also times I dreamt I was stripping bamboo and the knife cut all five fingers off one hand. When I ate rice I had to put my face into the bowl like a dog. That, in general, is what my dreams were like, with none of the more ordinary events of my life appearing in them. I thought that was because I had no imagination. But when I got wiser, I came to understand that, at sixteen years of age, I did not know anything.

I remember guarding the cane fields one July night when the moon was very bright. The moon beams illuminated the fields clearly, so that looking at the roots of the cane was like looking at the secondary roots that drop down from the notches in the trunk of a banyan tree. The row of sugarcane swept dark shadows along the surface of the soft, silky sand that had been dried by the wind. Every now and then, the wind gathered in gusts that rattled the cane field, giving me goose bumps. Then, I heard the sound of cane being toppled and, running towards it, I saw some of it lying flattened on the sand. I angrily fired a shot into the air. Five or six naked children rushed but. One girl, about twelve years old, who looked like the ringleader, ran out of the field dragging a clump of cane behind her. "Stop!" I yelled. The frightened thieves dived into the river and swam back as fast as they could in the direction of Noi Fields.

I threw down my gun, stripped off, and jumped into the river after them. I was determined to catch one of the children. If I caught one, it would lead to the rest—that was the method the police usually used.

The girl with the cane became separated from the others. She thrashed at the water as though she didn't know how to swim, and tried to move up-stream so that she made very slow progress. I swam after her. She turned around and, looking very mischievously at me, stuck out her tongue. I swam to head her off. She splashed water in my face. I dived, estimating the distance so that I could grab her legs. She pulled away from me. We swam on, with her maintaining a short distance between us.

For almost half an hour I kept after her, but could not catch her. I suddenly realized that my opponent was a very good swimmer, and that catching her was no joke. She had lured me along, so that the others could escape.

As she swam, the young girl teased me. I angrily thrashed the water an arm's length behind her. She burst out laughing and swam fast out into the middle of the river. "Turn around and go back," she called out to me, "don't lose your gun or it will be the end of you!" I was startled by this comment, because I knew that what she had said was true. The little girl added: "There's no way you can catch me; how are you going to catch Me Ca?"

My hair stood on end. Could this be the Water Nymph? The water slapped against my face. Momentarily, beneath the moon, I caught a fleeting glimpse of a supple, naked back frisking in the water before my face. It was both frightening and beautiful. In a flash, she disappeared, and I was suddenly alone in mid-stream.

It was as though nothing had happened. The river still ran as it had run for five hundred years. I felt ashamed of myself. There I was in the middle of the night, swimming naked in the river, splashing around, and for what reason? How much were a few sticks of sugar cane worth? When the cooperative harvests the cane, piles of it are thrown away. Or, in the wet season, it is normal for floods to destroy acres of the crop. I suddenly felt sad, ignored the stream of water, and swam back to the shore.

As it turned out, we hadn't lost much cane; just a few sticks. I sat down and bent a piece of sugar-cane in the middle so that I could eat it. It was tasteless. I threw it away and crawled back to the watch-tower where I lay awake till morning.

I tried to remember Me Ca's face, but couldn't. With my eyes closed, I pictured the faces of everyone I knew: there was Madam Hai Khoi's big round face with a nose pitted like orange peel; my sister Vinh's long face that looked as pale as a buffalo's scrotum; Miss Hy's face as red as a boiled prawn; my brother Du's face with the jaw bones of a horse. There were no human faces among them, just animal faces—not mean and deceitful, but full of shame and wrinkled with suffering. I found a piece of a broken mirror and took a look at my own face. The piece of mirror was too small, and the reflection was unclear; all I saw looking back at me was a pair of stupid, dull eyes like those of a wooden statue in the pagoda.

At the end of the year, I left the village guard and went to work in the irrigation unit. As people say: "Land comes first, crops second." Breaking the ground with a hoe was hard work, but I was young and strong and able to keep at it. This went on for over three years; over a thousand days. I would say that the earth I moved in that time amounted to a small mountain. But, then, my home region has no mountains: it consists of flat plains with leached fields where the earth is dry and cracked, despite all the canals that crisscross it.

Nineteen seventy-five: that was a year to remember. My village held a very big festival. There were swimming competitions in the river, wrestling contests, and the provincial theatrical company staged a performance. The wrestlers from Doai Ha emerged victorious in the region. The people of Noi Fields were daring enough to take up their challenge, and sent out four wrestlers; but, they went down in the first round. Having defeated Noi Fields, it was Doai Ha's day. The wrestler, Thi, goaded us by beating the drum and boasting loudly: "Since there's no one getting into the ring, I'll take the prize for Doai Ha." This angered the young men from my village who urged me into the ring. I must confess that I was not good at wrestling; but I was strong—if my hands got hold of something they were like pincers. Even though I did not know any of the holds, I could crush a brick with my hands.

I stripped off and put on a brown loin cloth. Everyone cheered. The referee gave a confused, long-winded interpretation of the rules. Generally speaking, if I wanted to take the prize I had to win five bouts. The young men in my village would not accept this condition and kicked up a row. In the end, it was agreed that I would have to beat two different wrestlers in preliminary bouts and then wrestle with Thi, the one who had the most points.

A wrestler named Tien entered the ring. I charged straight at him. He was fit and hooked himself around my legs. But, after more than a thousand days wading in the mud and carrying dirt, my legs were as firmly planted on the ground as a fence post. Tien screwed his body horizontally and vertically, but I remained immovable. Both my hands gripped his shoulder blades and maintained pressure on them. After about three minutes Tien went limp. His face was pale and he slumped to the ground. The referee proclaimed me the winner of the bout.

It was Nhieu's turn. He was a small, nimble wrestler who jumped like a warbler and was very slippery. After only a few moves, I knew Nhieu planned to trick me. He was waiting for me to lose my balance, so that he could lower his shoulder and then lift it to knock me down. Once I worked this out, I stood with my legs well apart and my body inclined slightly forward. Nhieu responded by bending down and lowering his head with the intention of bringing it up into my groin. I changed the position of my legs and brought my knees together, seizing his rib cage with all my strength. He wriggled like a snake. As soon as I felt him stop squirming, I put him on his back and hit him hard in the belly. There was thunderous applause. Someone stuffed a short piece of sugar-cane into my hand for me to suck. Everyone gathered around, fanning my face with their shirts like the seconds in English boxing matches do.

The drum sounded again. Thi was very big, with eyes like a boiled pig's. He tried a very skillful short feint. There were many grunts and snorts. I glared at Thi as he stood threateningly in front of me: "If you want to live, give up and now, my boy." "We'll see about that!" I retorted. "Son-of-a-bitch!" cursed Thi. "Hold on to your nose! I'm going to bloody it!" He rushed straight at me lifting his knees very dangerously.

Ten minutes later, Thi had still not thrown me. He changed his tactics. He used his elbows and knees to strike me. As he was from Doai Ha, the referee ignored Thi's fouls, instead of penalizing them. I asked angrily as I parried his blows: "Are we wrestling or boxing?" "Son-of-a-bitch!" growled Thi, "I'm going to thrash the life out of you!" The drum beat fast, everyone was shouting, but no one moved to stop the bout. Many cries of encouragement came for Thi: "Thrash him! Thrash the living daylights out of him!" In a wave of fury, my vision blurred. Thunder roared in my ears, and blood tasted salty on my lips. Thi attacked me with a high kick. I avoided the kick and seized his ankles. He pulled away, but my hands were like steel pincers. He rolled around on the ground, howling: "That's enough, that's enough." The referee said my hold was illegal. I said nothing. I pulled Thi out of the ring and went up to the dais where I picked up the trophy and stepped down. There were many cheers. Someone slapped me on the shoulder: "Very good! What a ruffian!" I did not understand the meaning of that word, but I was sure it was praise. I left the ring and went to the stalls. There I bought a packet of sweets for my young brothers and sisters and a comb for my mother, before taking a short cut home through the fields. When I reached the river it was twilight. At the bend in the river, a band of thugs rushed out at me with the wrestlers Thi, Nhieu, and Tien in the lead. "Stop if your life's worth living!" snarled Thi. "So this is a robbery, is it?" I responded. With this they leapt forward and attacked me. I fought back as best I could, but could not beat them off on my own. I was soon knocked unconscious.

When I came to, I found myself in a straw litter, aching all over. My mother asked: "Are you in pain?" I nodded. My mother cried: "Oh, Chuong, what do you go around fighting the world for? Is it shameful to make people happy?" I felt very miserable, because I knew my mother was right. "Promise me you'll never get into trouble like that again," begged my mother. I loved her, and so I promised— although I thought later that I should carry a knife. "Who saved me?" I asked my mother. "Me Ca saved you," she smiled. I wanted to ask my mother to tell me more, but she went outside to boil some medicinal herbs for me.

I quickly recovered my strength, because of my youth, rather than the medicine which was nothing but a wad of boiled leaves from which I squeezed the liquid. When I was back on my feet, my first thought was to get a knife and find Thi. However, the cooperative sent me on a specialized trade planning course in the district capital, and, being burdened with my studies, I lost interest in my plans for revenge.

The course was for six months and my class numbered thirty people. We studied various aspects of scientific socialism, history, political economy, management accounting. This was the first time I had heard about nouns and concepts and been taught some very strange technical words. I was extremely enthusiastic, but, after a few days, I was pained to find that I was not good at my lessons. The meanings of words faded from my memory. I could not work out the principles of accounting any more than I could understand the concepts of idealism and materialism. According to me, the dialectic was an unimpeded advance, much like my dreams of ploughing Ma Nguy Hill. I thought the law worked like the mean revenge that Thi's thugs had taken out on me. Since I hated them and the law meant revenge, I had to trample them harder than they had trampled me. I studied history and completely confused the periods. My teachers were annoyed with me and told me I had no aptitude for study.

No one in the class liked me. I lost emulation points. I was the odd one out. No one else dressed like me. They all dressed smartly in the latest town fashions which I also liked very much, but did not have the money to buy. I wore brown working trousers and a blue shirt. As for eating, everyone else ate together, while I ate by myself. There was a limit to what one could eat communally, and I had to eat eight or nine bowls of rice, three times a day.

In class I sat in a corner and nodded off to sleep. This discouraged the teachers who gave up on me and awarded me a five, the average mark for every examination paper. Not long before the class was about to break up, a Miss Phuong unexpectedly came to teach us accounting. She had a happy personality and had returned from studying overseas, wearing jeans with a blouse tucked into them, she carried a bag over her shoulder and reminded me of a movie star.

"Who is Chuong?" she suddenly asked one day, as she returned some examination papers. "That's me, Madam," I said with great respect. The whole class broke out in gales of laughter to hear me call her Madam, because Miss Phuong was only the same age as me. Miss Phuong stopped laughing and said: "I don't understand your paper at all. Your method of accounting is very mysterious." The class started laughing again. "See me after class," Miss Phuong said. "I'll go over the principles of accounting with you again."

After the afternoon class, I went to find Miss Phuong. People said she had just sped off to the river on her motor scooter. I sadly put my bag over my shoulder and wandered off.

I ambled along aimlessly and took a turn down by the river, where I unexpectedly came upon Miss Phuong sitting beside her motor scooter. With the cane fields coming down to the river, the area was identical with that near my home.

I went up to her and saw she was crying. Her head was in her hands and her shoulders were heaving. I mumbled an awkward hullo. She gave a start, looked up at me, and said angrily: "Go away! Men are miserable creatures!" I stared at her fearfully, riveted to the spot. She took off a shoe and threw it at my face. I was not able to avoid the shoe with its high heel and buckle. My face began to bleed profusely, I collapsed into a squat, and my eyes glazed over. Miss Phuong ran up to me and took my hands, as she knelt down and said: "Are you all right? Good heavens, I must have been out of my mind!"

I went down to the river and washed my painful wound. Miss Phuong fussed over me and apologized nervously. I showed her the scars that Thi had given me on my shoulders and arms. "It doesn't matter, Miss," I said. "Wounds like that are nothing." Miss Phuong said: "I'm so sorry. I've just had an awful quarrel and I couldn't restrain myself."

Miss Phuong plied me with bread and bananas. "Please forgive me. I was betrayed by someone I loved. I couldn't stand it. If you fall in love, you will understand," she whimpered. "I haven't been in love yet," I said, "but I think that anyone who betrays love is very bad." "You don't understand," she smiled sorrowfully, "the traitor is a good person too, but he does not have the courage to make a sacrifice." Miss Phuong sat down looking small and sad with her arms wrapped around her knees. She looked all the more beautiful for that, and I felt a wave of compassion for her as though she were my little sister.

"What I said wasn't true," she remarked. "It's true he wouldn't sacrifice himself for me. But I'm a bad girl, aren't I?" I shook my head. I thought anyone who could love Miss Phuong would really be happy. "Not at all, you are very beautiful," I said to her.

Miss Phuong laughed and took hold of my bag. She tapped it and asked, "What have you got in here, Chuong?" "Books, money, a travel certificate, an identity card," I replied awkwardly. "Chuong, if you loved someone, would you sacrifice yourself for that person?" she asked. I was confused and did not know what to say. "Take this for example, OK," she said. "If I loved you, would you be prepared to throw this bag to the bottom of the river for me?" I nodded, "then throw it," she said. I stood up, took the bag, and threw it into the river. It sunk like a stone. Miss Phuong was so astonished she went pale. "Would you dare to break down that fence over there?" I went quietly over to the fence around the cane field, snapped the barbed wire, and uprooted the steel pickets. I then bent them and threw them at her feet.

"Come here, Chuong," Miss Phuong said. She put her arms around my neck and kissed my lips. I was helpless. "Do you know that I was sad because of a selfish man? It's really not worth it!" Miss Phuong said very sweetly. She got on her motor scooter and, as she sped off, she turned around to say: "Chuong, make sure you forget all about those principles of accounting!"

I was astounded. I was still transported by the thrill of that unexpected kiss and, with a feeling of great elation, I waded into the river where I swam to the other side and back again. Swimming in the bright moonlight, I felt that life was absolutely beautiful.

Two days later, the class ended. Miss Phuong did not return, and I heard she had business that took her to Hanoi. I sadly collected my things, said goodbye to everyone, and returned to the village.

Back at the village, I was told I would now be a bookkeeper. A month later, Mr. Hai Thin said: "All you do is eat." I was sacked, but it did not bother me. I returned to the ordinary work that I had been doing for ten years: ploughing in the morning, digging laterite in the afternoon, and stripping bamboo in the evening. The work was heavy; but it gradually took my mind off Miss Phuong.

On one occasion, I seized an opportunity to go up to town and took a turn around the old school on the off chance that I might meet Miss Phuong. Nobody there recognized me. The school principal said: "Which Phuong are you after? There are many Phuongs at the school: Tran Thi Phuong, Quach Thi Phuong, Le Thi Phuong. There was a Miss Phuong the same age as you, but she has already left the school. She used to live at the convent. Her religious name was Johanna Doan Thi Phuong." I was stunned, as I remembered the fables that people used to tell me about Me Ca.

The principal could not tell me any more. It was the summer break, and the schoolyard was deserted. I wandered around the town not knowing whom to ask. Finally, I had an idea that I should go to the convent.

The Mother Superior received me. She was middle-aged and had very dark, sad eyes. "Johanna Doan Thi Phuong lived at this convent from the time she was six years old until the time she was twelve. Her father and mother relied on me to raise her," she said. "Why do people say that Johanna Doan Thi Phuong is Me Ca, the Water Nymph?" I asked with surprise. "Johanna Doan Thi Phuong's father and mother are from Hanoi. She is the only child of Mr. Doan Huu Ngoc, a fish sauce merchant," replied the Mother Superior. I was disappointed and got up sadly to go. The Mother Superior said: "I don't know your Me Ca, but Johanna Doan Thi Phuong is a child of the Lord. Mr. Doan Huu Ngoc sent his child to the house of the Lord, as though he was sending her to an orphanage. But the Lord is not angry. He is forgiving and charitable."

That night, I sat outside the walls of the convent. With the traffic running noisily through the streets of the town, I could not sleep. Early the next morning, I went down the street to find Tia Temple.

It was down on the river, perched precariously on top of a rock-face that had been shorn up and reinforced with timber by laborers. The man who looked after the temple was named Kiem. He was a fisherman of about sixty years of age, and he lived in the temple.

I went into the temple and saw that the courtyard was covered by fish that had been spread out to dry. Mr. Kiem gave me some wine and roasted some fish for me to sample. "I've looked after this temple for more than forty years—lived by myself and raised turtles for my friends," he explained, pointing to a chained turtle that was lying under the bed. I asked him about Me Ca. Mr. Kiem said: "I don't know. But I remember that storm; thunderbolts cut the tops of the mango trees at Noi Fields; you must go over there and have a look."

I stayed with Mr. Kiem all morning and helped him to fix a leak in the roof of the temple. At midday, I said goodbye to him and cut through the paddies to Noi Fields.

The road went past Doai Ha, where I asked about the house of Mr. Hoi who I had heard Me Ca once saved with his daughter. Mr. Hoi was old and confused. "Digging sand. Cave-in. Very dangerous. Blood flowed . . ." was all he could mumble each time I asked him a question. "The old man doesn't remember anything," his son told me. "He's been deaf for three or four years." I was again disappointed, as I said goodbye to the father and son and left.

I swam across the river and reached Noi Fields. The big tree that had been struck by a thunderbolt had been dead for many years. At the foot of the tree, children had burnt some of the roots, and hollowed out a deep, dark hole. I turned towards a tent made of nets that had been set up beside the hole. I peered into a dark corner of the tent and shuddered when I saw an old man lying on the ground in a straw litter. When he was aware of me, the old man asked: "That's Thi, isn't it?" He sat up like a ghostly apparition, terrifying me with his wild hair and smoky eyes. 1 guessed that he was paralyzed. His legs were shriveled beneath layers of dirt and hair that looked like pig's bristles. I greeted the old man and was surprised to find that he was unusually bright and well spoken. What he said soon confirmed that he was the father of my enemy, the wrestler, Thi, from Doai Ha. The old man had been crippled for twenty or thirty years and lay paralyzed in the tent.

We talked, and I asked him about the story of Me Ca. He held his belly and burst out laughing. The sight of his lifeless legs scared me. I had never seen anyone as frightening as him. "Did you see that large, flat winnowing basket that's torn to shreds over there?" he said to me. "The dragons coiled themselves around each other inside it." He laughed again. "I invented the story of Me Ca. At that time, I wasn't paralyzed. I invented the story of Me Ca. Everyone believed it. Her grave is over there. If you want to know what she looks like, dig her up and have a look!" The old man pointed to a mound near the foot of the mango tree. I took a spade from the tent and went over to the mound. I dug as though I were excavating a tomb. When I got down a meter, I pulled out a shapeless piece of rotten wood.

I sat down for a long time beside that piece of wood. The old ghost had stopped laughing and was now sleeping in his tent.

In front of me, the river flowed. It ran on to the sea. The sea is limitless. I had never seen the sea, even though I had already lived half my life. Time also flows on. In ten years it will be the year 2000.

I stood up and went home. Tomorrow, I'm going to the sea. Out in the sea there is no water nymph.

Painting the Eye

~ *2002, Singapore* ~

PHILIP JEYARETNAM

Although it is the smallest country in Southeast Asia, Singapore looms large for its economic success, and for the relative social and political stability enjoyed by its multiethnic population. Singapore was a British colony through the nineteenth and first half of the twentieth century, and developed as a major trade and administrative outpost in Southeast Asia. The island became an ethnically mixed place peopled by native Malays, larger numbers of ethnic Chinese, and modest numbers of Indian and European immigrants. Today the city-state is predominantly ethnic Chinese, who make up roughly 75 percent of its population, but the government is careful to protect the rights and cultural prerogatives of the other ethnic communities. Upon gaining independence, Singapore was briefly united with the newly independent Federation of Malaya in 1963, but political differences resulted in a separation of the two entities two years later. At the time, many were uncertain as to its prospects as an independent state, given its almost complete lack of natural resources, but the nation's leaders were able to parlay its strategic location and deep-water ports into economic success as it became a vital transshipment center in the region.

As a polyglot society, Singapore is home to a number of literary traditions produced in several languages. The best-known Singaporean literature is that written in English, a linguistic legacy of the colonial period and today the lingua franca of its society, but other tongues are also widely used. These are, moreover, carefully protected through Singapore's education policy, and indications of linguistic diversity are reflected both in literary production and, at a more mundane level, in public signage, which features all four official languages: English, Chinese, Malay, and Tamil.

This short story is by prize-winning author Philip Jeyaretnam, one of the most prominent writers of modern Singapore, but also an established and well-known lawyer. He has published several novels, including *First Loves* (1987), *Raffles Place Ragtime* (1988), and *Abraham's Promise* (1995), and numerous collections of short stories, all written in English. Among these is "Painting the Eye," which touches on many elements of the complex ethnic landscape of modern Singapore. The story's main character, Ah Leong, was the central figure of the earlier novel *First Loves*, in which he appeared as an adolescent growing up in a Singaporean high-rise apartment, exploring life in his immediate community and the larger city. Here we meet Ah Leong having entered the workforce. Like Jeyaretnam himself, he is a man with a day job—in his case selling insurance—but one with another passion, art, and specifically paint-ing portraits. "Painting the Eye" depicts the central character's passion for drawing faces, seeking to capture the rich ethnic diversity of the island's population. The focus on people's faces causes Ah Leong to recognize the distinctiveness of each—none readily classifiable, each more complicated than the overly simplistic ethnic categories delin-eated by the state. He probes behind the faces to reflect on the stories of his subjects' lives. His life as an insurance salesman also causes him to ponder people's stories, and the tale hinges on Ah Leong's attempt to discern the meaning behind a client's actions. While he tries to sell this person a policy, his curiosity about his potential client's story gets the better of him and ultimately prevents the sale.

Questions

1. How is the sense of place revealed in this story? How do you know that you are in Singapore?
2. What is the main character's passion, and how does he relate to the world in which he lives?
3. How do Ah Leong's occupation and his avocation intersect? How does his career as an insurance agent have an impact on his interests in painting?
4. What might the eye in this story represent? Who is watching whom, and why?

***

Painting the Eye

Philip Jeyaretnam. "Painting the Eye." In *Tigers in Paradise: The Collected Works of Philip Jeyaretnam*, (Singapore: Times Editions, 2004), pp. 124–130. Reprinted with the kind permission of the author.

Now that Song Jiang was abroad doing his doctoral thesis on some obscure branch of Chinese literature, Ah Leong suddenly felt his absence keenly. They had not really been together for a long time, eight or nine years, and especially once Song Jiang had entered the National University of Singapore, they had seen one another not more than once a month. Yet Song Jiang's being overseas, almost on the other side of the world at Harvard University, seemed to create a hole in Ah Leong's picture of his nation. He wondered why it was necessary for Song Jiang to disappear across half the world in order to study something that ought to be at the center of our lives, right here, and yet wasn't. He wondered whether all these scholars, streaming outwards from Singapore, brought more back when they returned than they took when they departed.

He worked as an insurance salesman, not a very good one, for just as he reached the crescendo of a sales pitch, his mind would wander. He'd wonder why his target, or victim, had chosen to paint the walls of her flat that luminous blue color; and drifting skywards, his thoughts would fly. And he'd see a thousand salesmen just like himself, all across the island, trying to convince people to buy, and then doubt would strike—was this policy really the best for her, could she really afford the policy—and he'd end up stumbling towards the door, mumbling apologies.

Of course, in the evenings there was his painting; he'd signed up for all the courses he could, wondering why they were termed extra-mural, imagining a course for vandals, spray-painting walls, and then finding himself squirming in his seat, as if the *rotan* were already making contact.* But the instructors were always pedestrian, teaching skills as if their purpose were merely to pass the time, and for his course-mates, often housewives, perhaps that was true. After all, what meaning could be found in the constant repetition of black branches and red blossoms?

---

*The *rotan* (from which the English rattan is derived) is a type of cane used to administer corporal punishment.

After a while though, he found his facility with ink and brush growing, and then with watercolors and oils. Then one day at the Substation, he came face to face with a collage, scraps of *The Straits Times*, and *peranakan* fabrics, and lurking behind them, a face—smoldering, a big Indian face, eyes deep-set and burning—that at first he thought was male, and only later when he saw the artist, large and silent in the middle of the gallery, did he realize was female.

From that moment on, he started painting only faces, and to do so observed everyone he came across, from passersby in the street to each and every one of his clients or potential clients, studying their eyes especially: were they calm or shifty, clear or clouded, profound or shallow, icy or warm? And then the same day or as soon as possible after, the canvas stretched tight across his easel, he would struggle to recapture the face, to fix himself with its remembered gaze. It was strange how different they all were—not just a young undergraduate girl's from that of the old *char kuay teow* man, or a middle-aged Indian doctor's from a Malay housewife's—but all of them. And he began to believe that all of the traditional classifications of faces (young or old, Chinese or Indian, happy or sad) helped not one bit in determining the true essence of faces, of people. Not that he could find new classifications to take their place. No pattern was discernible. Each face seemed to exist entirely unto itself, constituting its own universe. And in the course of a single observation, he would see a face transform itself a hundred times, as if to tell him that it contained at least in memory or in anticipation, all possible experiences of the human animal.

And then the faces began to speak to him and he to listen, rapt. He visited the woman in the house with the sky-blue walls again; and she told him of her husband, who used to visit prostitutes in Indonesia and Thailand but had now found a second wife in China, and her son away at the University, who hardly telephoned, even though she had made her husband buy a Telecom calling-card number that made calling from overseas cheap and convenient. He looked at the sky-blue walls and understood her desire to escape, and when he saw another prospect of his—a shy, timid teacher whom he imagined was bullied every day by students such as he had been ten years earlier—he put them in touch with one another. They both bought insurance and recommended him to others. And when she divorced and married the retiring teacher, he painted them both on their wedding day: two faces separate but together, their gazes joined. And suddenly Ah Leong was looking at his work differently, as something that brought him into contact with a thousand different unique individuals: people who talked to him, to whom he listened, people who sometimes helped him and whom sometimes he helped. And suddenly he was making a lot of money (from insurance that is, he had not yet sold a single painting), and wondering why the world had so intimidated him, why getting a good job had always seemed so hard, why he had seen people as a hurrying scurrying mass with no time or need for him.

A client of his, one day, told him that he had a friend who required life insurance. Could Ah Leong call him? Of course. The next day he did so, and although the man sounded less than friendly over the phone, Ah Leong was not surprised. It was often like that, the assumption being that a salesman was always out to con or cheat, that to be guarded and noncommittal was simple prudence. At least the man agreed to see him, so that his options could be explained further. It appeared Mr. Wee (for that was his name) worked from home, because the appointment, even though it was for 3 P.M., was at a residential address in Queenstown.

It was an ordinary enough, if somewhat old, HDB block with a lift that seemed to take forever, shuddering from one level to the next.* The window to the flat was shuttered, and the door, not the HDB original but a sturdy, almost armored-looking replacement, was further protected by a padlocked metal grille. Ah Leong took a deep breath and knocked. The door resonated, but nothing stirred within. Again he knocked, and again without response until, just as he was ready to give up, he heard metal grate on metal; and after a while, the door opened just an inch. At first Ah Leong could see nothing through the crack, and then lowering his gaze, he espied an eye and addressed it. "My name is Ah Leong. Are you Mr. Wee?" There was no reply, but the eye remained. Ah Leong tried again. "We spoke yesterday. About insurance. Your friend Mr. Lim recommended me."

The door swung open, and a man of half his height, dressed in a white cotton body suit, such as Ah Leong had only previously seen on babies, stood before him. "Identification please." Ah Leong fumbled in his wallet for his IC, and a name card, and then handed them to the man. The man held them up, one after the other, close to his face, and studied them intently. Then he held them back out towards Ah Leong. Ah Leong

---

*HDB stands for Housing and Development Board, the Singaporean government agency that builds and manages large apartment building complexes in which the vast majority of Singapore's population resides. The term HDB has come to serve as shorthand for the apartment buildings themselves.

retrieved his IC and told the man in a hurried nervous stammer that he could keep the business card.

"Thank you," the man muttered as he unlocked the padlock. Ah Leong hesitated over whether to pull open the grille, for the man made no attempt to do so and was already turning back into the flat. Then he remembered what he had been taught ("A foot in the door is half the battle won") and pulled it open. He stepped into the dark interior, his eyes struggling to adjust after the sunlit corridor. "Lock the grille after you."

Ah Leong flinched. A quick getaway would be impossible if he obeyed the man, whom he was still not certain was even Mr. Wee. But if he refused, he could forget about the sale. Focus on the face, he thought, but the man's back was towards him, and all he could remember was the eye: large, round, and opaque. An eye whose size was concentrated on seeing, and kept its owner's soul quite hidden. "Are you Mr. Wee?" he stammered, one hand on the grille.

"Yes."

Ah Leong's relief was so complete that he closed the grille and fastened the padlock in one short fluid motion.

"Sit."

The man was sitting in an armchair and gesturing towards the sofa. Ah Leong obeyed, noting that a dusty TV was the only presence in the room other than the man.

"Now I've worked out a couple of possibilities, based on the age you told me over the phone, thirty-six wasn't it? And you're a non-smoker, right?" Ah Leong removed the plans from his folder. "Perhaps a light would help you see?"

"No. Tell me the difference between the plans."

"Well, I know you wanted just insurance payable on death, but I've taken the liberty to work one out that also pays an assured sum at age sixty-five, as well as providing for certain partial payments in the event of certain illnesses . . ."

"No, just death."

"I see." Ah Leong was struck by the suspicion that something lay behind Mr. Wee's obstinacy.

"May I ask why, sir?"

"No."

"Suicide in the first year is an excluded event." The words had rushed out as they formed in his brain, before his tongue could restrain them. Now he waited trembling as the man stared at him, his eyes seeming to bulge threateningly. How he regretted padlocking the grille! But surely he could fend off this pint-sized fellow, if the worst came to the . . .

"I understand. No question of suicide. Have you brought the proposal form?"

"Yes. Now the insured amount is only $100,000, am I right?"

"That's the maximum without a medical, isn't it?"

"Yes, but you know the policy won't pay out if death occurs from any preexisting medical condition."

"Understood."

Ah Leong went through the form with him and was relieved when the man's doctor turned out to be on the company's panel anyway, and that the man was happy to authorize the doctor to release his medical history.

But in bed that night, he puzzled over Mr. Wee. The beneficiary of the policy was to be his mother, a choice Ah Leong had vainly cautioned against, suggesting someone younger, someone more certain of outliving him. Although Mr. Wee never said so, it was obvious that he was sure of an imminent demise. Yet a planned suicide did not, judging by Mr. Wee's rejoinder, seem the explanation, unless the man thought he could disguise it as something else, some natural cause. Nor did he seem to be ill. Anyway, it wasn't his job to rate the risk. That was for the girls in the backroom, who had suddenly become a good deal more friendly, even respectful, now that his business was booming. One of them was particularly cute, Lee Hua, and his mind turned to the question of whether she might or might not agree to go out with him. Someone as pretty as her must surely have a boyfriend already. But then she always worked late . . . never seemed in a hurry to rush off . . . no indication at all that she was attached . . .

He woke the next morning with a headache and a pounding conviction that Mr. Wee was in grave danger. He wanted the insurance because he expected to be murdered. Gambling . . . that was the answer. Poor Mr. Wee must owe too much money to one of the betting syndicates. He knew he would be rubbed out, and so for the first time was taking a sure bet: insurance on his life.

But what could Ah Leong do? Persuade the man to seek protection from the police? Would that help? There was so much betting money around these days that one could never tell. The syndicate had probably covered that angle already. Or could he protect Mr. Wee? No, he could hardly stake out the place night and day, even if he could persuade Selvam or anyone else to help. And to be honest, he didn't really fancy a life-and-death struggle with a couple of knife-wielding hoodlums. But could he just sit back and do nothing? He thought of the man's eye and how unyielding his gaze had been. He could not leave him to his fate.

That day and the days that followed, he found himself chasing Lee Hua for the company's acceptance of Mr. Wee's proposal, and for the insurance policy. He felt if he could only talk to the man again, he could offer his help, and together they might find a solution. But first, he needed the policy to provide an occasion for his returning to the flat. He comforted himself that Mr. Wee would only have troubled to obtain insurance if he knew he had enough time for the policy to be issued. And sure enough, when policy in hand he returned to Mr. Wee's apartment a week later, it was to a familiar unflinching scrutiny that the door opened a crack. Moments later he was within, and after a stuttering presentation of the policy, he knew it was now or never.

"I believe you are in danger . . . I want to help."

"Danger . . . how? What do you mean?"

"The betting syndicate. The gangsters."

"Betting . . . what do you mean?" The man stood up . . . Ah Leong imagined the man's heart pounding faster and faster as he realized that at last someone had arrived to help him.

"I understand, sir. I know why you need insurance for death only . . . someone's going to kill you, right?"

"You're mad. From the moment you first came in here, I thought there was something wrong with you. Get out of here now."

Ah Leong left, confused and ashamed. His imagination had run away with him again. Interfering, nosy, insensitive—his mind raced to find the appropriate condemnation of his flawed character. Yet he had only been trying to help. What surely could be wrong with that? And if his concern had been ill-founded, then what explained the man's distrust of anyone who came knocking at his door? At home he began a painting of an eye peering through a door opened no more than an inch. He made the door the standard HDB fitting, but the eye, just as he had seen it, larger than life, and lower than one would ordinarily expect. He filled the eye with fear and suspicion, with all the things that make a man turn in upon himself and away from his neighbors. It was the city, this city that he loved so much, that made men like that. His reaching out to face after face could make no difference, if the faces turned away, if the eyes were shuttered. This city would make him the freak, the one who poked his nose into

Shophouses such as these, with stores below and living quarters above, are increasingly scarce in Singapore, but were once common features of the cityscape. Most had been constructed during the period of British colonial control, which began in the early nineteenth century. *(Author's collection)*

other people's business. And his own rage and helplessness filled the painting, till it was saturated with the hues of his emotions.

The painting took him a week. Its creation so consumed him that he took time off work, postponed his follow-up of contracts and clients until his anger, channeled into this painting, left him. When it was finished, he went downstairs to the coffee shop, where he liked to sit and watch the faces of others. Today, however, he was still too demoralized for such observation, and he kept his eyes upon the floor as he walked. Thus it so happened that he came across the front page of a several-days-old *New Paper* and its sensational brazen headline: "You Bet You'll Die." There was the man, those same eyes staring up from a blown-up passport photograph. The report was on page three, and there was no page three.

Weariness descended upon him. He no longer wished to solve the mystery. It was as if all his curiosity had been extinguished by the realization that the distance between two individuals was sometimes too great for anyone, even Ah Leong, to overcome. It was almost worse that the man had not been irrationally afraid and suspicious and that he had good cause for his locks and caution. Ah Leong had correctly understood the man's fears, and yet those fears had been so great that his offer of help had been rejected, as if the man thought Ah Leong, even Ah Leong, might be another of his enemies.

It was only much later, months later, after the painting of "The Eye" had been bought for a deliciously large sum of money at an exhibition of young artists he participated in at Boat Quay, that Ah Leong realized it was possible that the man might have been motivated by concern, the desire not to involve him in a problem that in all honesty he would not have solved. And then, with more money in his pocket than he'd ever had before, Ah Leong returned to walking the streets and studying the faces of the city that he loved.

Bibliography

Allot, Anna J. "Continuity and Change in the Burmese Literary Canon." In *The Canon in Southeast Asian Literatures*, ed. David Smythe, pp. 21–40. London: Curzon, 2000.

Archaeological Survey of India. Taw Sein Ko and Emanuel Forchhammer, comp. *Inscriptions of Pagan, Pinya and Ava*. Rangoon: Superintendent of Government Printing, 1899.

Aung-Thwin, Michael. *Myth and History in the Historiography of Early Burma*. Athens: Ohio University Center for International Studies, 1998.

Botan. *Letters from Thailand*. Bangkok: DK Books, 1994.

Boon, James A. *Affinities and Extremes: Crisscrossing the Bittersweet Ethnology of East Indies History, Hindu-Balinese Culture, and Indo-European Allure*. Chicago: University of Chicago Press, 1990.

Bounyavong, Outhine. "Sacrifice." *Mother's Beloved: Stories from Laos*, ed. Bounheng Inversin and Daniel Duffy, pp. 45–55. Seattle: University of Washington Press, 1999.

Braginsky, Vladimir. *The Heritage of Traditional Malay Literature: A Historical Survey of Genres, Writings and Literary Views*. Leiden: KITLV Press, 2004.

———, ed. and comp. *The Classical Civilisations of South East Asia: An Anthology of Articles Published in the Bulletin of the School of Oriental and African Studies*. London: RoutledgeCurzon, 2002.

Brown, C.C. *The Sejarah Melayu or Malay Annals*. Oxford, UK: Oxford University Press, 1970.

Charney, Michael. *Powerful Learning: Buddhist Literati and the Throne in Burma's Last Dynasty, 1752–1885*. Ann Arbor, MI: Center for South and Southeast Asian Studies, 2006.

Cheong, Fiona. *Scent of the Gods*. New York: W.W. Norton, 1991.

Coedes, Georges. *The Indianized States of Southeast Asia*. Honolulu: University of Hawaii Press, 1968.

Durand, Maurice, and Nguyen Tran Huan. *An Introduction to Vietnamese Literature*. New York: Columbia University Press, 1985.

Florida, Nancy K. *Writing the Past, Inscribing the Future: History as Prophecy in Colonial Java*. Durham, NC: Duke University Press, 1995.

The Glass Palace Chronicle of the Kings of Burma. Trans. Pe Maung Tin and G.H. Luce. London: Oxford University Press, 1923.

Harvey, G.E. *History of Burma from the Earliest Times to 10 March 1824, the Beginning of the English Conquest.* New York: Octagon Books, 1983; reprint of 1925 edition.

Hellwig, Tineke, and Eric Tagliacozzo, eds. *The Indonesia Reader: History, Culture, Politics.* Durham, NC: Duke University Press, 2009.

Hla Pe, Anna J. Allott, and John Okell. "Three 'Immortal' Burmese Songs." *Bulletin of the School of Oriental and African Studies*, vol. 26 (1963), pp. 559–571.

Hsiou, Miao. "Return." In *An Anthology of Modern Malaysian Chinese Stories.* Trans. Ly Singko. Singapore: Heinemann Educational Books, 1976.

Hubbard, A.H. *Verhandelingen van het Bataviaasch genootschap der kunsten en wetenschappen* (Papers of the Batavian Society of Arts and Sciences), vol. 8. Batavia: Government Printing Press, 1816.

Jeyaretnam, Philip. *First Loves.* Singapore: Times Books International, 1988.

———. *Tigers in Paradise: The Collected Works of Philip Jeyaretnam.* Singapore: Times Editions, 2004.

Johns, Anthony H., trans. *Rantjak Dilabueh: A Minangkabau Kaba, A Specimen of the Traditional Literature of Central Sumatra.* Ithaca, NY: Cornell University Southeast Asia Program, 1958.

Kartini, Raden Adjeng. *Letters of a Javanese Princess.* Ed. Hildred Geertz and trans. Agnes Louise Symmers. Lanham, MD: University Press of America, 1985.

Kumar, Ann. "Dipanagara (1787?–1855)" *Indonesia*, vol. 13 (April 1972), pp. 69–118.

Leyden, J., and T.S. Raffles. *Malay Annals.* London: Longman, Hurst, Rees, Orme, and Brown, 1821.

Linh Dinh, ed. *Night Again: Contemporary Fiction from Vietnam.* New York: Seven Stories Press, 1996.

Ly Te Xuyen. *Departed Spirits of the Viet Realm.* Trans. Brian E. Ostrowski and Brian A. Zottoli. Ithaca, NY: Cornell University Southeast Asia Program, 1999.

Ma Sandar. "An Umbrella." In *Virtual Lotus: Modern Fiction of Southeast Asia*, ed. Teri Shaffer Yamada and trans. Than Than Win. Ann Arbor: University of Michigan Press, 2002.

Myint, Thein Pe. "Oil." In *Selected Short Stories of Thein Pe Myint.* Trans. Patricia M. Milne. Ithaca: Cornell University Southeast Asia Program, 1973.

Nguyen Dinh Hoa. *Vietnamese Literature: A Brief Survey.* San Diego, CA: San Diego State University, 1994.

Nguyen Du. *The "Kim Van Kieu" of Nguyen Du (1765–1820).* Trans. Vladislav Zhukov. Ithaca, NY: Cornell University Southeast Asia Program, 2012.

———. *Tale of Kieu.* Trans. Huynh Sanh Thong. New Haven, CT: Yale University Press, 1983.

Nguyen Huy Thiep. *The General Retires.* Trans. Greg Lockhart. Oxford: Oxford University Press, 1993.

Nguyen Khac Vien, and Huu Ngoc, eds. *Vietnamese Literature.* Hanoi: Red River Press, n.d.

Owen, Norman G., ed, *The Emergence of Modern Southeast Asia: A New History.* Honolulu: University of Hawaii Press, 2005.

Phillips, Herbert P. *Modern Thai Literature: With an Ethnographic Interpretation.* Honolulu: University of Hawaii Press, 1987.

Reamker (Ramakerti): The Cambodian Version of the Ramayana. Trans. Judith Jacob. London and New York: Routledge, 2006.

Ricklefs, M.C. *A History of Modern Indonesia Since c. 1300.* Stanford: Stanford University Press, 1993.

Rizal, José. *An Eagle Flight: A Filipino Novel, Adapted from "Noli me tangere."* New York: McClure, Phillips, 1900.

———. *Noli Me Tangere, a Novel.* Trans. Soledad Lacson-Locsin. Honolulu: University of Hawaii Press, 1997.

Sandalinka, Shin. *The Maniyadanabon of Shin Sandalinka.* Trans. L.E. Bagshawe. Ithaca, NY: Cornell University Southeast Asia Program, 1981.

Smyth, David, ed. *The Canon in Southeast Asian Literatures.* London: Curzon, 2000.

Sneddon, James. *The Indonesian Language: Its History and Role in Modern Society.* Kensington, Australia: University of New South Wales Press, 2003.

Sri Daoruang. *Married to the Demon King.* Trans. Susan Kepner. Chiang Mai: Silkworm Books, 2004.

The Tale of Prince Samuttakote. Trans. Thomas John Hudak. Athens: Ohio University Center for International Studies, 1993.

Tantular, Mpu. *Sutasoma: The Ancient Tale of a Buddha-Prince.* Trans. Kate O'Brien. Singapore: Orchid Press, 2008.

Tarling, Nicholas, ed. *The Cambridge History of Southeast Asia.* 4 vols. Cambridge, UK: Cambridge University Press, 1999.

Taylor, Jean Gelman. *Indonesia: Peoples and Histories.* New Haven, CT: Yale University Press, 2003.

Taylor, Keith. *A History of the Vietnamese.* Cambridge, UK: Cambridge University Press, 2013.

Toer, Pramoedya Anata. *This Earth of Mankind.* Trans. Max Lane. New York: Penguin Books, 1996.

———. *The Mute's Soliloquy.* Trans. William Samuels. New York: Penguin Books, 2000.

Vu Trong Phung. *Dumb Luck.* Trans. Nguyen Nguyet Cam and Peter Zinoman. Ann Arbor: University of Michigan Press, 2002.

Yamada, Terry Shaffer. *Virtual Lotus: Modern Fiction of Southeast Asia.* Ann Arbor: University of Michigan Press, 2002.

Zinoman, Peter. "Declassifying Nguyen Huy Thiep." *Positions,* vol. 2, no. 2 (1994), pp. 294–317.

About the Editor

George E. Dutton is an associate professor in the UCLA Department of Asian Languages and Cultures. He is also the director of the UCLA Center for Southeast Asian Studies. He is a specialist in early modern and colonial Vietnamese social history, and has written on topics ranging from eighteenth-century Vietnamese Catholicism to 1930s newspaper culture. He is co-editor of *Sources of Vietnamese Tradition* (2012), as well as the author of *The Tay Son Uprising: Society and Rebellion in Eighteenth-Century Vietnam* (2006).

Made in the USA
Lexington, KY
02 January 2018